**Library**

5801 Wilson Avenue
St. Louis, Missouri 63110

**In Memory of
SAM MYERS**
1913-1978
Historian of the American West
and the American Indian
Member of the Florissant Valley
History Department 1968 to 1978

# MENOMINEE DRUMS

*Menominee Indian Thunderbird.* Courtesy of Menominee Indian Tribe of Wisconsin, Keshena, Wis.

# MENOMINEE DRUMS

Tribal Termination and Restoration, 1954-1974

# By Nicholas C. Peroff

University of Oklahoma Press : Norman

Library of Congress Cataloging in Publication Data

Peroff, Nicholas C.
  Menominee drums.

  Bibliography: p.
  Includes index.
  1. Menominee Indians—Government relations.   2. Indians of
North America—Government relations—1934-        I. Title.
E99.M44P47          323.1'197          81-43641
                                       AACR2

Copyright © 1982 by the University of Oklahoma Press, Norman,
Publishing Division of the University. Manufactured in the U.S.A.
First Edition.

*To Linda, Amanda, and Deidre*

# CONTENTS

# ILLUSTRATIONS

## MAPS

# PREFACE

NATIONAL INDIAN POLICY is in a state of dangerous uncertainty. Rising anti-Indian sentiment and increasingly unsympathetic congressional reaction to several controversial court decisions on Indian land and water claims in Maine, Washington, and elsewhere suggest that the federal government may again disregard the treaty-guaranteed rights of Native Americans and search for a new solution to the "Indian problem." American Indians have not fully recovered from the last solution of Congress—the Indian termination policy. That ill-fated policy was advanced in the 1950s and early 1960s to abolish Indian reservations and terminate any special rights accorded Indian tribes because of their distinct identity as legally independent Indian nations. The goal of termination policy was the eventual assimilation of all Native Americans into the larger American society.

Congress launched its experiment in Indian termination by passing the Menominee Termination Act of 1954. In socioeconomic and psychological terms the immediate effects of the act on the Menominee tribe were disastrous. It did not promote rapid assimilation of the tribe. Eventually, individual dissatisfactions coalesced and became an organized campaign to achieve restoration of the Menominees' reservation and federally protected tribal status. Twenty years after passage of the Menominee Termination Act, Congress responded to the Menominee demands for the reversal of termination and passed the Menominee Restoration Act of 1974.

Although termination has been discredited and formally abandoned, there is a menacing possibility that a comparable national Indian policy will emerge, possibly under a different name but with the same goals as those of the original policy. The Menominee experience suggests that a return by Congress to policies dedicated to the forced assimilation of Indians would be indefensible. Future policies must not deny Native Americans their legal, treaty-defined rights to the cultural and political autonomy they desire.

The aim of this book is to explain how termination policy evolved and was applied to the Menominees, and also why it was reversed. The political and social forces that shape the evolution of Indian policy in the United States comprise an extremely complex process. Within it are the activities of a myriad of public officials in all levels of government, and an untold number of private citizens. As the need arises, several theories and concepts associated with the study of public policy will be introduced to help explain how the Indian policy process works (see appendix 1). It is hoped that the resulting synthesis of theory and fact will provide the reader with something beyond merely a descriptive account of the Menominee experience.

Data collected for this case study span a period of nearly thirty years and consist of media coverage, census records, congressional and state legislative hearings, and many studies and reports compiled by the tribe, the University of Wisconsin, the state of Wisconsin, and private individuals interested in the history and lives of the Menominee people. In 1974 and 1977, I conducted eighty open-ended interviews and follow-up interviews with key individuals involved in Menominee termination and restoration. The list of persons interviewed includes federal, state, and local political leaders and administrative officials; Menominee leaders and other tribal members; and several non-Menominee private citizens involved in the controversy. I have respected the requests of several individuals who have asked that some of their comments remain confidential. Selection of those interviewed was based on their documented or ascribed role in the tribe's termination and restoration.

My thanks to the following interviewees for their time and cooperation: D. Boyd, T. Boyd, D. Brizizinski, M. Buzard, G. Caulkins, S. Daly, A. Deer, C. Deer, R. Deer, A. Dick, G. Dickey, A. Dodge, C. Dodge, C. Egan, J. Fossum, J. Freshette, J. Gauthier, B. Granum, J. Grignon, R. Grignon, H. Grover, H. Harder, J. Hawkins, J. Heinz, A. Iadarola, N. Isaacson, T. Jacobs, W. Kackwitch, G. Kenote, Y. Knight, F. Leon, N. Lurie, B. Miller, G. Miller, F. Moulin, P. Nash, G.

Orfield, J. Preloznik, A. Pyatskowit, V. Ray, R. Rieter, S. Skubitz, M. VanGemert, H. Waukaw, A. Waupochick, M. Weso, S. Wilber, C. Wilkinson, and G. Wilkinson.

This book would not have been possible without the aid and cooperation of the Menominee tribe. My special thanks to Delores Boyd, Shirly Daly, Ada Deer, George Kenote, Silvia Wilber, and Al Fowler. Thanks are also extended to those involved in the research and preparation of this book, including Dennis Brizizinski, Bernard Granum, Jim Hawkins, Nancy Oestreich Lurie, Faith Moulin, Philleo Nash, Bob Herman, and Henry Hart. Special thanks goes to Martha Gresham, who typed the equivalent of at least three drafts of the manuscript. Finally, the value of the editorial and substantive comments on the manuscript of my wife, Linda, are surpassed only by the motivational support she gave me to finish the manuscript.

Nicholas C. Peroff

# MENOMINEE DRUMS

# 1

# INTRODUCTION

*We accepted our present reservation when it was considered of no value by our white friends. All we ask is that we are permitted to keep it as a home.* — Neopit, Menominee chief, 1882

FROM the earliest archaeological traces of the tribe, dating back over five thousand years, the forest has remained central to the lives of the Menominee Indians. Although ancestral claims of other Indian societies, such as the Potawatomi, Winnebago, Ottawa, and Chippewa, make it difficult to distinguish early tribal boundaries, Menominee lands once may have encompassed nearly ten million acres of forests within Wisconsin and Upper Michigan. When the first Euro-American explorers reached the region in the early seventeenth century, four to five thousand tribal members were subsisting on game, fish, and wild rice obtained from surrounding lakes and woodlands.

In the eighteenth and early nineteenth centuries French, British, and American exploration and settlement severely challenged, but did not destroy, the Menominee Nation. The tribe allied itself with several Euro-American powers as each attempted to achieve domination in the Great Lakes region. Menominees acted as suppliers of raw materials and troops to the French during the battle for Quebec in 1759, the British in the War of 1812, and the Americans after the Treaty of Ghent in 1814. By trading with the ever-increasing numbers of Euro-Americans and allowing non-Menominees to marry into the tribe, the Menominees retained their tribal identity. Retention of their forest was another matter.

Beginning in 1821 and ending in 1848, the Menominees signed a series of treaties that eventually ceded all of their virgin white pine forest to the United States. Political pressures exerted by lumber barons and the influx of pioneers moving steadily westward motivated the federal government to attempt a relocation of the Menominees to unsettled land in Minnesota. The tribe, led by Chief Oshkosh, resisted and, in 1854, after several years of negotiation, obtained approval for a reservation within its homeland. The 275,000 acres of sandy soil allotted to the tribe were considered poor farmland and of little value to Wisconsin settlers. In 1856 the Menominee Reservation was further reduced when the tribe was pressed to cede 40,000 acres for the creation of the Stockbridge Reservation.

Confined to 235,000 acres, the Menominees could no longer live by hunting, fishing, and gathering wild rice. Attempts to grow crops in the sandy soil of the reservation were generally futile. The fur trade, which had provided significant income, collapsed in the later 1800s. Fortunately the tribe still possessed nearly 350 square miles of prime timber.

The defense of the remaining forest from exploitation by lumbermen, who harvested nearly all of the available timber in the north-central states, became the key to preservation of the Menominees' tribal existence. Aided by the United States Forest Service, the tribe initiated sustained-yield management of their forest. With selective cutting, seedling replacement of harvested timber, and proper management the reservation could produce timber and other forest products into perpetuity. In 1908 the Bureau of Indian Affairs (BIA) helped construct a sawmill that became the major source of income and employment for the Menominee people. The BIA, however, failed to train Menominees for higher-level positions in supervision of sawmill operations or forest management. Alleging mismanagement of their timber resources, the Menominees in 1934 filed a suit against the federal government in the United States Court of Claims. After seventeen years the court ruled in favor of the tribe and awarded the Menominees $7.65 million.

In 1951 the Menominee Indians were among the most self-sufficient Indian tribes in the United States. They owned a 220,000-acre forest and a sawmill representing a capital investment of $1.5 million. Moreover, the tribe had accumulated $10 million on deposit in the United States Treasury. Unfortunately, the Menominees' image as one of the most "advanced" Indian tribes in the nation marked them as prime targets for one of the most ill-considered congressional experiments in the history of national Indian policy.

Beginning with the establishment of Indian reservations in the early eighteenth century, the federal government's consistent objective in national Indian policy has been the assimilation of Native Americans into the larger American society. Despite changes in presidents, congressmen, and BIA commissioners, the belief has persisted that assimilation is the best and only realistic future for American Indians. While disagreement has arisen over the means of achieving assimilation, national policymakers have rarely differed on the ends of Indian policy, total assimilation. In 1953, Congress seized upon termination policy as a new strategy to achieve Indian assimilation. The policy was summarized in House Concurrent Resolution 108, which stated, in part:

> Whereas it is the policy of Congress, as rapidly as possible to make the Indians within the territorial limits of the United States subject to the same laws and entitled to the same privileges and responsibilities as are applicable to other citizens of the United States, to end their status as wards of the United States, and to grant them all of the rights and prerogatives pertaining to American citizenship; and

> Whereas the Indians within the territorial limits of the United States should assume their full responsibilities as American citizens; Now therefore, be it

> Resolved by the House of Representatives (the Senate concurring), that it is the sense of Congress that, at the earliest possible time, all of the Indian tribes and individual members thereof . . . should be freed from Federal supervision and control . . . . [U.S., House, Concurrent Resolution 108, 1953]

With this resolution Congress made clear its determination to dismiss promises pledged in a long series of treaties between the federal government and the American Indians. It would no longer protect the traditional tribal way of life or Indian lands formerly held in trust and protected by the federal government.

The impact of termination policy on Native Americans was enormous. Vine Deloria, a noted Native American writer, refers to the termination era in Indian policy as "the most traumatic period of Indian existence" (Deloria 1978, p. 87). By the time the last tribe was terminated in 1962, 13,263 tribal members had been "freed" by Congress, and over 1,365,800 acres of tribal lands had been removed from the protection of federal-trust status (Butler 1978, p. 52).

When President Dwight D. Eisenhower signed the Menominee Termination Act on June 17, 1954, the Menominee tribe became the first tribe slated for termination. Although the act was not fully implemented until 1961, many of the negative effects of termination policy came to the surface years before the formal termination began. Expenses involved in the preparation for termination, along with other factors, nearly exhausted the tribe's cash assets on deposit with the United States Treasury. When lack of funds forced the closing of the tribal hospital, tuberculosis became a major health problem. Menominee children were no longer legally recognized as members of the tribe if their birthdays fell after the date of closure of the tribal rolls in 1954. Badly needed sources of leadership were depleted when economic decline and rising anxieties about their future led many of the younger and better-educated Menominees to leave the reservation for the cities. When the Menominee Reservation was finally terminated on May 1, 1961, it became a new Wisconsin county. Quickly tagged by state officials as "an instant pocket of poverty," Menominee County and its residents faced an extremely uncertain and unpromising future.

One of the greatest ironies surrounding the termination of the Menominee Tribe was that the momentum behind termination policy had begun to dissipate long before 1961. As early as September, 1958, Secretary of the Interior Fred Seaton had asserted that "no Indian tribe or group should end its relationship with the Federal Government unless such tribe or group has clearly demonstrated, . . . first, that it understands the plan under which such a program should go forward, and second, that the tribe or group affected concurs in and supports the plan proposed" (Seaton 1958). Had Secretary Seaton's conditions been adhered to in 1954, the Menominee Termination Act would not have become law. Despite a continuous series of Menominee efforts to stop or delay termination, political inertia prevailed, and Congress refused to reverse the 1954 decision. Final implementation of the Menominee Termination Act occurred nearly three years after Secretary Seaton's speech.

As America moved into the decade of the 1960s, the federal government abandoned further pursuit of termination policy. One reason was a growing national sensitivity to the rights and special problems of all minorities in America, including Native Americans. Another, more direct reason was the negative effects the termination policy was having on all Native Americans. Even though money was being poured into Indian country from such programs as the Community Action Project for Indian Reservations of the Office of Economic Opportunity, the BIA's Division of Economic Development, and the Office of Indian Progress of the Department of Health, Education, and Welfare, American Indians were afraid to take full advantage of the opportunities offered (Butler 1978, p. 56). They feared that if, as a result of the programs, they became more self-sufficient they would become the targets of a renewed policy of termination.

To ease these fears and encourage greater tribal participation in his antipoverty programs, President Lyndon B. Johnson, on March 6, 1968, delivered a speech to Congress entitled "The Forgotten American." In it he called for an end to termination and the beginning of a new "'policy of maximum choice for the American Indian, a policy expressed in programs of self-help, self-development, self-determination'" (Butler 1978, p. 56). President Richard M. Nixon reaffirmed the words of his predecessor in 1970, when he recommended that Congress adopt a new policy to provide for Indian self-determination "without termination of the special federal relationship with recognized Indian Tribes" (Nixon 1970). While the words of presidents and other federal officials were appreciated, American Indians remained skeptical. As long as the Menominees remained a terminated tribe, they felt that termination represented a latent but real threat to their tribal way of life.

The 1960s were a decade of disorder for all Americans, but they were particularly chaotic for the Menominee people. The economic and social problems suffered by the tribe strongly suggested that the decision by Congress to terminate special protection had been a mistake. Menominee County and its residents continued to struggle with new problems that arose and old ones that refused to go away. The new county's tax base was totally inadequate to support needed government services, and the standard of living in the county remained the lowest in the state. After ten years of continuous direct and indirect federal and state aid, the county could not raise revenues necessary for matching federal grants-in-aid.

Faced with the near certainty of fiscal collapse, Menominee leaders made a momentous decision. They began developing and selling to non-Indians lakeshore lots on the county's lakes and rivers. Tribal reaction to the sale of land to whites, coupled with the possible loss of political control over their own affairs as large numbers of non-Menominees established year-round residences and became a voting majority within the county, triggered the rise of a new tribal organization called Determination of Rights and Unity for Menominee Shareholders (DRUMS).

It will be seen that this organization was eventually to be instrumental in gaining the repeal of the Menominee Termination Act. With the enactment of the Menominee Restoration Act on December 22, 1973, Congress acknowledged that the policy of termination had been a mistake. The act restored federal recognition and protection to the Menominees and reestablished nearly all of their former reservation. The act also provided concrete evidence to all Native Americans that the era of Indian termination was over.

The Menominee termination and restoration experience is ironic. It typifies one of the worst periods in America's often troubled relationship with her Native American population. Yet, after restoration, the Menominee people are at the forefront of a new era in Indian affairs that promises American Indians greater self-determination over their own tribal affairs and future.

# 2

# WHITE AMERICA TRIES TO
# ASSIMILATE THE INDIAN

*For almost four centuries the American Indian has been in contact with
the Euro-American but he has remained the Indian. A slow-moving but
inexorable solution to the problems of a minority within a majority has
been tried and tested a thousand times in history and it has yet to fail.
The solution and perhaps the only complete one: Absorption. The
minority must be absorbed into the majority. It is an automatic and
fundamental solution to the problem of man's unkindness to man.* —
Charles House, "Absorption of Menominees by Whites Already
Started," *Green Bay Press-Gazette,* August 19, 1959

ASSIMILATION of Native Americans into the dominant image
of American society has been the major objective of Indian
policy since the early nineteenth century. The actions of the
principal advocates and opponents of assimilation over the
years suggest how assimilation was pursued and why it failed.

Indian policy began with adoption of the United States
Constitution in 1789 and the creation of Congress.[1] Laws
enacted during the following two to three decades reflected
the largely independent status of American Indians, since
they were still beyond the reach of the United States legal or
military authority. Congressional policy making dealt with
the regulation of trade or "intercourse" between the United
States and Indian nations and established boundaries between Indian Country and white settlements. Legislation

---

[1] The third article of the United States Constitution charges Congress
with the responsibility to "regulate commerce with foreign nations, and
among the several states, and with the Indian Tribes." Actually, United
States Indian policy has its antecedents in British colonial policies which
established trade with Indians through government-authorized trading
posts and adopted treaties with various tribes for the acquisition of land
(see Lurie 1971).

during this period largely applied to whites rather than to Indians (Washburn 1973, p. 2133; Prucha 1962).

During the following fifty years, roughly from 1820 to 1870, many of the core concepts of Indian policy were developed. This period included the most extensive use of treaties with Indians, adoption of the policy of "removal" from areas coveted by white settlers, and establishment of Indian reservations—mainly west of the Mississippi River (Deloria 1969; Zimmerman 1957; Lurie 1971a, 1973). Over a century later policy debate for and against termination was still based on a controversy over the continued legitimacy of treaties and survival of reservations established during this period.

Indian policy became explicitly designed to promote "civilization and education among Indians," that is, assimilation (Prucha 1962, p. 6).[2] Because the establishment of reservations was such a central factor in these policies and in the policies of termination and restoration decades later, it is necessary to pause to contrast Indian and non-Indian perceptions of Indian reservations.

Treaties establishing reservations were perceived in Congress and, more broadly, in the United States government, as a temporary administrative device for educating and civilizing Indians for their eventual assimilation into the larger American society. In addition reservations provided a mechanism for gathering and reeducating Indians to become Christians. Finally, reservations protected Indians from exploita-

---

[2] See, for example, a congressional act dated March 3, 1819 (3 Stat. 679) entitled "An Act Making Provision for the Civilization of the Indian Tribes Adjoining the Frontier Settlements." In part, the act stated that "for the purpose of providing against the further decline and final extinction of Indian tribes adjoining the frontier settlements of the United States, and for introducing among them the habits and arts of civilization, the President of the United States shall be, and he is hereby authorized, in every case where he shall judge improvement in the habits and condition of such Indians practicable, and that the means of instruction can be introduced with their own consent, to instruct them in the mode of agriculture suited to their situation." The provision for "their own consent" would be very loosely interpreted, however, since the United States always assumed it knew what was best for Indians, including the assumption that they should be trained as farmers.

tion by the dominant society while they were being "reconditioned." Reservations were considered temporary not only because assimilation was considered inevitable but also because the Indian population was declining rapidly during the nineteenth century, and Indian tribal organizations were expected simply to die out.

Indians viewed treaties as solemn political contracts which guaranteed that the United States would always protect the limited lands remaining to the Indians in exchange for the vast portion of territory already ceded to the United States. They expected to be left alone to adapt to the presence of white culture and even to become interdependent with white civilization, while maintaining their survival as identifiable communities. Nancy Oestreich Lurie perceptively summarized these two contrasting perspectives when she observed:

> The white man has grown increasingly impatient with the Indian's stubborn refusal to avail himself properly of the privileges extended by generous and benevolent governments to help him enter the white world. The Indian, in turn, has grown increasingly angry with the white man's willful refusal to honor governmental promises to provide meaningful wherewithal to build economically sound and socially comfortable communities to cope with the white world. Each has been disappointed by the other's apparent failure to live up to the presumably mutually agreed-upon terms. [Lurie 1971a, pp. 427–28][3]

After 1880 congressional impatience with the slow progress of assimilation forcefully asserted itself in new policy alternations that directly attacked the continued existence of Indian reservations. An act of Congress dated March 3, 1871, ended treaty making with Indians. The subsequent use of congressional "agreements" and, later, executive orders of the president, represented a further erosion of the status of Indian tribes as independent "nations" (Lurie 1971a, p. 431; Vogel 1972, pp. 162–65; Svensson 1973, p. 22).[4]

[3] For a more complete discussion of Indian and non-Indian perceptions of reservations see Lurie 1971a, 1971b, 1973.
[4] The act of March 3, 1871 (Sec. 2079), stated, in part: "No Indian Nation or tribe within the territory of the United States shall be acknowledged or recognized as an independent nation, tribe or power with whom the United States may contract by treaty; *but no obligation or any treaty lawfully*

The most forceful direct attack on the continued existence of reservations occurred with the passage of the General Allotment, or Dawes, Act of 1887. The Allotment Act authorized the president to "individualize" Indian reservations by allotting 160-acre plots to tribal members. After allotment, surplus lands were made available for white settlement. The act received support from two groups—"friends" of the Indians, who believed that vesting Indians with private property would remove the reservation as an obstruction to their natural course toward assimilation, and those individuals who wanted to acquire the reservation land for commercial purposes, mainly land speculation. Allotted lands were to be tax-free and held in trust by the federal government for twenty-five years or until the Indian allottee was considered legally "competent" to hold clear title to his land. Many Indians, however, were soon urged to ask for their papers of competency, and their land was then purchased by white land speculators at prices far below market value. Thus thousands of additional acres of allotted lands were lost to Indians.[5] When the Allotment Act was finally discarded in 1934, only about 35 percent of the 140 million acres held by the Indians in 1887 remained under federal trust in reservations, and approximately ninety thousand Indians had become landless.

Finally, the sovereignty of Indian tribes as separate "nations" was dealt an additional blow with the passage of the Citizenship Act of 1924. Although Congress was motivated in part by a recognition of the valor of those Indians who had volunteered for service in World War I, the act represented one additional facet in the continuing policy of assimi-

---

made and ratified with any such Indian nation or tribe prior to March third, eighteen hundred and seventy-one, shall be hereby invalidated or impaired" (Kappler, ed. 1904, 1:8; emphasis added). Since the Menominee Reservation had been established by treaties enacted before 1871, this act became a supporting argument for those opposed to termination in the 1950s.

[5] For further discussion of the Allotment Act and its consequences for Indians see Lurie 1971a, pp. 432–34, 1973, pp. 22–23; Svensson 1973, pp. 22–24; Haas 1957, pp. 13–16; Deloria 1969, pp. 51–53; Zimmerman 1957, pp. 39–40; Prucha 1973; Otis 1973; "Annual Report of the Secretary of the Interior," 1933.

lation. About 125,000 native-born Indians who had not become citizens previously were unilaterally declared citizens by the act. As recently as 1956, some states still refused Indians the right to vote despite passage of the Citizenship Act (Haas 1957, p. 16).

The end of the use of treaties, adoption of the Allotment Act, and even, to some extent, the granting of citizenship were all actions taken without consultation and often despite the strenuous objections of most Indians. Congress abandoned the principle of bilateralism or mutual agreement that was followed in treaty making before 1871. Moreover, while prior laws considered cultural differences among various Indian tribes, the Allotment Act set an important precedent by imposing a uniform legal pattern for Indians in general. Following the new pattern, the government largely bypassed tribal organizations and Indian leaders and dealt directly with individual Indians. Declining tribal leadership caused by the weakening of tribal governments was systematically replaced by the steadily expanding authority of the federal government in the form of hundreds of new laws and regulations relating to Indian affairs (Haas 1957, pp. 15–16). Congressional policies were aimed at assimilation and the subsequent solution of the "Indian problem." In fact, those policies expanded both federal authority over Indian affairs and the bureaucracy to administer that authority. Ironically, congressional chances of "getting out of the Indian business" were declining with the passage of every new act and statute.

Passage of the Indian Reorganization Act, also known as the Wheeler-Howard Act (46 Stat. 984), in 1934 began the next major cycle in federal Indian policy. The act grew out of recommendations from a study completed in 1928 by the Brookings Institution entitled "The Problem of Indian Administration," also called "The Meriam Report." It strongly criticized the unsatisfactory economic, educational, and health conditions on reservations and stressed the impossibility of integrating Indians directly into white society through allotment of Indian lands (Burnett 1972, p. 564).

Also contributing to the act were previous policy initiatives taken by the Hoover administration and the active support of New Deal appointees in the Department of the Interior (see the discussion of the BIA below). Although President Herbert C. Hoover made several public statements indicating his concern for the treatment of Indians under the Allotment Act, the Depression halted development of administration policies to deal with the situation (Svensson 1973, p. 27).

In essence the act curtailed further allotment of Indian lands, promoted consolidation of fragmented Indian lands and federal repurchase of land for landless Indians, and allowed Indians to organize under tribal constitutions, establish tribal corporations, and determine their own form of tribal government.[6] Support for the act was based on a belief that assimilation would be accelerated if Indians retained their special services, privileges, and rights until they were economically secure and adequately trained for life in white society and until they gradually acquired the values of the American cultural system (Tyler 1964, pp. 17-18).

By contrast, opposition to the act was based upon several diverse factors, including a continued desire by non-Indians to acquire Indian land protected by the act and a belief that the act encouraged "communistic tendencies" inherent in Indian culture. Noting that twenty-five thousand Indians had served in the armed forces during World War II and almost fifty thousand had worked in industry, opponents of the act concluded that Indians could fight and work like everyone else and, therefore, should join the mainstream of society and live like everyone else. With a logic that escapes comprehension, the belief of the act's foes that assimilation would be speeded by the removal of special services and

[6]Additional powers granted to tribes included the rights to administer justice (subject to congressional limitation), determine tribal membership, regulate inheritance, levy taxes and fees, exercise the usual authority of a landlord, and regulate domestic relations—including the adoption of children. A provision for preferential hiring of Indians for the Indian Service was also included in the act (Svensson 1973, pp. 27-28; Tyler 1964, 17-18). Acceptance of the act was determined by the tribes in formal elections. Ultimately 181 tribes accepted the act, 77 rejected it (including the Menominee), and 14 came under it because of a failure to vote. Alaska and Oklahoma groups were covered by the act without a vote (Haas 1957, pp. 19-22).

federal administrative agencies for Indian affairs often was accompanied by lingering skepticism about the ability of Indians to govern their own tribal communities.[7]

Byron Brophy offered the most penetrating criticism of the act when he stated:

> The Reorganization Act has the merit of encouraging organization of Indian tribes for consideration and action of their own affairs. If it then gave them responsibility for the administration of their reservations, it would be good. There is no such provision, however. The superintendent and his staff remain totally independent of the people they serve. Such a fundamental institution as the schools for their children are entirely independent of the Indian people. . . . Even on those matters over which they are supposed to have some choice, they are subject to the pressures which the powerful Indian Bureau representative in the person of the reservation superintendent can apply as the need may arise. [B. Brophy 1945, pp. 445–46]

Congress began expressing the opinion that, at best, the act was advancing assimilation far too slowly and, at worst, was ensuring perpetual government supervision and control of the Indians. Instead of changing certain provisions of the act, however, Congress discarded the act entirely and adopted the most extreme alternative policy available, total termination of any special federal responsibility for Indians.

Actually congressional eagerness for termination was apparent long before passage of the Menominee Termination Act in 1954. In part, because of growing dissatisfaction with New Deal officials and policies and the desire to save federal dollars, several House and Senate committee reports from 1943 to 1953 advocated or presented data supporting liquidation of the BIA and termination of its services (Watkins 1957, pp. 52–53; Burnett 1972, pp. 566–70; Tyler 1964, pp. 43–44). Many BIA reports (for instance, "The Zimmerman Report," 1947) and correspondence, all solicited by Congress, outlined criteria and procedures for terminating the "more advanced" Indian tribes (Deloria 1969, pp. 60–65; Tyler 1964,

---

[7] For additional discussion of the IRA see Lurie 1971*a*, pp. 436–38; Deloria 1969, pp. 51–53, 1971, pp. 64–69; Burnett 1972, p. 546; W. Brophy 1966, pp. 22–23.

p. 49; Robertson 1961, p. 1). Congress began repealing several federal laws containing special provisions to regulate Indian conduct, such as statutes prohibiting firearms and liquor on reservations (Lurie 1961, pp. 478–500; Haas 1957, p. 17). In 1949 a special Hoover Commission report submitted to Congress advocated a policy of "integration of the Indian into the rest of the population as a solution to the 'Indian Problem'" (Commission on the Organization of the Executive Branch 1949, pp. 1–81). With the passage of Public Law 280 in 1953, Congress authorized five states (California, Minnesota, Nebraska, Oregon, and Wisconsin) to extend their civil and criminal laws to Indian reservations within their borders (W. Brophy 1966, pp. 184–85; Svensson 1973, p. 33). Passage of the Indian Claims Commission Act of 1946 not only extended to Indian tribes the right to sue the government but also cleared the way for termination by providing for the final settlement of all alleged obligations of the federal government to Indian tribes (Watkins 1957, p. 50; Tyler 1964, p. 30; Lurie 1957).

The clearest indicator of the growing movement toward termination was represented by House Concurrent Resolution 108 (1953). The resolution stated:

> . . . it is the policy of Congress, as rapidly as possible to make the Indians within the territorial limits of the United States subject to the same laws and entitled to the same privileges and responsibilities as are applicable to other citizens of the United States, to end their status as wards of the United States, and to grant them all of the rights and prerogatives pertaining to American citizenship.

The resolution rapidly passed through both houses of Congress with almost no debate in support or opposition (Orfield 1965, chap. 1, 2). One senator described it as "nothing more than an expression of the sense of the Congress that we should end trusteeship and wardship" (D'Ewart 1953, p. 9262).

The subservience of the BIA to the House and Senate Subcommittees on Indian Affairs is well documented in J. Leiper Freeman's study of the politics of Indian Affairs (Freeman 1965). More recently Vine Deloria asserted that the bureau should be characterized as "fear-ridden." "The Commissioner," according to Deloria, "has one basic task—to keep the members of the Interior and Insular Affairs Committees of the House and Senate happy—not to serve Indians or even to run his own bureau" (Deloria 1969, pp. 134–35). A key product of this relationship has been parallel policy positions in Congress and the bureau since the bureau's creation in 1834.[8]

Review of the annual reports of the commissioner of Indian affairs from 1824 to 1953 readily supports this proposition (see Washburn 1973, pp. 5–991). For example, in 1829, Commissioner Thomas L. McKinney dealt with the merits of Indian removal, as well as with the problems involved in its execution. In 1876, Commissioner J. Q. Smith argued that the use of treaties to set aside reservations should be dispensed with, and, instead, United States civil law should be extended to cover Indians in Indian country. By 1890, Commissioner T. J. Morgan could state that "it has become the settled policy of the Government to break up reservations, destroy tribal relations, settle Indians upon their own homesteads, incorporate them into national life, and deal with them not as nations or tribes or bands, but as individual citizens" (Washburn 1973, p. 435). Commissioner Cato Sells's report in 1919 recognized the contribution of Indians in World War I and advocated the extension of citizenship to Indians.[9]

Examination of commissioners' reports during the tenure

[8]Actually, the post of superintendent of Indian affairs was first established within the War Department in 1789. The first "official" commissioner of Indian affairs was appointed without a bureau in 1832. The chief responsibility of the bureau while in the War Department was removal of Indians from the advance of white settlement. In 1849 the Department of the Interior was established, and the BIA was placed under civil control. The major duties of the bureau in its early years included negotiation and implementation of treaties, regulation of Indian trade, and supervision of educational and religious activities (Orfield 1965, chap. 4, p. 1; Lurie 1971a, p. 472).

[9]In Commissioner Sells's previous report for 1918 he discussed his opposition to the creation of separate Indian army units. The contrast between white America's treatment of its Indian and of its black minorities is significant. White society denied the Indian his desire to be separate but at the same time argued that blacks remain segregated. For Sells the creation of separate units of Indian soldiers would constitute a definite setback for the progress of assimilation (Washburn 1973, p. 873).

of Commissioner John Collier (1933 to 1945),[10] who—with the strong backing of President Franklin D. Roosevelt and Harold Ickes, secretary of the interior—was primarily responsible for congressional passage of the Indian Reorganization Act, at first seems to suggest a major variation in the previously parallel policy positions of the BIA and Congress. It has been argued, for example, that Collier "literally reversed the direction of the Government's Indian policy" (Washburn 1973, p. 905). Under Collier the BIA moved to rebuild the Indian land base, revitalize tribal organizations, and reestablish respect for Indian cultural traditions. Congress gradually became so disenchanted with Collier's policies that by 1944 the Senate Indian Affairs Subcommittee had proposed a long-range program to liquidate the BIA and the House began an investigation of the bureau (Tyler 1964, p. 56).

Although congressional attacks on Commissioner Collier's administration were certainly real, their differences were over the means of attaining assimilation, not the desirability of assimilation as such. Congress was impatient and did not believe that reestablishment of the Indians' political and cultural base was a practical strategy for integrating Indians into American society. There can be little doubt, however, that Collier believed in a long-range policy of assimilation. In defense of the act and his administration Collier stated: "If we think of the tribes as communities and of tribal self-government as local civic government, in the modern democratic sense, we can divest ourselves of the lingering fear that 'tribalism' is a regression and can look upon it as the most important single step in assimilating Indians to modern democratic life" (Collier 1943, pp. 1–2).[11]

[10] Collier's departure from the BIA corresponded, to the month, with President Roosevelt's death in March, 1945 (Washburn 1973, p. 905).

[11] Further discussion of the BIA's successes and failures in the implementation of the act is readily available from several sources: Collier 1953; Cohen 1971; Tyler 1964; Zimmerman 1957; Schusky 1970. Not everyone agrees that Collier's ultimate objective was Indian assimilation. Some argue that Collier saw Indian *communities* eventually fitting into the fabric of American life as entities which interacted with the larger culture without loss of their separate tribal identities (Lurie 1978; Butler 1978, pp. 51–52).

With the resignation of Commissioner Collier in 1945, Congress moved rapidly to force the BIA back into line by threatening and then executing cuts in BIA appropriations and staff positions (Warne 1948; Tyler 1964, pp. 29–30). In 1947 the Senate Public Lands Committee "compelled" Acting Commissioner William Zimmerman to produce a classification of tribes with target dates for "freedom from wardship" (*New York Times,* March 6, 1950). Using such criteria as "the degree of acculturation, economic resources and condition of the tribe, the willingness of the tribe to be relieved of federal control, and the willingness of the State to take over," the commissioner responded with a list dividing the tribes of the United States into three groups: group one, which "could be released now from federal supervision"; group two, which could be released "in 10 years"; and group three, which would require "indefinite time" before release (U.S., House, Report 2503, 1947, pp. 164–65). The "Zimmerman Report," as it was later called, was based largely upon the impressions and opinions of the bureau's superintendent and other officials, together with limited economic data on tribal physical and monetary resources. It was used extensively by Congress to formulate the provisions of the Termination Act.

The 1952 report of Commissioner Dillon Myer not only reveals total bureau compliance with the termination mood of Congress but also reflects an effort to anticipate congressional policy desires. The commissioner discussed the creation of a Division of Program within the bureau's central office to prepare tribes for a "step-by-step withdrawal of the Bureau from their affairs," the transfer of Indian health services from the bureau to state and local agencies, and the transfer of jurisdictional responsibilities for civil law from the federal government to the states. A program to encourage Indians to seek loans from banks and other private credit institutions rather than the bureau was also discussed (Myer 1952, pp. 389–95).

In addition Commissioner Myer, whose previous experience in government service included a position as director of the World War II Japanese-American Relocation Program (Burnett 1972, p. 567), vigorously pursued a "Voluntary Relocation Program" designed to move Indians off the reservation into selected major cities across the country. Each "volunteer" was provided with a one-way fare to a relocation center, a small subsidy, and limited social-welfare services for a year. He was also encouraged to merge with the non-Indian work force in the cities. The program proved to be a disaster for the Indians. Too many of those who relocated moved to the worst sections of large cities, where, unable to find work, they became "ghettoized" and subject to a kind of racism they had previously been spared (Lurie 1973, p. iii).[12]

By 1953 the policy of the BIA "from Commissioner to field clerk was to get rid of Indians as quickly as possible." Continuing in Deloria's words, "When the termination hearings were later held, the bureau had much to say. It gave every possible excuse to get rid of the particular tribe which was under consideration" (Deloria 1969, p. 67).

Historically a general lack of interest in Indian affairs by United States presidents indirectly constituted support for proponents of Indian assimilation in Congress and the BIA. With the exception of Andrew Jackson few presidents are well known for their contributions to the evolution of American Indian policy. Moreover, the recognition accorded to President Jackson is of doubtful distinction, since he is considered responsible for development of the "removal policies" of the early 1800s (Schusky 1970, pp. 22–23). Presidents Theodore and Franklin Roosevelt made less dramatic but important contributions to the sharply contrasting Indian policies of their respective administrations. President Theodore Roosevelt applauded the General Allotment Act as "a mighty pulverizing engine to break up the tribal mass" (Roosevelt 1901). President Franklin Roosevelt strongly backed Commissioner Collier's administration of the Indian Reorganization Act, which was designed to arrest the negative impacts of allotment (Tyler 1964, p. 48).

---

[12] Corresponding stagnation and destabilization occurred on several reservations when many of the younger, better-educated urban Indians began opposing tribal leaders and favoring the termination of their home reservations and the division of tribal assets (Svensson 1973, pp. 34–35).

In general, because of the power of his office, a president always plays an important role in Indian policy, even when he fails to take an active part in Indian affairs. For example, President James A. Garfield felt compelled to say that "no branch of the national government is so spotted with fraud, so tainted with corruption, so utterly unworthy of a free and enlightened government, as this Indian department" (Orfield 1965, chap. 4, p. 1). Unfortunately, subsequent presidential inaction directly contributed to a persistence of the conditions described by President Garfield.

In 1953, on the eve of termination, President Eisenhower assumed office, carrying with him Republican majorities in both houses of Congress. He shared with Congress a concern about the dangers of an excessive concentration of power in government and a desire to reduce the federal budget (Grodzins 1961, p. 5). Although he questioned the wisdom of certain congressional policy initiatives,[13] he considered emerging legislative trends in Indian affairs to be necessary steps toward complete Indian equality (W. Brophy 1966, p. 186).

National public opinion in the early fifties also provided indirect support for policies promoting accelerated Indian assimilation. Over the years the attitude of white Americans toward Indians suggests a kind of national schizophrenia. One side of the personality is characterized by ruthless greed for Indian land, total disregard for Indian culture and tradition, and an almost maniacal desire to hammer the Indian into his own image. The other side is represented by glossy-paged historical images of the noble savage, endless well-meaning but naïve solutions to "the Indian's plight," and used-clothing drives.

In the 1950s there was a growing unitary conception of the American way of life: "Mass Society was foreseen as a rather homogenously shared culture in which most persons would share values and beliefs, would hold to common aims, would

[13] Upon signing Public Law 280 into law in 1953, the president noted that it "was unfortunate" that the act did not include a provision for consultating the tribes before criminal and civil jurisdiction over their reservations was transferred from federal to state authority (W. Brophy et al. 1966, p. 186).

follow similar life styles, and thus would behave in similar
ways" (Rittel and Webber 1973, pp. 167–68). Most American
Indians, however, persistently adhered to an "unrealistic"
desire to maintain a separate identity. Such behavior was
incomprehensible. Assimilation simply had to be the right
answer. Give Indians the incentive and some initial assistance, a chance to succeed, and they would adopt the superior values of white culture (Orfield 1965, chap. 1, p. 1, chap.
4, p. 1). Separation from their reservations was viewed as
one way to instill in Indians the required incentive.

Over the years non-Indian criticism of federal policies
promoting rapid Indian assimilation was heard sporadically,
particularly in the federal courts.

The most important legal decisions affecting Indian policy
were handed down by the Supreme Court over 120 years
before passage of the Termination Act. In 1831 the Court
defended tribal sovereignty by ruling that the state of Georgia
had no authority to extend arbitrarily its jurisdiction over
the Cherokee Nation. Rather the tribe must be considered
a sovereign domestic dependent nation empowered to regulate its own affairs, limited only by acts of Congress (Burnett 1972, p. 559).

This decision (*Cherokee Nation* v. *Georgia*, 30 U.S. [5 Pet.]
1 [1831]) also produced the famous descriptive analogy char-
acterizing the Indian's relationship to the federal government as that of a "ward to his guardian." Unfortunately the
analogy is misleading. Although the federal government is
a trustee of Indian property, it is not the legal guardian of
individual Indians.

The Court reaffirmed and amplified its decision the following year in a second landmark case (*Worchester* v. *Georgia*,
31 U.S. [6 Pet.] 515 [1832]). Chief Justice John Marshall,
speaking for the Court, expressed

> the universal conviction that the Indian nations possessed a full
> right to the lands they occupied, until that right should be ex-
> tinguished by the United States with their consent; that their
> territory was separated from that of any State within whose char-
> tered limits they might reside, by a boundary line, established
> by treaties; that within their boundary, they possessed the rights
> with which no State could interfere.

Moreover, concerning the Indians' right to self-determination as communities, the chief justice argued:

> The very fact of repeated treaties with them recognizes it; and the settled doctrine of the law of nations is that a weaker power does not surrender its independence—its right to self government, by associating with a stronger and taking its protection. A weak State in order to provide for its safety, may place itself under the protection of one more powerful without stripping itself of the right of government and ceasing to be a State. (Lurie 1971a, pp. 428–29).

In ensuing years Congress, the BIA, and the states gradually eroded the Court's affirmed principle of tribal sovereignty to the point where Indians retained jurisdiction only over minor offenses committed on their reservation (Burnett 1972, pp. 558–64).[14] Yet despite considerable abridgment, the two decisions were never overturned. They are still widely cited to support Indian claims to the right of tribal sovereignty.

Another branch of the federal-court system, the United States Court of Claims has also become significantly involved in Indian affairs. In the 1860s, Indian tribes began appearing in federal courts to argue for compensation for alleged injustices by the government. Congress responded by passing legislation to forbid Indian tribes standing to sue (Deloria 1971, p. 142). Then in 1946, partly because of the pressure

---

[14]While the Seven Major Crimes Act (1885) removed such major offenses as murder, manslaughter, and rape from trial jurisdiction, to say that "Indians only retained jurisdiction over minor offenses" may be somewhat misleading. Today Indian tribes retain the power to make laws and regulations for the administration of justice and also have the authority to maintain law-enforcement departments and courts. Generally Indian courts have jurisdiction over cases involving tribal affairs, over civil suits brought by Indians or non-Indians against tribal members arising from matters occurring on the reservation, and over prosecuting violations of the tribal criminal code. Federal and state courts do not have jurisdiction over matters involving violations of tribal ordinances. In cases within their jurisdiction the decision of tribal courts cannot be appealed to state or federal courts. In 1968, Congress passed the Indian Civil Rights Act, which further limited tribal jurisdiction by confining the jurisdiction of Indian courts to criminal offenses punishable by fines of less than five hundred dollars or six months in jail (M. Smith 1973, p. 13).

of mounting claims, Congress reversed itself to pass the Indian Claims Commission Act. Despite subsequent complaints
about the fairness and speed of the commission, tribal access
to the court of claims did result in many awards, often total-
ing millions of dollars, to compensate Indians for illegal
seizures of their land and mismanagement of tribal affairs
by the BIA.

The function of the courts is to determine the constitu-
tionality of actions taken by the other branches of government. In doing so, they have provided Indians an avenue for
obtaining compensation for some of the more harmful consequences of past assimilation strategies. To a limited extent
they have also checked the federal government's historical
tendency to employ flagrantly unjust tactics to force Indian
assimilation.

Before 1954 the most strongly expressed opposition to policies promoting rapid Indian assimilation came from Indians
themselves. Eventually their opposition broke out of the
boundaries of the reservations to reach the Washington offices
of the BIA and the United States Congress.

Indian views of assimilation before the advent of termination policy can be summarized in three categories: assimila-
tionists, antiassimilation traditionalists, and antiassimilation
moderates. Conceivably a fourth category also exists representing the views toward assimilation of an unknown number
of Indians already assimilated into the larger society. Their
assimilation, however, makes it all but impossible to identify
or examine this category. Discussion will be confined to the
first three categories.

During the eighteenth and nineteenth centuries political
representation of Indians in the national political arena was
largely restricted to non-Indians who identified themselves
as "friends of the Indians." As many Indians became more
politically sophisticated, however, they also became increasingly dissatisfied with non-Indian representation of their interests. The Society of American Indians (SAI), formed in
1911, represented the first nationally based expression of this
dissatisfaction. Composed of Indians from several different
tribes, the SAI proclaimed two major themes: pan-Indianism
—a belief that because Indians share a common destiny they

should be guided politically and socially by that destiny—and assimilation—a belief that Indians "should adopt the culture and life style of the dominant non-Indian majority, while retaining a pride in their racial identity and those of their values which most closely approximated 'European' ones" (Svensson 1973, p. 29).

Oddly enough, the SAI opposed the BIA not because its members wanted improved services from the bureau but because they thought that the bureau was doing too good a job of perpetuating tribalism and traditional Indian cultures. The BIA, they believed, was needlessly prolonging the amount of time needed to transform Indians into typical "Americans" (Svensson 1973, pp. 28–29).

Although the SAI soon declined as tribalism began emerging as a political force, the proassimilation stand of the society requires an explanation. Previous studies of the society's membership reveal that they were typically of part-white or intertribal descent, often married whites or members of other tribes, spoke English when few Indians could, had at least a few years of formal education (usually in BIA schools), engaged in occupations typical of those of white society, and often belonged to Christian churches and other non-Indian organizations (Svensson 1973, p. 29). In other words, the first Indians to acquire the education and sophistication necessary to survive in white society favored assimilation. When the sophistication required for survival gradually reached the greater mass of Indians still maintaining traditional lifeways on reservations, however, it was not used to further the assimilation of individual tribal members. Rather it was used to promote the survival and integrity of Indian communities apart from white society.

Two kinds of national Indian organizations, both opposed to assimilation, evolved with the decline of the SAI. The first, represented by the League of Nations–Pan American Indians (LN–PAI), took an uncompromising "traditionalist" policy position. Citing a "trail of broken treaties," the traditionalists argued for recognition of Indian tribes as virtual nations or mini-states in peaceful treaty relationships with the United States. Tribal grievances should be referred not to Washington but to the United Nations. They also sought to restore customary tribal forms of self-government to manage their internal affairs (Lurie 1971a, pp. 453–55).

A contrasting "moderate" position on assimilation is represented by the National Congress of American Indians (NCAI). In part growing out of an effort to capitalize on the positive qualities of the Indian Reorganization Act, the NCAI's primary purpose was to lobby in Washington, D.C., for Indian programs and against legislation contrary to Indian interests, to provide legal services in the pursuit of litigation on Indian rights, and to establish a national Indian political movement based upon a coalition of tribal organizations (Svensson 1973, p. 30). The NCAI position on assimilation was summarized as follows:

> 1) Indian groups residing on reservations will continue indefinitely as distinct social units; 2) although Indian communities resist assimilation, they are constantly making adjustments to life around them; 3) although Indian cultures, as self-contained systems will probably disappear eventually, this fact does not seem to many Indians to be a reason for abandoning their present way of life; 4) optional assimilation on an individual basis, unlike forced assimilation, would leave the way open for assimilation to occur at the speed and in the direction which the people themselves desire; 5) even though many Indians continue to live in separate communities with some distinctive cultural patterns, integration into the life of the larger society can still take place. [Dozier et al. 1957, pp. 163–65.]

The moderates thought that the traditionalists' position was unrealistic and irresponsible. If seriously pursued, they argued that it would so seriously alienate public sympathy that even moderate forms of self-determination would become impossible to achieve. On the other hand, while traditionalists recognized that Indians must make adjustments and work with respected sources of power to survive in the modern world, they did not believe it was necessary to accede to all the white values and organizational structures implicit in the moderates' position (Lurie 1971a, pp. 454–55).

Although the traditionalists and moderates disagreed over the amount of accommodation necessary to survive within an assimilation-minded white society, they were quick to unite in vehement opposition to the passage in 1953 of House Concurrent Resolution 108. In their view the Indian's special legal status represented a continuing acknowledgment that they were the aboriginal owners of North America and that the United States had entered into a formal contractual arrangement with them to extinguish their title and acquire the land. The various services provided by the government were simply part of the continuing legal obligation of the United States to compensate the former owners (Svensson 1973, pp. 31–32). The stated determination of Congress to terminate all federal responsibility for special services for the Indians and end federal protection for remaining Indian land represented an attack on their land, their treaties, and their right to be Indian (Lurie 1973, p. 24).

3

# THE MENOMINEE GOVERNING ELITE

*All available evidence of reports on this tribe, and statistics on its
economic and social condition, reinforce the conclusion that the Tribe
is fully ready for removal from Indian Bureau tutelage. In fact most
of the available reports put the Menominees about at the top of
advancement among the individual Indian tribes. As long ago as 1930
the Menominees were five-sixths assimilated to modern American way
way of life.* — Senator Arthur V. Watkins, Congressional Debate,
1953

By the early 1950s, Congress and the BIA were moving
rapidly toward termination as a new strategy for vigorously
pursuing Indian assimilation. To assure a successful launch-
ing of the new policy, federal officials wanted to begin by
terminating tribes that were the most prosperous and, therefore, the most likely to integrate with ease into non-Indian
society. The Menominee tribe seemed a likely candidate.
National policymakers correctly concluded that the Menominees were one of the most "advanced" tribes in the nation
but incorrectly assumed that their relative prosperity, compared with that of other tribes, adequately prepared them for
successful economic and social advancement without their
reservation. The assumption that the Menominees were "highly
advanced" and "five-sixths assimilated to modern American
way of life" was the dominant factor in the congressional
decision to single out the Menominee tribe for termination.

This congressional image of the tribe was based upon
limited contact with a small governing minority of the tribal
elite. The Menominee elite appeared ready for rapid assimilation. The tribal membership as a whole, however, was criti-
cally ill prepared for abrupt integration into the larger social
and political system. Elite theory suggests several reasons for
this mistaken perception of the Menominee tribe.[1]

According to elite theory, complex patterns of human political and social behavior collectively determine a society's structural characteristics. Society is divided into the few who have power and the masses who do not. Governing elites are not like the masses who are governed. The governing elites are drawn disproportionately from the upper socioeconomic levels of society. They generally agree on the basic values of society and the need to preserve the social system. The shared values of elites in the United States include a dedication to private property, limited government, and individual liberty. While nonelites can become elites, the movement upward is slow and restricted so that social and political stability can be maintained. Only nonelites who have accepted basic elite values are admitted to governing circles. Finally, elite theory suggests that a small number of elites define public policy for the entire society. The apathetic masses exert very little influence on governing elites.[2]

The creators of elite theory were thinking about a national governing elite in a major political system like the United States. The Menominee Reservation was a very different community. There were 3,059 enrolled Menominees in the United States in 1952, 80 percent of whom lived on tribal lands. The 233,902-acre reservation was largely undeveloped, with 95 percent of its acreage covered by mixed hardwood and softwood forests. A tribally owned sawmill and other subsidiary industries accounted for almost the entire economic base of the reservation. The total estimated replacement value of the combined forest operation was $6 million.[3] Employment opportunities on the reservation were inadequate for full employment, and the economy of the area was wholly dependent upon an unstable national market for raw forest products.

[1]The existence of political elites was first suggested in the works of Aristotle, Duc de Saint-Simon; Gaetano Mosca; and Vilfredo Pareto (Keller 1963; Bacharach 1967). For subsequent revisions and additions to the theory see Lasswell and Kaplan 1950; Kornhauser 1959; Bacharach 1967; Dahl 1961; Dye and Zeigler 1970; Parenti 1978.

[2]This summation of elite theory was taken from Dye 1973, pp. 24–26; Dye and Zeigler 1970, pp. 1–6; Bacharach 1967, pp. 1–9.

[3]By 1954 capital investment for industrial development on the reservation totaled $1.5 million (Joint Hearings 1954, pp. 589–91).

In physical and economic terms few parallels exist between the Menominee Reservation and the United States as a whole. Moreover, the Menominees' cultural and historical traditions are those of Native Americans, not those of the larger American society. Despite these and other dissimilarities, elite theory still provides a useful framework for examining the social and political features of the tribe before termination.

Only a few Menominees are members of the tribal elite. Using the level of acculturation or adaptation to the dominant white society and economic status as differentiative criteria, two anthropologists, George Spindler and Louise Spindler, identify five major "cultural divisions" within the Menominee tribe: "native-oriented," "Peyotist," "transitional," "lower-status-acculturated," and "elite-acculturated" groups (Spindler and Spindler 1971, pp. 2–5).[4]

More specifically, the Spindlers established the relative position of the cultural groups statistically, employing indices of occupation, education, and language, as well as such indices as possession and kind of household furnishings, display of native objects, and participation in religious activities. Their data were derived from extensive interviews conducted during summer field-work with the Menominees from 1948 to 1956. The Spindlers' book *Dreamers Without Power: The Menominee Indians* is the most penetrating anthropological study of the tribe currently available.

Diminishing numbers, or a "handful," of native-oriented tribal members live in and around a small reservation community cailed Zoar. This group has most closely adhered to aboriginal Menominee traditions, including the Dream Dance (conducted in native language), the Medicine Lodge, the War (or Chief's) Dance, and other rituals—all of a religious character. Spindler and Spindler suggest that the latescent, quiescent, enduring self-control of the native-

---

[4]Before termination the Menominee governing elite were members of but did not comprise the entire membership of the elite-acculturated category. Since, however, the governing elite and elite-acculturated categories shared the same background, attitudinal, and socioeconomic characteristics, the two groups will be treated as one until discussion turns specifically to the political leadership of the tribe.

oriented group is not functional in the socioeconomic and political context of white society. They conclude that, although the group has shown "some signs of continued vitality, . . . their future seems very doubtful" (Spindler and Spindler 1971, p. 193).

The Peyotists, although more dispersed, also live in the Zoar area, interact with the native-oriented more than any other group, and share many common traditional beliefs and values. They differ from the native-oriented group in their more extensive contact with non-Indian culture, their membership in the Native American church, and their distinctive rituals, which incorporate the eating of peyote. Like the native-oriented, however, the Peyotists are also declining in numbers, and Spindler and Spindler conclude that it is also difficult to see how the Peyotists can survive long as a culturally distinct group.

Most Menominees, particularly those over thirty, are transitionals. Included in the division are "individuals loosely joined together in informal groupings, such as drinking groups, people who are almost wholly isolated, and people who are striving toward fuller participation in the non-Menominee world" (Spindler and Spindler 1971, p. 2). Transitionals generally share a common early experience with more traditional cultural divisions but have moved away from a strong identification with either the native-oriented group or with the Peyotists. Many have become nominal, or, to use their term, "lukewarm" Roman Catholics. Described as being in "a kind of cultural no-man's land," Spindler and Spindler conclude that transitionals have experienced a deterioration of their native-oriented backgrounds without any corresponding cultural or psychological assimilation into the cultural patterns of white society.

The last two categories identified by Spindler and Spindler, the lower-status-acculturated and elite-acculturated groups, differ mainly in terms of the higher socioeconomic development of the latter. Both groups have become overtly assimilated into Western cultural patterns. Neither group identifies strongly with the more traditional cultural divisions. Both groups are predominately Roman Catholics, although the elite acculturated "tend to be more devout in their partici-

pation in the church" (Spindler and Spindler 1971, p. 185).
A major distinction between the two groups is their respective occupational status. The lower-status acculturated are
generally confined to jobs that, while not menial, are not
managerial or professional positions. The distinction is, in
turn, reflected in the style, size, condition, and furnishing
of the homes of the two groups. Today elite-acculturated
homes tend to be indistinguishable from the homes of non-
Menominee business and professional people in surrounding
non-Indian communities.

Spindler and Spindler concluded their analysis of the five
Menominee acculturative divisions by observing that the
elite-acculturated group "holds power and wealth disproportionate to its number. . . . The heads of elite-acculturated
families are 'the people who run things'" (Spindler and Spindler 1971, pp. 177, 184). Before termination the elite acculturated held the highest-level positions available to Menominees in the lumber industry and tribal government supervised by the BIA. In a real sense their status within Menominee society was very similar to the theoretical position
of an elite minority in the greater American society.

Elite theory assumes that elites generally agree on the basic
values of society, such as a shared dedication to private property, limited government, and individual liberty. They also
agree on the need to maintain the social system that supports their elite status. While the Menominee acculturated
elite agree on certain societal values, the bases for agreement on those values were distinct from those suggested for
the elite in the United States as a whole. Before termination
the sanctity of private property, limited government, and
individual liberty had limited relevance for Indians whose
land was held in trust by the federal government and whose
life was supervised by the Bureau of Indian Affairs.

The Menominee elite acculturated represent those who
have "made it" in white society. To adapt and even prosper
from contact with the dominant American society, the Menominee elite have tried to become like the members of that
society. Consequently, they have assumed a "cultural stance
that . . . is essentially small town, middle-class, middle-West-
ern White, with something else added, almost indefinable,

that is 'Indian,' and more cosmopolitan" (Spindler and Spindler 1971, p. 189).

The Menominee elite share a corresponding set of societal values that include reverence for hard work, progress, and material status. High value is also placed upon respectability and orderliness. "Above all, the elite avoid associations and behaviors that, as they see it, would identify them with stereotypes whites have of Indians, such as public drunkenness, irresponsibility, or slovenly behavior or appearance" (Spindler and Spindler 1971, p. 185).

In sum, the Menominee elite, before termination, shared a consensus on societal values; however, that consensus was based upon a middle-class white American model rather than on the traditional society of the Menominee Indian. Moreover, the elite acculturated were more concerned with admittance into the dominant white society than with the preservation of their own traditional social system.

While nonelites can become elites, elite theory suggests that the movement upward is slow and restricted so that social and political stability can be preserved. Only nonelites who have accepted basic elite values are accepted into governing circles. Before termination upward mobility into the Menominee elite acculturated clearly conformed with the theory. Spindler and Spindler noted that most of the elite-acculturated group "were born into families that had already substantially adopted the white man's way" (Spindler and Spindler 1971, p. 185). In fact, 76 percent of the Spindler sample of twenty-one elite-acculturated Menominees were born into the elite—five of thirteen men and eight of eight women (Spindler and Spindler 1971, p. 185). All those who made the transition to elite-acculturated status during their lifetimes also adopted elite characteristics previously discussed, including the loss of contact with traditional Menominee culture, use of English in the home, and "superior Catholicism."

The elite acculturated also maintained a distinct social distance between themselves and other cultural groups, preferring to associate with their own kind or whites in nearby towns. Unlike other groups, the elite acculturated tended to be active "joiners" in various social clubs, including conservation groups and a saddle club. It is clear that upward mobility into the Menominee elite community was difficult but did sometimes occur. The integrity of Menominee cultural divisions and stability of Menominee society as a whole was safeguarded, with the elite acculturated maintaining the dominant social position in the tribe.

Elite theory proposes that only a small number of elites formulate public policy for society. Governing elites are subject to relatively little direct influence from the apathetic masses. Elites influence the masses far more than the masses influence elites.

At first glance the presence of the BIA reservation superintendent and his non-Menominee administrative staff would appear to nullify the basic theoretical requirement that the elite must formulate public policy for the masses. While the Menominees acquired a certain measure of control over their own affairs, including the right to review and approve in advance the bureau's reservation budget, the primary responsibility for tribal affairs remained with the BIA (Orfield 1965, chap. 4, pp. 2–3).

Despite the Menominees' obvious lack of policy-making autonomy, elite theory is still a useful device for examining tribal politics and policy-making processes. While the tribal elite did not retain exclusive control over tribal affairs, they did establish a symbolic relationship with the Bureau of Indian Affairs which, in practical terms, allowed the elite to maintain their dominant policy-making position over the tribal membership.

The curious alliance of the local representatives of a dominant external political power and members of a local native elite is nothing new to those familiar with European colonization of native populations in subjected colonial territories.[5] Colonists established control by subduing native leaders, either directly through military action or indirectly by removing their basis of power. For example, by converting a native population to Christianity, colonists often weak-

[5] By no means a radical idea, the analogy between reservation and colony has recently been advanced by the United States government. See United States Commission on Civil Rights, "The Navajo Nation: An American Colony," September, 1975.

ened or destroyed a native leader's authority over his subjects. After several years of colonization a new native elite gradually emerged. Its authority was based on adaptability to the colonists' superior authority. By adopting the colonists' language, religion, and many of their values, the native elite maintained a position of co-existence with colonial authorities. The relationship between colonist and native elite was symbiotic because the colonists used the native elite to maintain order within the colony, usually by training them as lower-level administrators or petty public officials. The native elite, in turn, was dependent upon the presence of the colonists since the native elite's authority was based upon the artificially imposed values and requirements of the colonist, not the values and needs of the native society. Many tribes, living on reservations, underwent a pattern of evolution similar to that of a colonial experience.

Between 1827 and 1848 most of the Menominee land base which encompassed much of central and northeastern Wisconsin was ceded to the United States through a series of treaties (see figure 1). In 1890 the federal government weakened the traditional authority of the tribal chiefs by persuading them to exchange their titles for appointments as tribal judges. This action converted the position of tribal chief into a federally appointed position (Orfield 1965, chap. 3, pp. 1–3). By the beginning of the twentieth century the modification and disintegration of the historic Menominee tribal culture was nearly complete (Keesing 1939).[6]

Gary Orfield suggests that the end result of the experience for the Menominees was the emergence of a "reservation culture." Reservation life, with its dependence upon federal supervision, fostered a distinct new system of values and expectations. Tribal members grew to expect a wide variety of services without charge. They expected government care when they were in need, or jobs when they needed money, despite high job absenteeism, especially after paydays and during the hunting and fishing seasons. Only a few of the Menominees had any drive to save and invest to improve

[6]The early history of the Menominee tribe is available from several studies. See Keesing 1939; Shames, ed., 1972, pp. 1–17; Ray 1971, pp. 4–28.

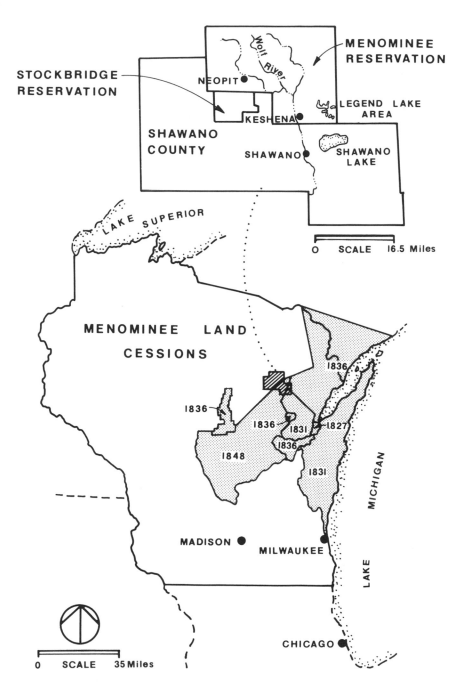

STOCKBRIDGE
RESERVATION

MENOMINEE
RESERVATION

NEOPIT

Wolf River

LEGEND LAKE
AREA

KESHENA

SHAWANO
COUNTY

SHAWANO

SHAWANO
LAKE

0    SCALE    16.5 Miles

LAKE SUPERIOR

MENOMINEE   LAND

CESSIONS

1836

1836

1836    1831    1827

1836

1848

1831

MICHIGAN

MADISON

MILWAUKEE

LAKE

0    SCALE    35 Miles

CHICAGO

*Menominee County and Menominee land cessions, 1827 to 1972.*

their economic status. Most tribal members were satisfied as long as they could support themselves from day to day. Orfield concludes his characterization of reservation culture by noting that "only a small elite shared the middle class values common to a small town" (Orfield 1965, chap. 6, p. 2).

The "small middle-class reservation elite" cited by Orfield and the "elite-acculturated group" discovered by Spindler and Spindler both suggest the existence of a small number of Menominees who are uncharacteristic of the tribe as a whole. Orfield's middle-class reservation elite are not captives of the reservation culture but rather are able to adapt and prosper in that culture. Spindler and Spindler's elite acculturated have evolved from the traditional Menominee culture, beyond the transitional stage, to become the most prosperous division in Menominee society. Both studies refer to a Menominee socioeconomic elite. The Menominee governing elite can be distinguished from this larger group of elites.

In his studies of colonialism James S. Coleman notes that native colonial societies generally undergo a period of "elite differentiation" characterized by continuous interelite tension and conflict. Politics tends to be almost an exclusive phenomena of competing elites (Coleman 1971, p. 81). Nancy O. Lurie, an anthropologist, describes a similar pattern of interelite conflict and differentiation on American Indian reservations:

> Tribesmen who became cynically astute in manipulating the reservation system for personal gain were often favored by bureau personnel because they appeared enterprising in white terms. Many Indian people came to see poverty and uncompromising negativism toward any bureau suggestion as badges of personal integrity. Other people, who for various reasons had become effectively self-supporting and could have been prosperous, curtailed conspicuous evidence of their well-being and shared their wealth with sufficient generosity to maintain community respect and cooperation. To whites these natural leaders . . . appeared to encourage sloth by supporting "lazy" relatives rather than acting as exemplary models of competitive white acquisitiveness with their houses and other possessions. They often left home, weary of the struggle between bureau and community. Thus a great deal of potentially qualified leadership was regularly spun

*Location of Menominee County in Wisconsin.*

off the reservations . . . [and] reservation life fostered an amazing
skill in political maneuvering of sources of power. . . . Such negotiating had an old history, but the reservation situation cor-
rupted and narrowed it until it became almost an end unto itself.
[Lurie 1971a, p. 435]

The direct and indirect impact of the BIA on elite differentiation on American Indian reservations is readily apparent. On the Menominee Reservation those who developed
the political skills necessary to survive the demands of the
Bureau of Indian Affairs and those of their own society
evolved into the Menominee governing elite. The political
power and policy-making influence exercised by the governing elite can best be understood when placed in the context
of Menominee tribal politics before termination.

Even before the complete decline of the traditional authority of the tribal chiefs, the Menominees established a "business committee" to govern certain tribal activities; however,
before 1928 the committee was discarded as an unsatisfactory
governing mechanism. In 1934 the Menominees rejected the
self-governing provisions of the Indian Reorganization Act,
partly because of the tribe's satisfaction with its existing system of tribal government (Ray 1965, pp. 10–11).

A constitutionally defined tribal government was first established in 1928 as a mechanism for making suggestions to
the Bureau of Indian Affairs. Formal political power was
placed in two bodies, the General Council and the Advisory
Council. With a voting membership of all adult Menominees,
the General Council was designed as the principal political
voice of the tribe. By contrast, a majority of the twelve-mem-
ber Advisory Council were acculturated elites.[7] Advisory
Council members were elected by the tribe and exercised
formal governing authority between meetings of the General

[7]This statement is based on tribal records of the Advisory Council's
membership and interviews with former Advisory Council members. Six
of the members were elected as representatives of designated voting districts in the reservation, and six were elected at large. One of the voting
districts comprised the "native-oriented" community of Zoar, thereby assuring at least one Advisory Council member from this group. For a detailed discussion of the Advisory Council's acquisition and use of its powers,
see Sady 1947.

Council. The General Council retained the authority to repeal any decision of the Advisory Council within sixty days
of the Advisory Council's action.

Before termination formal political power on the reservation lay with the majority of adult Menominee tribal members in the General Council. In practical terms, however, the
General Council's inability to execute its own legislative authority led to a default of policy-making power to the elite-
dominated Advisory Council.

There were many interrelated reasons for the General
Council's ineffectiveness. Problems caused by an unwieldy
size (a quorum of seventy-five was required), unpredictable
composition, and an irregular meeting schedule were com-
pounded by tribal reluctance to appoint a permanent leader
to chair council meetings. A new chairman was appointed
at each session. Many of the distinctive values and related
behavior of Native Americans played a part in the council's
ineffectiveness. Such behavior included a preference for decisions by consensus.[8] "Decision by consensus" refers to the
aboriginal practice of discussing an issue until everyone was
aware of the consensus, at which time all, or nearly all, of the
members vote with the majority, regardless of individual
preferences or convictions (Ray 1971, p. 50). Such behavior
placed a high value on oratory as pure artistry, a "respect
for people" (which translated into a tolerance for unlimited
discussion of any issue raised by any member regardless of
the agenda), a tendency to vote with the recommendations
of tribal leaders even when one is in personal disagreement
with the leader, and a belief that no council action was irrevocable because any decision could be reversed at a later
meeting. One other kind of behavior which further detracted
from the council's effectiveness was absence: it could be used
as a means of withdrawal from an anxiety-producing situation
if an unacceptable issue came up for discussion or as a sign
of protest over a pending issue (Ray 1971, pp. 50–51; Lurie
1971a, pp. 444–47).

[8] As one example of this common pattern, the controversial Menominee
tribal vote on adoption of the Indian Reorganization Act (1934) was 596
no and 15 yes out of a total voting population of 1,020 (Haas 1947, p. 20).

High interfactional rivalries within the tribe also carried over into the General Council. Such rivalries represented ongoing conflicts between various large Menominee families, competition among the followers of several self-appointed tribal leaders, and a mutual distrust among the several socio-economic and cultural divisions within the tribe. General Council meetings provided a readily available arena in which interfactional disputes could flourish (Spindler 1955, p. 5406; Orfield 1965, chap. 3, p. 4). Finally, a chronic disinterest in the General Council's activities created problems. Orfield notes that the Menominees were "overwhelmingly apathetic toward tribal government. They were suspicious of the leaders and easily swayed by popular opponents" (Orfield 1965, chap. 3, p. 3). Obtaining General Council quorums for meetings was thus extremely difficult.

Orfield notes that even during a later twenty-eight month period, which was highly charged with debate over termination, only about one-half of the thirteen called General Council meetings drew a quorum of seventy-five adult Menominees, despite free transportation and free meals (Orfield 1965, chap. 3, p. 3).

While the Menominee Advisory Council certainly did not operate without conflict, it was, in relative terms, a much more effective policy-making organization than the General Council. Its membership contained a majority of acculturated elites who met at regularly scheduled monthly meetings and at additional meetings if required by pressing tribal business.[9] Moreover, the Advisory Council functioned as the primary link between the tribe and the BIA superintendent. Policy was initiated and formulated either in the Advisory Council or was conceived by the BIA and transmitted to the tribe through the Advisory Council.[10] In either case, the

[9] The suggestion that the smaller, more homogeneous Advisory Council operated as the more effective policy-making body is also supported by the literature on collective decision making. See, for example, Mancur Olson, *The Logic of Collective Action.* (Cambridge, Mass.: Harvard University Press), 1965; Robert L. Bish, *The Public Economy of Metropolitan Areas.* (Chicago: Rand McNally), 1971, pp. 35–62.

[10] A third alternative involving joint formulation of tribal policy through bargaining and negotiation between the BIA and the Advisory Council

governing elite within the Advisory Council, not the Menominee masses within the General Council, functioned as
the primary policy providers for the tribe. Before termination threatened the tribe's existence, the tribal masses within
the General Council exerted little influence on the policy-
making coalition of the governing elite and the BIA.[11]

White society's knowledge of the Menominee Indians was
primarily acquired through political interaction with tribal
governing elites on the Advisory Council or, more generally,
through limited contact with the larger group of acculturated
"middle-class" elites. Opinions and judgments based upon
limited contact with the Menominee elite led to an erroneous
assumption that the Menominee tribe, as a whole, was prepared for assimilation, or more absurdly, was already "five-
sixths assimilated to modern American way of life."

Contacts with whites, particularly those living in towns
and on farms adjoining the reservation, were much more
extensive, reaching to every Menominee group, with the
possible exception of some of the most traditional residents
of the Zoar community. Interestingly enough, there was (and
still is) little support among many local whites for the assertion that the Menominees were prepared for assimilation.

Policy "inputs" are various factors that directly or indirectly bear upon a governmental decision to change an
existing policy or develop a new one. A thorough study of
the Menominees' readiness for termination was never initiated by Congress or the BIA. A 1947 Bureau of Indian
Affairs study entitled the "Zimmerman Report" considered

---

may also have occurred, though no evidence of this pattern was available.
Any action by either the Advisory Council or the General Council had to
meet the approval of the BIA superintendent.

[11] Data on the number and nature of Advisory Council decisions actually
overturned by the General Council for a sample number of years before
termination would have provided the best basis for determining the relative power of the two councils. Unfortunately such data were not available. Personal interviews conducted in Menominee County in 1974 and
some limited data from several issues of the tribal newspaper, *Menominee
News,* for the years 1954 to 1960 support these observations.

the relative readiness of various tribes for termination and concluded that several tribes, including the Menominees, "could be released now from federal supervision" (U.S., House, Report 2503, 1947, pp. 164–65). The study, however, was not thorough or complete. Its conclusions were based mainly on the impressions and opinions of reservation super-intendents and other bureau personnel.

Without such a study the faulty assumption by Congress that the Menominees were ready for immediate assimilation was the dominant policy impact on congressional consider-ation of Menominee termination. Undoubtedly, such a study would have provided some additional inputs to support the congressional assumption that the tribe was ready for termi-nation. For example, the Menominees undeniably possessed abundant natural resources. Ninety-five percent, or 221,696 acres, of their reservation consisted of mixed hard and soft-wood forests. Sustained-yield principles of forest manage-ment were adopted in 1908. Under sustained-yield practices selection of cutting timber is based on a tree's age and over-all condition. Seedlings are regularly planted to replace har-vested trees. In 1951 a Department of Interior report opti-mistically concluded that "the timber resources of the Me-nominee Reservation have made the Menominee Tribe prac-tically self-sustaining. . . . By the selective cutting of timber, the Menominee Forest is managed on a sustained yield basis, conserving this source of income for future generations" (U.S., House, Committee on Interior and Insular Affairs, Report 642, 1961, p. 2).

Compared with that of other reservation tribes, the Me-nominees' industrial development was also quite advanced. The tribe operated a sawmill and related subsidiary indus-tries with an estimated capital investment of $1,544,740 and a replacement value of approximately $6 million. Also in-cluded as tribal assets were a small garment factory, utili-ties, community facilities, and other improvements (Joint Hearings 1954, p. 590). One white visitor to the reservation enthusiastically described the sawmill as "a two million dollar a year industry [which] not only provided employment for 550 workers, but also pays nearly the entire expense of run-ning the Reservation" (Ritzenthaler 1951, p. 1).

A pretermination study of the Menominees would also have noted the tribe's substantial monetary reserves. The tribe had approximately $10 million on deposit in the United States Treasury in 1951. A major portion of that amount ($8.5 million) was awarded to the tribe by the United States Court of Claims as a settlement for a suit alleging BIA mismanagement of tribal forest and mill operations before 1910.[12] In addition, the tribe realized enough revenue from its sawmill to pay for the cost of bureau services, including the reservation superintendent's salary. Combined federal and state assistance to the tribe represented only about 11.4 percent of the tribe's 1953–54 budget of $1,855,042 (Wisconsin Legislative Council Report 1965, p. 17). The Menominees also earned approximately $200,000 a year interest on tribal funds held by the United States Treasury (Congressional Debate 1953, p. 2039).

Although these and other inputs would have supported termination of the Menominee tribe, other information would probably have emerged from the study to argue against termination. In sociocultural terms the aboriginal characteristics of most Menominees suggest that the tribe was not prepared for rapid assimilation. Spindler and Spindler note that most of the Menominee people belonged to either the "native-oriented," "Peyotist," or "transitional" cultural divisions. Only the acculturated elite demonstrated attitudes and behavior necessary for successful integration into society outside the reservation.

The debilitating effects of life on an Indian reservation, collectively referred to earlier as "reservation culture," also lessened the probability for successful termination. The ingrained sense of dependency cultivated by the protective presence of the Bureau of Indian Affairs provided a very poor basis for successful adaptation to life outside the confines of the reservation.

The economic base of the reservation was fragile and nondiversified. While the sawmill and related industries were extensive (with a capital investment of $1.5 million), the

[12] For additional historical information on the claims case, see Nichols 1956, pp. 7–34.

tribe's economy centered solely around this industry. The economy of the area was completely tied to fluctuations in the national market for raw forest products.[13]

The Menominees possessed limited experience in nonreservation politics and business management. While the level of education reached by tribal members was similar to that of whites in neighboring Wisconsin counties,[14] the Menominees had almost no professional training in the skills necessary to a viable community. There were no local business leaders. The managers of the sawmill had always been white (Orfield 1965, chap. 6, p. 2; Ritzenthaler 1951, p. 1).

Most tribal members were opposed to or ignorant of the implications of termination. Commenting on their research conducted between 1948 and 1954, Spindler and Spindler note:

> The overwhelming majority of the Menominee were either apathetic about termination or were very much against it. When we interviewed the sixty-eight men and sixty-one women in our original sample, while termination was first being considered and discussed, there were four people in favor of it. Some people thought that eventually termination would have to come in some form, but that the phasing out should take years, along with a well-planned program of economic development, in order to avoid chaos and loss that they felt were bound to come if termination occurred all at once. The majority feared and resented termination, with varying degrees of understanding of what it was. [Spindler and Spindler 1971, p. 195]

In 1952 the chairman of the Menominee Indian Advisory Council warned that the tribe was "reaching a very critical period in [its] history" because of the intention of Congress

[13] In 1953 the estimated total income from the mill operation and miscellaneous collections (utilities, community facilities, and other) was $2,195,000. Total expenditures for the year were $2.8 million. The deficit was covered by withdrawing tribal funds from the United States Treasury (Wisconsin Legislative Council 1966, p. 13).

[14] In 1954 median education for Menominee males was 8.5 years and for females, 8.3 years. In 1952, 24.4 percent of the Menominee people were attending school, either in public schools, mission schools, or bureau boarding schools (Joint Hearings 1954, p. 590). Only 10 percent (328) of the tribe had graduated from high school, however, and only 0.3 percent (9) had graduated from college (Debo 1970, p. 309).

"to relieve either in full or in part, Federal jurisdiction and responsibility over the Menominee Reservation" (*Shawano Evening Leader,* June 19, 1952). The following response by another Menominee reflected the commonly held attitude within the tribe:

> Congress is not threatening to cut the Menominees adrift right away, neither is the Commissioner of Indian Affairs forcing the issue. . . . Anyone with common sense knows that this is a big job and will require a lot of work and planning and both Congress and the Indian Office . . . will be the first to admit that this work will not be completed in one year, nor two, nor maybe longer. When a group of people . . . have lived like the Menominees have for over a hundred years certainly no one is going to have the answers to the many problems that will face the Government and the Indians when a change is suggested. [*Shawano Evening Leader,* June 26, 1952]

Finally, data available on the tribe for the period from 1950 to 1954 reflect a population with socioeconomic problems far more severe than those of the white population in surrounding Wisconsin counties. The estimated median annual income for mill employees was $2,300, about 82 percent of that earned by surrounding non-Indian families. The balance of the population earned a median of $650 annually. Birth rates averaged 36.9 per thousand as compared with the state rate of 25.2. Infant mortality rates for the same period were 62.7 per thousand births compared with 23.5 for the state. The ratio of Menominees under the supervision of the State Division of Corrections was 10.8 per thousand population versus 2.0 per thousand for the state. Approximately one-third of the Menominees received public assistance from welfare, while one-thirty-sixth of the Wisconsin population received similar aid (Wisconsin Legislative Council 1966, p. 13).

This list of potential policy inputs, compiled almost thirty years after the decision by Congress to terminate the Menominee tribe, is undoubtedly incomplete. Much of the necessary information was never recorded or has been lost over the years. Nevertheless, a brief examination of the data that were potentially available to Congress suggests that, on balance, the tribe was a less-than-promising candidate for any new policy designed to promote rapid Indian assimilation.

*Menominee forest and Wolf River.* Capital Times, *Madison, Wis.*

*Menominee sawmill, early 1950s. Courtesy of Menominee Self-Determination Office, Keshena, Wis.*

*Spirit Rock of the Menominees.* Menominee Tribal News, Keshena, Wis.

*Legend of Spirit Rock.* Capital Times.

*An example of tourism on the Menominee Reservation before termination.* Capital Times.

# 4

# THE MENOMINEE TERMINATION ACT OF 1954

*After all, the matter of freeing the Indian from wardship status is not rightfully a subject of debate in academic fashion, with facts marshalled here and there to be maneuvered and countermaneuvered in a vast battle of words and ideas. Much more I see this as an ideal or universal truth, to which all men subscribe, and concerning which they differ only in their opinion as to how the ideal may be attained and in what degree and during what period of time.* —Senator Arthur V. Watkins, "Termination of Federal Supervision," 1957, p. 47

The decision to terminate the Menominee tribe was made entirely in Congress, or, more specifically, in the House and Senate subcommittees on Indian affairs. The first clear indicator of a congressional interest in Menominee termination occurred on February 8, 1947, when acting BIA Commissioner Zimmerman, in congressional testimony, declared that the Menominees were one of ten tribes in the United States that could be released from federal supervision (U.S., Senate, Committee on the Post Office and Civil Service, 1947). While Zimmerman stated that BIA services could be terminated, he also argued that tribal lands should remain in federal trust for fifty years to relieve tax burdens on the tribe during the transition to independence. On July 21, 1947, Senator Raymond Butler of Nebraska, apparently acting on Zimmerman's recommendation, introduced a bill in the Senate Subcommittee on Public Lands to terminate federal trusteeship of the Menominee Reservation. Senator Butler's bill was designed "to remove restrictions on the property and moneys belonging to individual enrolled members of the Menominee Indian Tribe in Wisconsin, to provide for the liquidation of Tribal property and distribution of the proceeds thereof, to confer complete citizenship upon such Indians and for other purposes" (Robertson 1961, p. 1). No congressional action was taken on the proposed legislation.

The termination issue was then dormant for three years but returned in 1951, when Congress appropriated $8.5 million to be placed in the United States Treasury for the Menominee tribe. The money represented the compromise settlement of a suit filed by the tribe in 1935 alleging mismanagement of tribal assets by the BIA. A special committee of the Menominee Advisory Council developed for submission to Congress a $9.5 million program for reservation development, using the claims-case award and previous tribal funds already on deposit in the United States Treasury. The program included a plan to underwrite and expand the tribe's lumber operation; develop other plans for industrial diversification, conservation, social and village improvements; and provide for a per capita payment of $1,000 to each enrolled tribal member. In January, 1953, the Menominee General Council superseded the Advisory Council and changed the program to request a $1,500 per capita payment. The pressure for an increased per capita payment came from tribal members acting through their votes in the General Council. This fact has been distorted in some accounts of termination. For example, Kirke Kickingbird and Karen Ducheneaux have argued that Congress "had to sweeten the pot a little to get the tribal delegates to accept the termination law, and so, instead of a per capita payment of $1,000, the legislation authorized a payment of $1,500 per member" (Kickingbird and Ducheneaux 1973, p. 149). Legislation was then submitted in both the House and the Senate authorizing the per capita payment but not the tribe's development program.[1]

In late 1951 the Bureau of Indian Affairs began urging the Menominees to prepare for termination. In October, 1951, the acting commissioner of the BIA warned the tribe that "pressure was being placed in Congress and the government to eliminate the Indian Bureau and it was generally believed that this would happen" (Robertson 1961, p. 1). Several Advisory Council members stated that they were aware of the

---

[1] A per capita withdrawal of tribal funds from the United States Treasury required congressional approval.

trend but did not feel the Menominees were prepared to take over their own business affairs. In January, 1952, upon receipt of the tribe's development program, the BIA suggested that the tribe "formulate a more comprehensive program and that the program should be directed toward termination of Federal trusteeship responsibilities for the Menominees in line with the thinking of Congress" (Robertson 1961, p. 2). In March, 1952, a tribal delegation to Washington responded to BIA Commissioner Myer in a memorandum stating its willingness "to recommend to the tribe that it consider taking over all of its own affairs within two years except operation of the Menominee Indian Mills" (Robertson 1961, p. 3). The BIA was not satisfied, however, and recommended against passage of the tribe's proposed legislation, including its per capita payment, until "a comprehensive program for termination was developed" (Joint Hearings 1954, p. 608).

In January, 1953, the Menominee General Council unanimously adopted a resolution authorizing tribal representatives and attorneys to develop legislation to transfer to the tribe "certain supervisory and administrative responsibilities and activities now vested in the Federal government," including forestry, education, health and medical services, conservation, agricultural extension, credit, relief, and welfare. The General Council recommended that the transfer of responsibilities be completed by 1958. The General Council also directed that the legislation "shall be so worded as to preserve the existing basic principle of Federal trusteeship over the affairs of the Menominee Indians" (Robertson 1961, pp. 4–5).

By early 1953 the Menominee governing elite found themselves in an extremely difficult position. On the one hand, the tribe's general membership was exerting pressure to obtain a $1,500 per capita payment. On the other hand, the leaders were under mounting pressure from Congress and the BIA to formulate concrete plans for termination, an action unfavorable to both the leaders and the tribe in general. Unfortunately, termination appeared to be inextricably tied to receipt of the per capita payment. Accordingly the tribe's governing elite, although personally opposed to termination, adopted a strategy of grudging acquiescence to the idea of termination, while pushing energetically for the per capita payment. Congressional pressure was exerted mainly by Senator Watkins of the Senate Subcommittee on Indian Affairs. This evaluation of the earlier phases of the termination decision is based on several interviews with former Menominee leaders in 1974. Referring to the dilemma of one of the tribal leaders, one respondent noted: "The $1,500 share payment was most important to Menominees. —— figured at the time that he could work on changing things later on. —— was pressed from both sides for termination—from the Menominees for money and from Watkins."

On February 9, 1953, Congressman Melvin Laird of Wisconsin introduced a bill (H.R. 2828) authorizing a $1,500 per capita payment to the Menominees. The bill quickly passed the House without amendment or objection. On March 27, 1953, Senator Watkins held hearings on a bill (S. 1014, the Senate counterpart of H.R. 2828) before the Senate Subcommittee on Indian Affairs. Representative Laird, several tribal delegates, and a tribal attorney testified in favor of the per capita payment. No opposing testimony was given. Throughout the hearings Senator Watkins, chairman of the subcommittee, vigorously pressed the question of Menominee preparedness for termination.

After the hearing the tribe's representatives invited the members of the Senate Subcommittee on Indian Affairs to the reservation. On June 20, 1953, Senator Watkins and two BIA officials met with the General Council to discuss termination. Watkins stated that he was not willing to approve a per capita payment until a program to complete termination within three years was adopted. One hour after the departure of Senator Watkins the General Council adopted a resolution instructing tribal representatives and attorneys to present to Senator Watkins for introduction in Congress amendments to the per capita bill to terminate federal trust responsibilities for the tribe. The resolution, however, called for a five-year rather than a three-year transition period before complete termination.

The resolution, which was prepared by the Advisory Council, read as follows:

RESOLVED, that the Menominee General Council instruct the tribal attorneys and the tribal planning officer to present to Senator Watkins for introduction in Congress as an amendment to the per capita Bill a draft containing the following: 1. A Three year period during which the tribe may arrange for such planning as it deems desirable; 2. Authorize the Secretary of the Interior, at the end of such three year period, to transfer so-called agency functions to the Tribe in accordance with a plan to be submitted by the Tribe and as amended by the Secretary; 3. Authorize the Secretary to transfer to the Tribe, or an organization designed by the Tribe, responsibility for operation of the Menominee forests and mills in accordance with a plan submitted by the Tribe and as amended by the Secretary after five years following the enactment of the bill; 4. Authorize the disbursement of such tribal funds as may be requested by the tribe for the planning necessary to carry out the intention of the legislation; 5. Provide for the closing of the Menominee rolls as of a date to be designated by the Menominee General Council; 6. Provide that individual interests in the tribal assets shall pass by inheritance under the laws of Wisconsin; 7. Provide that the Tribe may, within the five year term provided, indicate its desire that the Reservation be sold in one or several units, and that such request shall be carried into effect by the Secretary. [Ray 1971, pp. 19–20]

The resolution passed by a vote of 169 to 5, with 28 abstaining.

On July 15, 1953, the Senate Committee on Interior and Insular Affairs filed Senate Report No. 590, Eighty-third Congress, amending House bill 2828 to provide "for orderly termination of federal supervision over the property and members of the Menominee Indian Tribe of Wisconsin." The report contained Senator Watkins's demand for the completion of termination in three years. Within two days in a special open session the Advisory Council unanimously passed two resolutions to make every effort "to block passage *of the proposed amendments* to House bill 2828 by Senator Watkins and the Indian Office" (emphasis added) and ask Representative Laird to introduce termination legislation conforming with the resolution that had been passed by the General Council on June 20, 1953 (Robertson 1961, p. 8). It is important to note that the tribe did not ask for the blockage of legislation to authorize the per capita payment, which was still strongly desired by the tribal members.[2] Although several differences between the General Council's resolution and Senator Watkins's proposed legislation remained, the primary difference was over the three-year versus five-year period to complete termination.

Senator Watkins's amended version of House bill 2828 passed the Senate July 24, 1953. The House, primarily because of Representative Laird's efforts, disagreed with the Senate amendments and requested a conference committee of both houses. The conference committee recommended that the House suspend its disagreement with the Senate amendments to House bill 2828. On July 24, 1953, the Senate accepted the conference report, but the House rejected it. Opponents of the report argued that neither Representative Laird nor the Menominees had received adequate opportunity to be heard at the conference-committee hearings. In other words, House rejection of the proposed bill was based upon disapproval of the procedural methods employed, not the purposes of the legislation. House floor debate on the conference report indicated that if there had been an adequate hearing of the Menominees' requests and Representative Laird's representations the bill's chances of passing would have been greatly increased (Robertson 1961, p. 9).

From March 10 to 12, 1954, joint hearings were held before the subcommittees of the committees on interior and insular affairs to resolve differences between the legislative goals of Senator Watkins and those of the tribe.[3] Senator Watkins presided over the hearings. Testimony was heard from members of the Wisconsin congressional delegation,

[2] On at least two occasions the tribe's attorneys urged the Menominees to "forget" the $1,500 payment because of the "strings," or amendments, being attached to the original per capita bill (Robertson 1961, p. 8).

[3] The hearings on Menominee termination were part of a set of hearings stemming from the enactment of H.R. Con. Res. 108, 83rd Congress, 1st Session (see chapter 2). The entire series ran from February to April, 1954, with twenty days devoted to taking testimony from the Menominee and other tribes also under consideration for termination. In the Menominee hearings Senator Watkins's position was expressed in H.R. 2828 as amended, while the tribe's position was presented in two new bills, S. 2813 and H.R. 7135.

representatives of the state of Wisconsin, the Menominee tribal delegation, and the Department of the Interior. After the hearings ended, a series of informal conferences revealed a continuing difference of opinion, the Senate supporting Senator Watkins's three-year preparation period and the House favoring the tribe's and Representative Laird's insistence on a five-year period. After another conference a compromise was reached allowing four and one-half years before termination, or completion before December 31, 1958. With the signature of President Eisenhower on June 17, 1954, House bill 2828, as amended, became Public Law 399, Eighty-third Congress, the "Menominee Termination Act" (see appendix 2).

With the passage of the Termination Act the Menominee governing elite knew that they had lost a major battle, but they were not prepared to concede the war. Their immediate hope centered on a Democratic victory in the 1956 congressional elections. With new leadership in Congress and especially in the House Committee on Interior and Insular Affairs and its counterpart in the Senate, they thought they had a good chance of overturning the Termination Act.

A five-year preparation period before termination would have put the date for termination in July, 1958, and would, of course, have given the Menominee governing elite one more chance for a Democratic victory. A deeper basis of hope, however, underlay the governing elite's long-range strategy: the Menominees had a record of victories over the federal government. They had successfully retained part of their original land as their reservation; they had resisted the allotment of their reservation when so many other tribes lost their land; and they had won a multimillion-dollar damage suit against the federal government for the mismanagement of their reservation. Given the Menominees' record of past successes, they thought that they could again overcome the current threat to their tribal existence.

The preceding overview of the termination decision clearly dramatizes the predominant role of Senator Watkins. During his first year in the Senate in 1947 he held subcommittee hearings on the possible withdrawal of federal services and trusteeship for all Indian tribes. As chairman of both the

Senate Indian Affairs Subcommittee and the Joint Subcommittee on Indian Affairs, he dominated the evolution of Indian policy in Congress throughout the early and mid-1950s. His unabashed claim on termination as his own personal cause was apparent during his visit to the Menominee Reservation in 1954. Addressing the Menominee General Council, he said:

> I would be willing to [agree to] a three year program with the condition that it means action at the end of it. I want you to make a study. You can establish funds for that very purpose, and there must be some day when the property will be turned over to you. I am willing to go three years before you actually make the program effective, but at the end of three years, something has to be done. [Ray 1971, pp. 16–17]

At least three levels of explanation exist for the overriding influence of Senator Watkins. First, he dominated the termination policy-making process through his own sheer force of will, based upon his personal conviction that termination was the right and only answer to the "Indian problem." Second, his influence over Indian policy was, in part, a product of the powers available to a subcommittee chairman in Congress. Finally, public attitudes toward American Indians in the mid-1950s provided a political climate that was favorable to anyone advocating a national policy of "federal decontrol" and "freedom for the Indians."

As for the first explanation, Orfield concluded that Senator Watkins "was sincerely convinced that he had found the solution to the problem of the Indian people . . . [his] conviction had a religious quality and was held completely beyond doubt" (Orfield 1965, chap. 2, p. 5). Senator Watkins, who had a deeply conservative political philosophy, was a self-made man and strong adherent to the Mormon faith:

> He shared the conservative antipathy to governmental control and direction of human lives, and he abhorred the attitude of bureaucratic paternalism. The most fundamental freedom, he believed, was freedom from government. He exalted individual initiative and private property; and he looked with deep suspicion upon a policy putting group interests before those of the individual. [Orfield 1965, chap. 6, p. 1]

A noted scholar, Charles E. Lindblom, has observed that men who "know" what they want are one of the prime reasons why policy problems are rarely studied thoroughly to find the best possible policy solutions. As an example, he stated:

> . . . most taxpayers' councils scattered around the U.S. want only limited analysis of government fiscal policy: on their basic antagonism of government expenditures they have already made up their minds: on that issue, they feel the less discussion and the less study, the better. [Lindblom 1968, p. 16]

Scarcely a better example exists of a man who "knew" what he wanted than Senator Watkins. Throughout the debate over termination he considered new information irrelevant:

> . . . the matter of freeing the Indian from wardship status is not rightfully a subject of debate in academic fashion with facts marshalled here and there to be maneuvered and counter-maneuvered in a vast battle of words and ideas. Much more I see this as an ideal or universal truth, to which all men subscribe, and concerning which they differ only in their opinion as to how the ideal may be attained and in what degree and during what period of time. [Watkins 1957, p. 47]

The force of one's convictions, coupled with a mind closed to information not compatible to one's policy goals does not, however, give any one congressman a dominant influence over an entire national-policy issue. During interviews in Menominee County in 1974 a former tribal leader thought back to the debate over termination and said, "I don't understand why the other congressmen let Watkins do what he wanted to do." The answer to this will be sought by turning to an examination of the power accorded Senator Watkins as chairman of the Senate Subcommittee on Indian Affairs. More specifically, what can be said about the committee structure of Congress that would help explain Senator Watkins's domination of Indian policy?[4]

It is well known that the work of Congress is done in committee, not on the House or Senate floor. The use of sub-

[4]For further study of congressional committees and subcommittees see Matthews 1960; Lees 1967; Fenno 1973; Ripley 1975; Goodwin 1970; Rieselbach 1973.

committees within committees represents a further fragmentation and decentralization of power in Congress. While many subcommittees make the overall integration of policy more difficult, they do provide an opportunity for junior congressmen to exercise considerable influence over public policy. Because of their lack of seniority, such congressmen are denied a position of leadership within full committees. Several factors can affect the degree of policy-making influence of a subcommittee chairman, including the composition and goals of the subcommittee's membership, its prestige, the frequency of acceptance of its decisions by the full committee and Congress, and the national importance of its business.[5]

The composition of the Senate and House subcommittees on Indian affairs was dominated by western congressmen— 80 percent in the Senate and 60 percent in the House.[6] Despite the western location of most Indian reservations, the congressmen from the West, like most other congressmen, had little interest in Indian affairs. The members of the two subcommittees were motivated by two goals—secure floor passage of all constituency-related bills and reelection (Fenno 1973, pp. 165–66). If subcommittee business had nothing to do with affairs in their home states, they had little interest in subcommittee matters and usually deferred decisions to the subcommittee chairman.

Based on net-member transfers into and out of committees, the prestige of the parent committees of the Senate and House Indian Affairs subcommittees ranked comparatively low, eighth among fifteen Senate committees for the Senate Interior Committee and fifteenth among nineteen House committees for the House Interior Committee (Ripley 1975, p. 102; Fenno 1973, p. 150). Because members frequently give up seats for other assignments, the Senate and House Indian Affairs subcommittees tended to be staffed by newcomers. In 1952, Senator Watkins was still in his first

[5] In some instances data for the full Interior committees were incorporated into the following discussion when specific data on the two Indian Affairs subcommittees were unavailable.

[6] At the beginning of the Eisenhower administration the Senate Subcommittee on Indian Affairs comprised three Republicans and two Democrats; the House subcommittee, nine Republicans and six Democrats.

term. With turnover high, knowledge of committee business was often lacking, and morale was low, especially among members eyeing seats on more prestigious committees (Matthews 1960, pp. 143–69). Under such conditions subcommittee members are again likely to defer decisions to the subcommittee chairman.

In terms of national importance little of the work of the Senate and House Interior committees consists of major policy questions. The work of the Indian Affairs subcommittees is no exception. The reason is simple. Senator Watkins once noted: "You only have a few Indians in the United States compared to the 161 million people in the United States that are white [in other words] there are not enough Indians that vote, and those [senators] that maybe only have two or three hundred, which is true of a lot of States in the East, are not sympathetic" (U.S., Senate, Hearings, 1954, pp. 173–74). The attendance record of subcommittee members is a good indicator of the importance of committee business. Throughout twenty days of testimony the only member of the Joint Committee on Termination to attend all the hearings was Senator Watkins. One member, Senator Clinton P. Anderson of New Mexico, did not attend at all.

The high frequency of acceptance of subcommittee decisions by the full House and Senate interior committees and in Congress also contributed to Watkins's commanding influence in Indian affairs. Referring to the Senate Interior Committee, Richard Fenno has noted that "the overwhelming practice is for the full committee to approve and submit subcommittee reports" (Fenno 1973, p. 55). Moreover, Interior Committee reports are commonly accepted by the full Senate or House with only brief debate or sporadic attempts to amend the reports (Lees 1967, p. 26). Fenno also noted that the only real difference between the Senate and House Interior Committees is that the Senate acts with less deliberation and thoroughness than the House (Fenno 1973, pp. 177–80).

Senator Watkins's influence over Indian policy could have been reduced by less cooperation between the Senate and House Indian Affairs subcommittees. The continued need to compromise opposing policy views could have severely eroded

Senator Watkins's strong protermination position. In fact, George Goodwin noted that traditionally there has been very little cooperation between House and Senate Interior subcommittees (Goodwin 1970, p. 54). The Indian Affairs subcommittees were exceptions. The two subcommittees chose to hold joint rather than separate hearings on termination. An interesting result of this arrangement was that it avoided any discussion of the legislation between the two houses of Congress. The joint subcommittee could simply write up identical bills for each house and report them for the consent calendar. When the senator or representative answered roll call, the bills would pass, and probably fewer than a dozen congressmen would ever know what they had voted for (Kickingbird and Ducheneaux 1973, p. 141).

Orfield noted that there was little to distinguish the chairmen of the two subcommittees. Representative E. Y. Berry of South Dakota, the House Indian Affairs subcommittee chairman, shared Watkins's view that continued protection of the reservations retarded Indian progress. Orfield also noted that all the members of the joint subcommittee who took part in more than one hearing seemed to be in basic agreement with Senator Watkins (Orfield 1965, chap. 1, p. 15).

In sum, most of the members of the Senate and House Interior and Insular Affairs committees used their committee seats to pursue and protect constituent interests to achieve reelection. Other committee business was of little interest, particularly an issue of as little national importance as Menominee termination. Almost by the default of his fellow subcommittee members, Senator Watkins was given the freedom to advance his policy position on Indian termination. Moreover, the deference of the full Interior committees to the policy decisions of their subcommittees and, in turn, the full Congress to the Interior committees permitted the policy convictions of one subcommittee chairman to become the policy of the entire Congress.

A full assessment of Senator Watkins's policy influence requires a brief consideration of liberal white opinion regarding all minorities in the early and mid-1950s. Lurie has argued: "While former Senator Arthur Watkins and a few other active promoters of termination clearly considered Indians an unwarranted burden on the federal government, there is no question that termination and related legislation were strongly endorsed by well-meaning legislators who were influenced by analogies to the Negro movement for civil rights" (Lurie 1971a, p. 156). The terms used for termination by liberals and conservatives alike reveal the civil-rights tone of the debate. Termination was commonly called the "freedom program," "freedom for the Indian," "freedom of action for the Indian," or some similar phrase. Senator Watkins occasionally made the direct analogy between Indian termination and black civil rights. During the joint hearings on termination he stated: "See what the colored people have done . . . without reservations, without properties that come to them, they came here strangers. We forced them over here . . . and then suddenly upon the Emancipation Proclamation by President Lincoln, they were put on their own. . . . They have made remarkable progress as a race" (Joint Hearings 1954, p. 670). Three years later he proclaimed, "Following in the footsteps of the Emancipation Proclamation of ninety-four years ago, I see the following words emblazoned in letters of fire above the heads of the Indians — THESE PEOPLE SHALL BE FREE" (Watkins 1957, p. 55).

When Senator Watkins spoke of freedom, he did so with a conservative's emphasis on the freedom to hold private property. Liberals, on the other hand, tend to put a greater emphasis on the freedom to exercise the rights granted a citizen in a democratic political system. In the early and mid-1950s blacks were demanding equal rights within a white-dominated society. American Indians, on the other hand, were demanding their right to remain separate from that society. Because of a mistaken blurring of the vastly dissimilar demands of blacks and Indians, and mostly because they simply were not interested in Indian affairs, liberal congressmen and liberals in general accepted Senator Watkins's position that he was simply trying to "free" the Indians.

To help explain how public policy is made in our political system, social scientists have developed the incremental decision-making model.[7] Overall, incrementalism is a useful theoretical framework for explaining why Congress terminated the Menominee tribe.

According to the incremental model, policymakers want to maintain a stable society above all else. To maintain stability, they are more interested in finding political compromises between people in society with opposing objectives than in developing policies and programs to solve the problems underlying societal conflicts. Finding real solutions to society's problems may be too costly and time-consuming or may be impossible because of the nature of the problem. For example, labor and management continually disagree on the definition of fair wages and benefits. When government arbitrators are called in to mediate a labor dispute, they try to find a compromise strike settlement agreeable to both labor and management. They do not attempt to define what would constitute "fair" wages and benefits or what the proper relationship should be between labor and management in the production of goods and services. Such questions conceivably could renew major ideologically based conflicts between labor and management, such as those of the turbulent years when labor unions first organized in the United States. The arbitrator's main objective is simply to find some immediate way to avoid a prolonged strike that could undermine political and economic stability.

The behavior of Congress in the early 1950s largely conformed to the incremental perspective. Congress did not try to find or evaluate alternative solutions to the problem of Indian resistance to assimilation. Senator Watkins's solution —termination—was advanced with little or no debate. Moreover, the need for political compromise strongly affected the evolution of termination policy, particularly during the process of singling out individual tribes for termination.

Senator Watkins tried to terminate as many tribes as possible; however, he yielded to the opposition of several tribes who had been marked for termination, including the Seminoles of Florida, the Flatheads of Montana, the Turtle Mountain Chippewas of North Dakota, and the Osages of Okla-

[7] Literature on the incremental concept is voluminous. For further reading see Lindblom 1959, 1965, 1968; Braybrooke and Lindblom 1963; Wildavsky 1966; Gawthrop 1971; Sharkansky 1970b; Dye 1972, pp. 30–32; Davis, Dempster, and Wildavsky 1966; Natchez and Bupp 1973; Bailey and O'Connor 1975.

homa. During congressional hearings on Indian termination
the tribes' resistance to termination was backed by senators
from their respective states, including Senators George A.
Smathers of Florida, Mike Mansfield of Montana, Milton R.
Young of North Dakota, and Robert S. Kerr of Oklahoma.
Orfield noted:

> . . . in each of these cases the tribes had strongly opposed the
> legislation and there had been Congressional testimony in oppo-
> sition during the hearings. In each of these instances, state gov-
> ernmental agencies or well-organized local groups had made an
> effective presentation of the case against termination. In no in-
> stance was a bill to pass where either members of Congress or
> local governments were strongly opposed [Orfield 1965, chap.
> 1, p. 16][8]

Although he did it very grudgingly, Senator Watkins also
acceded to compromises with the Menominees. He granted
hearings for the Menominees because of Representative
Laird's opposition to the senator's methods of obtaining congressional approval for Menominee termination. He also
granted an extension of the preparation time for termination from three to four and one-half years to obtain House
approval of the Termination Act. Representative Laird's opposition evolved from Senator Watkins's revision of his one-
section, one-page bill (H.R. 2828), which simply called for a
$1,000 per capita payment for the tribe, to a thirteen-section,
seven-page bill, which called for the complete termination
of the Menominee tribe. That Representative Laird's objection was solely procedural was supported by Representative
Claire Engle when he stated:

> I think the objectives of the Senate substitute are sound and I
> believe that Mr. Laird thinks so, too, because he agreed to go
> along with it if certain amendments were adopted. . . . Mr. Laird
> has been made the victim of a procedural injustice. He has been
> given a new and different bill under his name for which he
> disclaims any responsibility, and on which *he has been denied
> a hearing before the appropriate committee of this House, which he*

---

[8] For further discussion of other tribes also facing termination in the
early 1950s see Orfield 1965, chap. 1, pp. 7–15; Debo 1970, pp. 304–11.

*should without question be entitled to have.* [U.S., House, Report 1034, 1953; emphasis added]

Note that the objection was to the omission of a hearing for Representative Laird, not a hearing for the Menominees.

Throughout the deliberation over termination Senator Watkins was certainly not opposed to compromise or the resolution of conflict between himself and the tribes he considered ready for termination, as long as it led to implementation of the policy somewhere. The stability of the political system was not of immediate concern to Senator Watkins because Indian termination was not likely to become the basis of a major national controversy. Still, political compromises were necessary to avoid the escalation of political conflict between him and other public officials who opposed the termination of tribes within their states.

Incrementalism stipulates that policymakers are political professionals who interact within a detached, nonemotional decision-making environment. The limitation of nonprofessional participation in the policy-making process is desirable because nonprofessionals are likely to be idealistic, politically naïve, and emotionally committed to their policy objectives. Such traits do not contribute to the achievement of political compromises.

Throughout the deliberation over Menominee termination, Senator Watkins "did not believe that Indian consent was a necessary condition for termination, contending that it would be 50 years before the tribes would agree" (Orfield 1965, chap. 1, p. 14).

In fact, at one point during the termination hearings Senator Watkins seemed to suggest that the American Indians might never voluntarily submit to termination.

I find this, which has been a surprise to me: that the more educated Indians, Indian individuals, object most strenuously to the withdrawal, because they will have to pay taxes. I don't find nearly as much objection from the other Indians as from these. And they are not always Indians of the full blood. In fact, most of the time they are more white than Indian biologically. . . . We educate them to a point where they should be prepared to take over the competent management of their own affairs and the response is most surprising because they become more and more vocal against termination of this trusteeship or guardianship. This is one of the disturbing things. [Joint Hearings 1954, pp. 673-74]

Before the 1954 termination hearings the senator argued that his visit to the Menominee Reservation constituted a sufficient opportunity for tribal contribution to the termination decision (*Weekly News Letter,* January 25, 1954, pp. 2-3; Larson, Andrews, and Milsap 1954, pp. 8-9). He eventually yielded to pressure by Representative Laird, however, and granted a formal hearing on the issue.

The Joint Indian Affairs Subcommittee hearings represented the only formal opportunity for direct Menominee participation in the termination decision. Congressional hearings are, however, a less than optimal environment for nonprofessional participation in the policy-making process. David Truman suggested that the most familiar, but probably also the least important, function of hearings is as a means of transmitting technical and political information from various individuals and interest groups to the committee. Two other functions are more important—its "use as a propaganda channel," usually for the committee, and its use as "a quasi-ritualistic means of adjusting group conflicts and relieving disturbances through a safety valve" (Truman 1951, p. 372).

The Menominee termination hearings easily conform with Truman's observations. Of the three potential functions, the subcommittee hearings on termination functioned most prominently as a propaganda channel for Senator Watkins's views on Indian assimilation. Most of the major policy deliberation occurred during the informal conferences outside the formal hearings and without the presence of the Menominee delegation. The most visible participants in the decision-making process were Senator Watkins, Representative Laird, Rex Lee of the BIA, and Ernest Wilkenson, a Washington lawyer retained by the tribe *(Weekly News Letter,* January 25, 1954, pp. 2-3; Joint Hearings 1954, p. 609). Nonprofessional participation was minimized throughout the entire debate over Menominee termination.

According to incrementalism, policymakers are extremely reluctant to abandon established public policies. One of the reasons for their reluctance is the presence of "sunk costs"; that is, expended or committed monetary and other resources, psychological dispositions, and established administrative practices tend to legitimize current policies, regardless of the merits of a particular policy. A second factor, uncertainty avoidance, is also important. Because of limited predictive capabilities the consequences of adopting new or different policies are often uncertain. While a new policy may represent the solution to a problem, it may also worsen the problem. Policymakers, therefore, tend to continue past policies or programs, whether or not they have proven effective.

Senator Watkins once observed: "Historically . . . the Congress, although perhaps more or less ineffectively until recent years, has sought in the nineteenth and early twentieth centuries to free the Indian. . . . Freedom for the Indian was the goal then, it is the goal now" (Watkins 1957, pp. 48–49).[9] Senator Watkins unquestionably accepted the legitimacy of the past policy goal of Indian assimilation. One might question, however, whether the presence of sunk costs was a compelling reason for that acceptance.

From one perspective it would seem that the exact opposite would be true. That is, complete assimilation would lead to dissolution of the Bureau of Indian Affairs and the many services and programs provided to Indians by the bureau. While it is true that millions of dollars and many programs were administered to Indians, most were provided by the federal government because it was believed that they would help Indians achieve assimilation. Reservation training and education programs are excellent examples. Taken from this perspective, the sunk costs of past Indian programs strongly supported the adoption of termination as a new assimilation strategy.

Psychological costs were also important; that is, the belief within white society that a tribal existence simply was not "natural" or "American" provided a solid basis for termination as a national Indian policy. For people like Senator Watkins to believe anything else would have required, in

[9] Senator Watkins's observation is supported by previous discussion of federal Indian policy before termination (see chapter 2).

psychological terms, an extremely costly reorientation of set values and beliefs. Depending on the depth of one's cynicism, it is possible to cite an additional direct cost to non-Indians if assimilation policies were abandoned — the lost potential for development of the land and other natural resources held by the Indians.

Finally, the need for uncertainty avoidance was also a factor in the Menominee termination decision. Senator Watkins and national policymakers conceivably could have declared a wholesale termination of all Indian reservations in the United States. That policy alternative, however, was fraught with extreme uncertainty. If the policy failed, the federal government would find itself responsible for special aids and services to thousands of Indians unable to adapt to white society. The safest strategy was a limited termination of a few tribes who appeared ready for rapid assimilation. If the experiment failed, the consequences of the failure would be more easily manageable. From an incremental perspective the Menominees were considered excellent candidates for the termination experiment.

The incremental concept suggests that debate over new policies or changes in existing policy focuses on the means of carrying out a proposed policy, not the ends of the policy; on policy details, not goals; on specifics, not the societal values underlying a choice between alternative policies. This situation occurs because of the difficulty of defining policy problems and solutions, a lack of adequate information, the need for minimizing emotionally charged debate, and the need for political practicality. While the incremental model generally characterizes congressional debate over Indian termination, the model tends to underemphasize the superficiality of that debate, especially limited consideration by Congress of policy details and the means available for implementing Menominee termination.

Reasons for the limited study of public policy by public decision makers can be elaborated upon in greater detail. First, it is extremely difficult to define policy problems and solutions. Society's problems are complex. Moreover, perception of those problems and their potential solutions vary over time, with the goals and values of the observer, and

with the position of the observer in the policymaking process. Second, policymakers always suffer from inadequate
information. The study of public policies is limited because
of the inadequacy of resources (for instance, money, time,
skills) to resolve effectively the ends or goals of public policies. As with the rest of us, decision makers' intelligence and
analytical capacities are finite and often inadequate (see Simon's discussion of "bounded rationality" 1966, pp. 19–21).
Third, the development of public policies requires a minimum of emotionally charged debate. If policies are evaluated
in terms of normative goals and values (for example, policies
to achieve "quality education" or "adequate housing"), the
intensity of commitment to opposing policy positions is increased. Conflict under such conditions is difficult to avoid
because major policy goals rarely have broad public support.
Political stability is endangered. Finally, policymakers must
exercise political practicality. The pragmatic politician seeks
a way that will work and does not insist on adoption of the
one best way of solving a policy problem. Other matters
which demand attention preclude any search for the best
solution. Moreover, the need to build political support for
any policy innovation usually requires a willingness to bargain away certain specific components of a favored policy innovation. Consequently, decision-making energies are often
absorbed by bargaining and compromise over details, not
policy goals.

Incrementalism suggests that decision makers debate the
details of a policy and the means of its implementation,
rather than its goals or ends, because they have difficulty
defining policy problems and solutions and because they lack
adequate information. This assumes that decision makers
prefer to search out various alternatives to find "the best"
solution and that they are interested in seeking adequate information to solve the policy problem but, for any of several
reasons, are prevented from doing so. There is no evidence
of any congressional interest in a search for the best Indian
policy in the early 1950s.

Senator Watkins and his supporters knew that the "problem" was the continuation of Indian reservations in America.
They also knew that termination was the solution to the "In-

dian problem." The solution was applicable to any of the tribes, no matter how prepared they appeared to be. Illustrations of this view are readily available. At one point in the termination hearings, Representative Jack Westland of Kansas argued that a Kansas tribe was prepared for termination *because* it was poverty-stricken and unable to support itself.

> How can it be worse than it is now? I mean, it seems to me that a tribe like this has reached the depths, then, and how could they be worse off than they are? Perhaps if they were given their, let us say, freedom, and do not have the idea of relying and leaning on somebody, and if they had thought that they had to get things for themselves, perhaps that would be better. [Joint Hearings 1954, p. 1383]

The values of protermination decision makers pervaded the entire decision-making process but were never challenged. For example, in response to the Menominees' claim that the continued existence of their reservation was guaranteed by treaty, Representative Engle offered the following opinion:

> Now, perhaps if I were an Indian and I were operating my property and living on it and managing it but having none of the responsibilities of taxation then I might look with misgivings on this legislation. But I would be less than frank if I did not say to the Indians here that you make a bad case for yourselves when you put it on the basis of absolute selfishness, that you want to remain under federal wardship and in the status of subservient citizenship. It is not an appealing argument either to this committee or the public generally, and I am perfectly satisfied that neither the Congress nor the public generally will accept it. [Joint Hearings 1954, p. 478]

Totally hidden from Representative Engle's observations is that "whatever we have given to Indians and whatever we give them today is not a matter of charity, but is a part of a series of real estate transactions through which about 90 percent of the land of the United States was purchased from the Indian by the Federal Government" (Cohn 1960, p. 255). Federal protection of the Indians' communal lifeways and federal provision of services promised to the Indians by treaty were abhorrent to Representative Engle, given his respect for private property and his belief in individualism unencumbered by a dependence on the federal government.

Antitermination arguments based on Indian treaty rights were totally ignored by Senator Watkins and his allies. During the hearings Watkins asked a BIA representative for a clarification of the statement in the Menominees' 1854 treaty, which said that the lands granted by the United States to the Menominees "shall be held as Indian lands are held." The BIA official responded that in his judgment "Indian lands are held in whatever manner Congress directs that they be held" (Joint Hearings 1954, p. 630).

As for lack of adequate information to make a thorough analysis of the feasibility of termination before passage of the Termination Act, Senator Watkins simply treated new information as irrelevant. Lurie noted that the federal government conducted no studies before the termination decision, not even to the extent necessary to gain some insight, however meager, into whether or not the Menominee tribe was ready for termination: "When 'termination' was applied to the Menominees there was no indication of how it was to be implemented. It was simply a word . . . and people in Washington were ready to terminate them without having defined, themselves, really what they meant by this word" (*Menominee Tribe et al.* v. *United States* 1967, p. 63).

Incrementalism also proposes that the details and means of public policies, rather than their ends or goals, are emphasized because of the need to minimize emotionally charged, often irresolvable, debate conducted in terms of normative goals and values. While the need to minimize such debate might be relevant, it was not a major factor in the decision to terminate the Menominee tribe. First, there was very little organized national opposition to Indian assimilation or to the new policy of termination. Even the National Congress of American Indians failed to organize a concerted effort to combat termination until after passage of the Menominee Termination Act (Lurie 1971*b*, p. 10; Orfield 1965, chap. 2, p. 3). Also, no real reason existed to avoid discussion of the goals or values underlying termination because most other Americans were in favor of assimilation.

Some members of the public, while in favor of the general

policy of assimilation, expressed doubts regarding the strategy of termination. On April 12, 1954, the *Washington Post* commented:

> In general we sympathize with the long range aims of the Administration to "get out of the Indian business." But it cannot be accomplished overnight. Certainly the Government ought not withdraw the special aid and protection it has given the tribes on reservations until they are prepared to manage their own affairs. The vice in some of the bills now being considered is that they disregard the wishes of the Indians as well as the illiteracy and unpreparedness of the members of some tribes to make a living in competition with other Americans.

In any case, the fate of American Indians has never been considered of sufficient importance to warrant national attention, and even if the goals of termination had been openly discussed, it is unlikely that such action would have led to irresolvable divisiveness or instability of the political system.

A greater chance existed that an open discussion of the goals of termination would have led to greater opposition to termination by the state of Wisconsin, but that opposition would not have occurred because state officials disagreed with the goals of termination. Rather, it would have occurred because a debate over the ends of the policy might have given state officials time to realize the problems that Menominee termination would create for the state after passage of the Termination Act.

The following excerpts were taken from Congressional debate on the termination bill:

> *Representative John Byrnes* (Rep. Wis.): "Let me make it clear that the Tribe itself and the Members of Congress who have that Tribe within their congressional district have no objection whatever to the termination of that Federal supervision. There is no resistance whatever on our part or on the part of the Tribe; in fact, we think it is indeed a step in the right direction, and that step should be taken at the earliest possible opportunity."

> *Senator Alexander Wiley* (Rep. Wis.): "There is little difference between us and Senator Watkins in relation to the matter which we understand is coming up." [That is, Menominee termination, Congressional Debate 1953, p. 2043]

*Representative Arthur Miller* (Rep. Neb.): "But I did think the gentleman said he was in agreement with the general principles of the [termination] bill, and I am pleased to know that."

*Representative Melvin Laird* (Rep. Wis.): "I am."

*Representative Miller:* "The gentleman does agree that the Menominee Indian Tribes [six] are far advanced and are ready for complete liberation?"

*Representative Laird:* "I agree to that. I believe the Menominee Indian Tribe is ready for complete emancipation as set forth in the resolution of the Tribe." [Congressional Debate 1953, pp. 2045, 2050]

Incrementalism suggests that policy debate is directed to the details and means of implementation of a policy because of the need for political practicality, that is, the need to build the political support necessary for the successful enactment of public policies. Because the specifics of a policy are much more amenable to bargaining and compromise, the ends or goals of a policy are rarely discussed. During the joint hearings on termination debate centered on a tribe-by-tribe review of the several tribes listed in House Concurrent Resolution 108 as ready for "freedom from federal supervision and control."[10] Senator Watkins and other proponents of termination compromised many of their objectives. Eventually only two major tribes (the Menominees and the Klamaths of Oregon) and four small bands of Indians were selected for termination.[11] Rather than defending termination in terms of the ends and goals of assimilation, Senator Watkins only terminated tribes that offered the least resistance to the new policy. By this means enough political

[10] H.R. Con. Res. 108 called for the end of federal supervision over all the tribes in California, Florida, New York, and Texas and also the Flatheads of Montana, the Klamaths of Oregon, the Menominees of Wisconsin, the Potawatomies of Kansas and Nebraska, and the Chippewas on the Turtle Mountain Reservation in North Dakota.

[11] The Menominee termination legislation was enacted in June, 1954. In August, 1954, the other five termination laws were enacted. The latter five terminated the Klamaths and several small groups of Indians in Oregon, four small Paiute bands and a mixed-blood population of Uintah and Ouray Indians in Utah, and the Alabama-Coushattas of Texas.

support was accumulated to begin advancing termination with a small but significant number of Indians.

The incremental model also indicates that public policy consists of a sequence of remedial policy changes, or increments, aimed at the alleviation of specific problems. Decision makers believe that the policy-making process would be destabilized by extreme and rapid policy change. They also recognize, however, that the process must be upset to achieve the policy change necessary for adaptation to a changing political and social environment. Therefore, decision makers generally produce small or incremental changes in policy, rather than major policy innovations. Adaptation can then be made with a minimum of political conflict and social divisiveness.

Termination of the Menominee tribe was an incremental change in Indian policy. If the experiment proved successful, termination would be applied as widely as possible to combat the problem of Indian resistance to complete assimilation. Referring to his demand that the Menominees be allowed only three years to prepare for termination, Senator Watkins stated: "This Tribe . . . sort of sets the pattern. If these people get 10 years or 12 years, the rest of them [the other tribes] will come in and want five times as much. And the present generation won't see termination" (Joint Hearings 1954, p. 656).

That Menominee termination was intended as only one step in the eventual assimilation of all Indians in the United States is apparent in the following excerpt of congressional debate over termination:

> *Rep. August Anderson* (Rep. Minn.): As I understand it, this bill applies to just one tribe of Indians."
>
> *Rep. Wesley D'Ewart* (Rep. Mont.): "That is correct."
>
> *Rep. Anderson:* "And this is a pilot project on which we are going to try the first experiment?"
>
> *Rep. D'Ewart:* "This is the most forward looking tribe, economically, socially, and otherwise in the United States. Therefore, we are proceeding with them first." (Congressional Debate 1953, pp. 2051–52)

Clearly the Menominee termination decision was conceived of as the first in a sequence of policy increments aimed at a solution to the "Indian problem."

# 5

# THE IMPLEMENTATION OF
# MENOMINEE TERMINATION

*You Menominee people have the strength. These white people have no
jurisdiction over our business. I'm telling you the whole truth. Band
together and throw out all these documents. I'm not going to give up.
I have backing by high spiritual power to understand my business.* —
Ernest Neconish, a Menominee Indian; quoted by Jerry Van Ryzin,
*Green Bay Press-Gazette,* January 19, 1959

THE Menominee Termination Act was passed by Congress
and signed by President Eisenhower on June 17, 1954. Full
implementation of the new assimilation strategy was not
achieved until May 1, 1961, however, with formal transforma-
tion of the Menominee Reservation into Wisconsin's seventy-
second county. The term "implementation" as used here
refers to the development of the means for carrying out or
"setting up the machinery" to carry out a public policy;[1]
that is, it refers to the process of creating or designating
organizations and assigning individuals to achieve the goals
of a policy. The process also includes the interpretation of
a policy's objectives, the reconciliation of conflicting interpretations of those objectives, and the expenditure of resources to set up the policy for operation.

Policy-implementation processes vary with the kind of
policy being implemented. In some instances little or no
government action may be required beyond the assignment
of a government spokesman to announce a new policy, which
was the case when President Jimmy Carter announced total
amnesty for all Vietnam War resisters. Implementation can

[1]For a good summary of various interpretations of the term implementation see Bunker 1972, pp. 71–75; Jones 1970; Anderson 1976*a,* 1976*b;* Pressman and Wildavsky 1973; Droz 1968; Van Meter and Van Horn 1975.

also be an elaborate process involving many actors in all
sectors of government—federal, state, and local—examples
are the Model Cities Program and the Equal Employment
Opportunity Act. In the latter instance many monitoring
organizations were set up and many individuals assigned to
new positions to assure that compliance was forthcoming at
all levels of government.

Implementation of the Menominee Termination Act covered seven years of interaction among many actors from all
arenas of the policy-making process. The exact identities of
"the implementers" of the Menominee Termination Act are
often unclear. Certainly Congress, the Wisconsin state legislature, the Menominee governing elite, and the tribe's attorneys all played important roles in the process. The Senate
Subcommittee on Indian Affairs provided the driving force
behind implementation, the state legislature strongly influenced the outcome of the process, and the Menominee governing elites, with help from tribal lawyers, wrote the final
termination plan. Others, including the Bureau of Indian
Affairs, the University of Wisconsin, and the Menominee
people apart from the governing elite made direct and indirect contributions to the implementation process.

The objectives of those involved in the implementation
of Menominee termination were varied. Congress wanted
to see the termination experiment implemented so that resources already committed to termination would not be
wasted and results of the experiment would be available
for new legislation to advance Indian assimilation still further. The state of Wisconsin, although opposed to termina
tion, decided that it was inevitable and became fully committed to its success. Failure would mean dissipation of the
region's fragile economic base and state responsibility for a
new poverty-stricken minority population. The Menominee
governing elite, like the state, opposed termination. When
its delaying tactics became futile, the governing elite accepted
termination and molded its implementation to protect its
status and power within the Menominee community. The
major implementation decisions—a separate county, dependence on local taxation for support of government services,
and creation of a management trust to control Menominee

assets—were all founded on the objectives of implementers of termination.

The principal source of pressure to implement termination came from Congress. Pressure, particularly from the Senate Subcommittee on Indian Affairs, was applied to the BIA, the state of Wisconsin, and the Menominee tribe. Ironically, the unswerving will of Congress to see Menominee termination through to the end was accompanied by a gradual turning away from termination as an assimilation strategy for other tribes in the nation. By 1957 a perceptible slowing down of the pace of termination of other Indian groups had begun. By 1958 the inadvisability of proceeding with further termination became clear to Congress, at least until results with already terminated tribes became known (Tyler 1964, p. 41; Josephy 1971, pp. 44–46). Even though termination of the Menominees was not yet implemented, Congress considered the tribe to be a part of its ongoing experiment in Indian assimilation and a plan that could not be abandoned.

The Menominees, backed by the state of Wisconsin, requested many postponements of the termination date, the last request coming one week before termination of their reservation. Two of their requests were granted by Congress, moving the date from December 31, 1958, to December 31, 1960, and then to the final date, June 31, 1961. By 1960, however, the patience of the Senate Subcommittee on Indian Affairs had worn noticeably thin. Responding to the statement of Democratic Senator William B. Proxmire of Wisconsin supporting a six-month extension of the final date of termination, Senator Anderson (Dem., N. Mex.), chairman of the Senate subcommittee, replied, "Do you know what the extension of 6 months is for? So they can come back to the next Congress and ask for some more time. They do not intend to terminate" (U.S., House, Report 1824, 1960, p. 38). The attitude of the subcommittee was summarized by a government witness who suggested that "if they ever are going to make it I don't see why they can't do it now" (U.S., House, Report 1824, 1960, p. 89).

The main reason for the adamant insistence by Congress that Menominee termination be implemented was to see the experiment through to completion. A second reason involved the mounting cost of implementation. From June 1, 1954, to December 31, 1960, the federal government allocated approximately $3 million to the tribe and to the BIA for termination expenses (Wisconsin Legislative Council 1966, p. 20). The original Termination Act, Public Law 399, made no provision for reimbursement of expenses, but the law was amended in 1956 to provide that the federal government would begin to pay the full cost of termination. In 1956, however, Congress again reversed itself and decided to pay only one-half the approved cost or $275,000, whichever was less (Robertson 1961). Insistence on this provision came primarily from Senator Maurine Neuberger (Dem., Ore.) and Senator Anderson, who argued for a cut in the federal share of termination costs because implementation was moving too slowly.[2] They argued that the federal government had already given the Menominees enough money to prepare for termination. Congress as a whole agreed, though it should be noted that Representative Melvin Laird vigorously opposed the amendment. He was defeated, however, in a Senate-House conference committee (*Milwaukee Journal,* July 17, 1958). Former Representative Laird is still well thought of among the Menominees, with most of them recalling that he helped the tribe as much as he could under the circumstances.

The forceful backing of implementation by Congress was based on two additional factors. The first was a widespread belief that it was the Menominees' idea to terminate and that the tribe was now trying to back out of that agreement. The second was the genuine optimism of several congressmen that termination was the best thing for the Menominees, if they would only get on with it. Indicative of the first view was a statement by Senator Barry Goldwater (Rep., Ariz.) as follows:

> It has been my recollection all along that this was instituted by the Tribe. . . . It was not thrust on them by Congress. . . . It was a result of a resolution being presented to this committee and this committee acting on that resolution. [U.S., Senate, Hearings 1961, p. 8]

[2]This conclusion is based on an interview with a former tribal leader in 1974.

As shown in the previous chapter, Senator Goldwater's recollection was clearly not supported by the history of the Termination Act.

Enthusiastic optimism for the eventual success of termination was, surprisingly, shared by the more liberal members of Congress. Senator Frank Church (Dem., Idaho), a member of the Senate Subcommittee on Indian Affairs, volunteered the following observations:

> I would venture to predict that once this termination is completed and the Indian people in this newly established county are thrown upon their own resources and on processes of self-government and look to these resources for the kind of further economic development that is required that you are going to be better off in the years to come than you have heretofore been under Government wardship.
>
> Your general standard of living and your general wage levels are going to improve and economic development will be facilitated and the standard of education you receive will go up faster than it has heretofore gone up under wardship. I think if that had not been the basic concept, the Termination Act would never have been enacted in the first place and the Menominee Tribe would not have approved it, if that was not the underlying confidence. I think you will find that to be your experience in the years ahead. [U.S., House, Report 1824, 1960, p. 59]

Senator Church's optimism was in part a reflection of the general liberal position on racial discrimination in the 1960s. How could freedom from oppressive federal paternalism be bad? Liberals felt that the cry for "black freedom" should be extended to freedom for all minorities. This was believed, even though blacks were arguing for full integration into American society while American Indians were arguing for the maintenance of a distinct tribal identity separate from the larger society.

Contrasting sharply with the persistent pressure by Congress to see Menominee termination implemented as quickly as possible was an almost total disregard for the "details" of implementation. In hearings before the Senate Subcommittee on Indian Affairs, Senator Anderson had no sympathy for a tribal member's statement that experienced Menominees were not available to fill positions immediately and assume the responsibilities of the new county government. The senator argued:

> The Government did not ask the Menominees to set up a county. The Menominees had this idea themselves. Even though they were urged not to do it, they said, "Oh no, we know how to do this. We will have our own county officials." But then they come back here and say, "We can't because we don't have anybody who is experienced." Why did they not think of that before they asked for the county? [U.S., House, Report 1824, 1960, p. 8]

As for the ability of the tribe to finance new and continuing government operations and services after termination, the Senate subcommittee was unimpressed with data presented by the state of Wisconsin and the tribe showing that the tribe's capital reserve had greatly diminished since passage of the Termination Act and that the new county was going to operate at a deficit in its first years of existence. Senator Anderson, replying again to Senator Proxmire, stated:

> The fact is, when the Termination Act was passed, these Indians had about $10 million. By the time they got down to 1958, that had been distributed, and dissipated down to $4 million. Now a good deal of the rest of that is gone I guess. They are proposing a loan fund. How long do you have to throw money away before you realize that maybe these people ought to be required to do something for themselves. [U.S., House, Report 1824, 1960, p. 38]

Regarding the feasibility of alternative methods for the management of the tribe's resources and economy after termination, the Senate subcommittee again offered little constructive advice to the tribe beyond suggesting that if the problems of managing their resources were too great they should hire a trustee to handle their affairs [U.S., House, Report 1824, 1960, p. 101].

On the eve of final implementation the Senate Subcommittee on Indian Affairs partly acknowledged that the tribe was not completely prepared for immediate termination. Although the subcommittee refused to change the termination date or go along with a previously approved House bill to provide grants as "phase-out" aid, it did authorize $1.5 million in loans to modernize the Menominee sawmill, diversify the tribe's lumber industry, and develop other resources. It authorized an additional $438,000 to complete the modernization of the reservation sanitation system. Unfortunately, the proposed aid did not materialize because the final termination date passed before Congress took final action on the legislation (Robertson 1961).

In sum, the primary objective of Congress was to see Menominee termination implemented. Little interest was shown in how it was done, as long as it was done. Many congressmen were sympathetic to the problems of the Menominees, particularly in the House, where Representative Laird's continuous support of the tribe's opposition to immediate termination received a receptive audience. In practical terms, however, the Senate Subcommittee on Indian Affairs, under the chairmanship of Senator Anderson, dictated the Menominees' fate, just as the same subcommittee had done under Senator Watkins in 1954. In the previous chapter it was pointed out that the Menominee Termination Act represented one increment in a continuing congressional policy to promote Indian assimilation. For the policy experiment to work it had to be tried. Relentless prodding by the Senate subcommittee assured the implementation of Menominee termination.

Like the Congress, the BIA also supported rapid implementation of the Menominee Termination Act. The most salient feature of the participation of the BIA in the 1954 Termination Hearings was its total support of the Senate Subcommittee on Indian Affairs under Senator Watkins. The subcommittee's domination of the BIA continued throughout implementation of the Menominee Termination Act. This occurred despite the BIA's grave doubts, beginning in 1958, about termination as an effective assimilation strategy (Tyler 1964; Josephy 1971, pp. 44–46; Wisconsin Peace Action Committee 1970, p. 11). In an interview with a former commissioner of the BIA in 1974, I was told that the BIA "termination decade began in 1948 and ended with the appointment of Rodger Ernst as commissioner in 1958."

The following excerpt from a speech by Interior Secretary Seaton in 1958 created considerable confusion over the future of termination as a continuing strategy for Indian assimilation:

(M)y own position is this: no Indian tribe or group should end its relationship with the Federal Government unless such tribe or group has clearly demonstrated—first, that it understands the plan under which such a program would go forward, and second, that the tribe or group affected concurs in and supports the plan proposed.

Now . . . it is absolutely unthinkable to me as your Secretary of the Interior that consideration would be given to forcing upon an Indian tribe a so-called termination plan which did not have the understanding and acceptance of a clear majority of the members affected. Those tribes which have thus far sought to end their Federal wardship status have, in each instance, demonstrated their acceptance of the plan prior to action by the Congress. I shall continue to insist this be the case and I hope and believe that Congress and its leaders will pursue the same course. To make my position perfectly clear, as long as I am Secretary of the Interior, I shall be dedicated to preserving the principle which I have just enunciated.

To me it would be incredible, even criminal, to send any Indian tribe out into the stream of American life until and unless the educational level of that tribe was one which was equal to the responsibilities which it was shouldering. [Seaton 1958]

By 1961 certain indications showed that the BIA was having doubts about the merits of Menominee termination. Bureau spokesmen voiced the opinion that "congressional modification of the act in some form or another" might be advisable and that a "phased extension" of termination might be appropriate (U.S., Senate, Hearings 1961, pp. 29–34). The rather meek dissent of the BIA was ignored, however, by the Senate Subcommittee on Indian Affairs.

Except during the years when it was headed by Commissioner Collier in the 1930s and early 1940s, the BIA remained dependent upon the goodwill of Congress for its continued existence (Josephy 1971, pp. 151–52; W. Brophy 1966, pp. 118–23). In an interview a former commissioner of the BIA suggested, "BIA policy is really made in congressional legislative and appropriation committees. The White House runs the BIA so it won't be an embarrassment to the President. The working assumption is that the executive always loses." From the end of World War II through the 1950s the BIA was particularly defensive because of a strong current of congressional opinion that the bureau ought to be eliminated and its operations absorbed into other government agencies. Under these conditions the BIA had little taste for arguing with a Senate subcommittee committed to Indian assimilation through termination.

The bureau's deference to the subcommittee was apparent during 1956 hearings on amendments to Menominee termination when a bureau official argued that "ultimate responsibility for determining when the time has arrived for terminating a Federal trust responsibility rests solely with Congress. The Indians have no vested right to the continuance of the trust relationship" (quoted in Orfield 1965, chap. 4, p. 12). In 1959, referring to Secretary Seaton's statement that no tribe would be terminated without its full consent, Commissioner Ernst wrote the chairman of the Menominee Advisory Council to clarify the bureau's position:

> Secretary Seaton's speech was intended to inform Indian Tribes of the standards which we would employ when proposing future legislation to the Congress. . . . Once the Congress has enacted the legislation, however, we have no alternative but to administer that legislation as it is written. Therefore, if the Menominee Indian Tribe does not propose a plan for [termination] . . . the Department must go ahead with the planning process; and we must divest ourselves of trust custody over your property. [Ernst 1959]

In other words, the consent of the Menominees was not required for the implementation of termination.

In almost all respects the bureau backed the Senate subcommittee's insistence that Menominee termination be implemented as quickly as possible. In hearings in 1957 the bureau argued: "We feel that the mounting costs of the transitional program emphasize the need for compacting it into the shortest reasonable period" (U.S., Senate, Report 1116, 1957, p. 6). during the same hearings the bureau also argued that no further studies were required because the tribe already had enough data to implement termination. In 1960 the BIA made the incredible argument that ill-preparedness of the tribe had nothing to do with the central question of implementing termination:

It should be noted and emphasized that the more important reasons advanced for delay relate to the desire for more financial assistance in the fields of education, health, and public utilities. These subjects are not directly related to the procedural processes of termination. If Congress is disposed to give this type of assistance it can be considered independently of termination and granted after termination is effective. [U.S., House, Report 1824, 1960, p. 7]

The bureau did little to support the Menominees in Congress. It also did very little to help the tribe implement termination. In the words of the BIA area director: "The Indian Service's heavy hand should not be on them at all. We should be in the background, ready with some guidance and suggestions and any help we can give" (Joint Hearings 1954, p. 617). The bureau took the position that it would provide no implementation advice to the tribe unless specifically requested to do so. Years later the tribe filed a suit in federal court alleging that they had needed BIA aid to implement termination but the bureau had done nothing to help (Ray 1971, pp. 24–28). The BIA argued that the tribe made no requests for assistance (*Menominee Tribe et al.* v. *United States,* 1973a, pp. 358–60). At the time of this writing a decision on the suit is still pending.

Setting aside the question of who was at fault, all of the available evidence clearly shows that from 1954 to 1961 relations between the tribe and the bureau could hardly have been worse.[3] In 1955 the Menominees immediately began complaining when the BIA made major staff cuts in the reservation superintendent's staff (*Menominee News,* January 27, 1955, pp. 1–3). In 1956 the tribe again complained when the reservation program officer, who was experienced in and sympathetic to the Menominees' problems, was transferred to another reservation and his position abolished (Robertson 1961). In 1957 the tribe demanded and got a new agency superintendent, after bitterly protesting the lack of help from the previous superintendent (Orfield 1965, chap. 4, p. 10). Two years later the Menominees again protested when the

[3]As late as 1974 a near-unanimous opinion still existed among the Menominees that the BIA was unhelpful or more harmful than helpful during implementation.

BIA decided that no work would be done to bring reservation roads up to state standards until a termination plan was completed, even though the time remaining between the date for final submission of the plan and the date for the final implementation of termination was insufficient to complete the work (Orfield 1965, chap. 4, p. 12).

Although the bureau did very little to help the tribe formulate plans for governing the reservation, obtaining government services, or managing their resources after termination, it did move vigorously on its relocation and adult-education programs.[4] These programs provided vocational and on-the-job training, as well as full moving expenses for entire families, one way, to any of several relocation cities in the United States (*Menominee News*, May 13, 1955, p. 4). The bureau downplayed the use of the programs as a strategy to accelerate assimilation of the Menominees (*Menominee News*, April 25, 1956, p. 5), but that clearly was the objective. The relocation and adult-education programs conformed with the secretary of the interior's position that the interests of the tribal group should not be given priority over the rights and interests of the individual Indian. "We believe," he said, "in the primacy of the individual Indian" (McKay 1955, pp. 1–7). By contrast, the Menominees tried to comply with the Termination Act and still preserve their *collective* identity as a tribe. The sharply contrasting views of the bureau and the tribe over the ultimate objectives of termination provided an exceedingly poor basis for cooperation during implementation.

Elsewhere in the national policy arena very little active interest in the Menominees was evident after completion of the Termination Hearings in 1954. President Eisenhower heartily endorsed Menominee termination when he signed the act into law and never again expressed an opinion on the subject. President John F. Kennedy opposed termination during his campaign for the presidency but did not intervene in the Menominee case after taking office. The Bureau of the Budget consistently supported implementation of Menominee termination. The bureau reasoned that the federal gov-

---

[4]The state of Wisconsin also sponsored an adult-education program for vocational education. Neither the bureau nor the state program initially provided money for college education (*Menominee News*, May 13, 1955, p. 6).

ernment should not continue to put money into the reservation because it would make life there more comfortable, thereby prolonging Menominee dependence on the government.[5]

While little national interest in Menominee termination was apparent beyond the involvement of Congress and the BIA, evidence of growing national opposition to termination as a strategy for achieving Indian assimilation was accumulating. National Indian organizations, such as the National Congress of American Indians, voiced strong opposition to termination (Josephy 1971, pp. 44–46). In fact, the termination issue served to join many tribes in a common effort to achieve more favorable Indian policies from Washington. Beginning in 1955 several other national organizations also expressed opposition to termination, including the National Council of Churches, the Religious Society of Friends (the "Quakers"), the Indian Rights Association, the Association of American Indian Affairs, and several national Protestant and Roman Catholic organizations (Debo 1970, p. 331). Several national figures were also "antiterminationists," including Sol Tax (Tax 1958) and Oliver LaFarge (LaFarge 1957).

Such opposition to Menominee termination had no direct impact on implementation of the process. The tribe simply was too small to draw national attention. Indirectly antitermination opinion may have encouraged the Menominees to seek congressional delays of final termination in the hope that the assimilation strategy might be reversed before they lost their reservation. The Menominees, however, needed little encouragement to pursue such delays.

Unlike Congress and the BIA, the state of Wisconsin was openly wary about the likelihood of successful implementation of the Menominee Termination Act. Although opposed to Menominee termination, the state never mounted a concerted effort to oppose the legislation. In 1954 the state was taken so unawares by the rapidity of events that the Termination Bill became law before the state could mobilize an effective response. After the act was a reality, the state

---

[5]The observation is based on an interview with a former commissioner of the BIA in 1974.

seemed to vacillate between a cautious optimism based on state pride that Wisconsin could "make it work" and a fatalistic view that termination was simply an inevitable fact with which to contend. In the words of one state spokesman:

> "Termination" is an ominous and ill-chosen word. We say this because there would be good occasion for the lapse of federal supervision only when the Menominees had achieved the individual, social and economic preconditions for successfully managing their own affairs, thereby rendering federal supervision superfluous. . . . The fact is that the cart having been put before the horse, transitional economic and governmental arrangements are required to even give minimum assurance of success. [Bowers and Fisher 1959, pp. 3–7]

Under these conditions the state had two objectives: (1) to avoid a drain on the state treasury for implementation expenses and (2) to mold implementation to assure the protection of state interests should the congressional experiment fail. The state's position on the form of government, the revenue for local government operations and services, and the methods of resource management for the reservation after termination can be interpreted in light of these two main objectives.

A major portion of direct state involvement in implementation was conducted through the Menominee Indian Study Committee (MISC). The committee was created in 1955 by the state legislature as an arm of the Legislative Council. Its membership included representatives from the tribe, the state agencies, the legislature, and the counties surrounding the reservation and was chaired by the state attorney general.

The membership of the MISC included three Menominees; one member each from two counties bordering the reservation; six members representing the state departments of taxation, public welfare, public instruction and highway commission; one state senator; two assemblymen; and the attorney general. The MISC was given a three-year life-span and was funded with $5,000 of state funds and $20,000 of tribal funds (Robertson 1961). It is noteworthy that the tribe's support of MISC functions was decided before the federal government agreed to reimburse the Menominees for termination expenses. The central function of the MISC was to report to the legislature on the progress of implementation so that appropriate state legislation could be drafted before the final termination deadline. It was also suggested that the MISC should disseminate information and interpret the implications of termination for the Menominees, develop leadership-training opportunites on the reservation, and "facilitate practical experience for the Menominee in assuming full citizenship responsibility" (Barton 1956).

In reality the MISC saw its function as elaborating and commenting upon the implementation options of the tribe, while always protecting the interests of the state (Orfield 1965, chap. 5, pp. 8-9). The committee contracted the University of Wisconsin to study the many problems involved in implementation (for example, Knight 1956; Loomer 1956; Brown 1957a; Ames 1958); however, Menominees responsible for implementation considered the studies of little value. In the words of one former tribal leader: "The University of Wisconsin took the position that they would provide information, but would not make recommendations. I don't think this was right."[6]

The MISC made many important recommendations to the state legislature which eventually were incorporated into state legislation.[7] Direct implementation aid to the tribe was less than satisfactory, however. The MISC conducted sporadic meetings throughout the implementation period, sometimes as much as six months apart. A review of the minutes shows a chronic attendance problem, lack of communication between the MISC and the Menominee people, and a general pattern of ineffective interaction between the MISC and the tribe. Recent interviews revealed that the Menominees had a very low opinion of MISC involvement in implementation.

[6]Quoted from an interview conducted in 1974. Most of the Menominees interviewed felt that the university studies were "not of much help" during the preparation for termination.

[7]For a concise summation of MISC's contribution to state termination legislation, see Robertson 1961.

In the words of one respondent: "The Menominee Indian Study Committee worked without Menominees to make decisions. Their primary concern was with the State of Wisconsin and the potential burden of the Menominees on the State."

In 1974, one Menominee recalled, "The MISC were good bureaucrats. They viewed the Menominees entirely in terms of the statutes on the books rather than changing laws to fit the Menominee situation. They thought about how they could change the Menominees." As an example of the MISC's inflexible position on innovation, Orfield notes that in the committee's review of possible organizational forms for tribal government after termination "those clearly not allowed by state law were eliminated. Thus novel arrangements such as leaving the reservation an unorganized area with no local government, or organizing the whole area as a village or city were rejected" (Orfield 1965, chap. 5, pp. 6–7).

The MISC worked most closely with the tribe in those areas where interests of the state and the Menominees merged. For example, the MISC consistently advised the legislature to support the Menominees' efforts to secure congressional postponements of the final date of termination and other tribal requests for federal aid.

In general, the state supported the tribe's desire to maintain its reservation intact as a separate county. The state legislature, however, wanted assurance that if the "experiment" failed the state would have other organizational alternatives, such as possible merger with or division among existing counties surrounding the reservation. To that end legislation was passed requiring two state evaluations of the county's success in five-year intervals after final implementation of termination.

If it should eventually be concluded that Menominee County was a failure, the state already had its alternatives planned, as indicated in this excerpt from an MISC report:

It is noted that Art. 13, sec. 7, Wis. Const., provides that a county of less than 900 square miles cannot be divided by the legislature, *except upon approval of the majority of the residents of the county by referendum.* Since the proposed county of Menominee would be 367 square miles in area, the question arises as to extent of legislative control once the county is created. The two issues which arise are legislative authority to dissolve the new county and legislative authority to divide the new county.

Under Art. 13, sec. 7, it would appear at first glance that subsequent division is prohibited. However, *State ex rel. Haswell v. Cram,* (1863) 16 Wis. 343, is authority for the legislature to attach a county of less than 900 square miles to a portion of a county of more than 900 square miles, making the first county total more than 900 square miles and thereafter to divide the county. [Bowers and Fisher 1959, p. 15; emphasis added]

The legislature wanted assurance that it could end the county experiment with or without the approval of the Menominees.

Regarding alternative sources of revenue to support new government operations and services after termination, the legislature's main concern was that the provision of required services should not become a burden on the state. The state's interest in selection of alternative management methods for the new county's resources and economy was founded on the same concern. In 1959 a MISC report noted, "It is a simple fact that the Menominees are not ready each to take full control of his property and collectively to manage their own economic affairs—regardless of Congress' assumptions in passing P.L. 399." The report went on to warn: "If the county becomes a deficit area as a consequence of management policies, the state will have to contribute" (Bowers and Fisher 1959, pp. 4–7).

The state's central concern in regard to natural resources was for the Menominees' economic base, their forest. The MISC warned that "neither the federal government [nor] the state of Wisconsin . . . can afford to sit by supinely and see the forest butchered into oblivion" (Bowers and Fisher 1959, p. 10). The state reasoned correctly that long-term preservation of the forest was the key to the Menominees' future. The legislature was determined to see that the forest was protected from all danger, including the possibility that the Menominees might themselves wish to sell or otherwise expend their property after termination. One cynical observer of the state's role in the implementation of termination remarked, "There has been a concern over the future of the magnificent trees on the reservation which, unfortunately, has not been matched by a concern for the people who live under them" (Ames 1959, p. 4).

State administrative agencies active in the implementation of termination tended to reflect the objectives and fears of the legislature. In addition, each agency worried about the implications of termination for their respective policy areas. The Department of Taxation worried about revenue; Public Welfare worried about increased caseloads; and the Conservation Commission worried about the Menominee forest. Most of the agencies participated in MISC studies or conducted implementation research on their own. In almost every case the research was designed to help the respective agency prepare for possible contingencies arising from state acquisition of a somewhat problematic population of Indians. The agencies were less-than-effective providers of direct problem consultation to the Menominees, although information generated from their studies was sometimes of value to the tribe.

Officially the office of governor remained opposed to termination throughout its implementation. Governor Vernon W. Thompson consistently endorsed MISC requests to Congress to postpone termination until the state was prepared to take over the additional responsibility (Honeck 1957). Some evidence exists, however, that toward the end of implementation, Governor Gaylor Nelson became somewhat irritated by the delaying tactics of the tribe and privately advised the tribe to "get on with it." This observation is based on a confidential interview with a former state official active in the implementation of termination. The official went on to suggest that the Menominees' delaying tactics probably would have worked out and termination would have been avoided if it had not been for the state Democratic administration's covert protermination position before final implementation of the act.

In any case, the main objective of the governor's office was to see implementation through smoothly to avoid problems for the state. The governor's office was not instrumental in providing direct aid to help the tribe implement termination.

Throughout implementation the state press remained generally indifferent and remarkably uninformed about termination. Although there was an appreciation of the problems pending for the state and the tribe, the media generally favored businesslike implementation of the legislation. In 1959 the state's leading paper commented:

> For the state a 72nd county is not an attractive prospect. But its creation seems to be the practical thing and what the tribe overwhelmingly wants. . . . Unless there is overwhelming evidence that the (termination) plan is faulty, the legislature ought to quit dilly-dallying . . . so that termination steps can proceed in the orderly way that has been laid out. [*Milwaukee Journal*, June 22, 1959]

Overall, the state's media exercised an almost negligible influence on the implementation process.

Two of the three counties surrounding the Menominee Reservation were the last remaining state policy subarenas to participate actively in the implementation of termination. Since combinations of merger with or division of the reservation among the surrounding counties were considered before agreement on a separate Menominee county, all three counties had a reason for participation. Shawano and Oconto counties had representatives on the MISC. Shawano, the county seat of Shawano County, was the closest large non-Indian population center to the reservation and clearly stood to be importantly affected by termination. Oconto County was particularly interested in acquisition of the Menominee forest, which county officials considered a "potential goldmine" (Ames 1956a, p. 3).

White residents of both counties tended to be more pessimistic about the outcome of termination than the people of the rest of the state. Their principal fear was that "the Menominees will fritter away their individual and/or collective assets and become paupers who will have to be supported by the county or state." There was also "a widespread concern over the future of the Menominee forest, equalled only by the concern over a potentially heavy welfare load" (Ames 1958, p. 11). Under these conditions the implementation objectives of county officials were twofold. If an opportunity emerged to gain some benefit for their county (for example, acquisition of the forest without responsibility for the people) they would attempt to seize it. Second, they would participate in implementation to assure that county interests were not harmed by implementation. Neither county was interested in adding to their own population the Menominees, with all of their potential problems.

State participation in the implementation of the Menominee Termination Act was marked, more than anything else, by a prevailing concern for the implementation objectives of the state. Various state officials often reinterpreted these objectives in terms of their own positions in the state policy process, yet the central objective of protecting the state from a political and fiscal disaster, should the Menominee experiment fail, remained salient throughout implementation.

The main objective of the Menominee people during implementation was to block termination. Soon after passage of the Termination Act, the BIA reservation superintendent wrote the BIA commissioner to say that "the Menominees, or at least their leaders, are violently opposed to withdrawal and have repeatedly stated in meetings 'The government and Congress want withdrawal, now let them do it as we don't want any part of it'" (*Menominee Tribe et al.* v. *United States* 1967, p. 43). A year later the BIA program officer on the reservation wrote:

> We are experiencing non-acceptance, resistance and a considerable bewilderment, irritation and conflict among the Menominee people. The mental state of the people is contrastingly different than you would expect from a group with their reputation. . . . Almost no one wants withdrawal and most are seriously confused. [*Menominee Tribe et al.* v. *United States* 1967, pp. 43–44]

Throughout the implementation period the Menominee General Council regularly passed unanimous resolutions favoring the postponement of termination. The last postponement resolution was voted only three weeks before termination took effect. Despite warnings from Representative Laird that "any chance for extension of termination . . . was very remote" and that the Senate "does not want to hear about any extension" (Robertson 1961), the Menominees continued to hope that, given more time, Congress might change its mind and repeal termination.

With a potential voting membership of all adult Menominees, the General Council was a good barometer of tribal attitudes toward termination. Besides voting many resolutions to postpone termination, the General Council became increasingly dissatisfied with the Menominee leaders, charging that they did not aggressively or effectively pursue the delay of termination. In 1960 such allegations were the basis for a successful General Council vote to replace the tribe's delegation to Congress and a narrowly unsuccessful motion to censure and remove the tribal chairman (Robertson 1961).

In addition to active opposition the General Council also reflected considerable passive opposition to termination. From October 1, 1955, to February 16, 1960, the General Council failed fourteen times to reach a quorum of seventy-five tribal members, despite the need for action on several important implementation decisions. The usual motivation for nonattendance was expressed by one Menominee woman: "Somehow they feel that if they don't attend the meetings, termination won't come" (Orfield 1965, chap. 5, p. 7).

Underlying the Menominees' opposition to termination was a deep apprehension about their fate as individuals and as a tribe. Many tribal members argued that over one hundred years of life within a "reservation culture" made a successful integration into the "white man's" world extremely difficult or impossible. Others feared that individually held property would be lost after termination through tax delinquencies and through liens placed on the homes of welfare recipients. Concern about the possible bankruptcy of the tribe's lumber industry because of the additional burden of state and local taxes also prompted considerable anxiety. Finally, many Menominees felt that the tribe was so hampered by internal divisions and ineffective leadership that it would never develop a workable plan to manage tribal affairs after termination (Ames 1958, pp. 4–11).

Concern about tribal factionalism was certainly well founded. Apprehension over termination tended to enliven old rivalries within the tribe and create new bases for division and conflict. Nearly all the cleavages cut across factional divisions; any individual was a potential claimant to membership in two or more factions. The result was a highly unstable environment for the effective planning and implementation of termination.

The separation between Menominee elites and nonelites was the most important of approximately eight divisions within the tribe. In 1958 about 90 of 500 Menominee families had at least one member in an important reservation position, such as an administrator in the tribal logging industry or a member of the board of trustees of the tribe's credit-and-loan program. Nearly all the "governing elites"—those people in leadership positions in tribal politics—belonged to the same families.[8] Elites tended to own the best homes and usually conformed to the white-middle-class stereotype. The nonelites represented most of the population. Generally they were laborers or were economically dependent upon the government. A large portion of the nonelites tended to be "unreliable" workers, led "unstructured" family lives (for example, allowed their children to "eat whenever they are hungry and go to bed when they please," Ames 1958, p. 36), and in the common estimate were not considered "responsible" individuals. "In their view, money is meant to be spent *now* for a good time; after enough money is made to satisfy their needs, they choose to stop working because other activities, such as hunting or fishing, are more highly valued by them than earning money" (Ames 1958, p. 36).[9] Usually elites tended to be more favorable to, or at least less threatened by, termination than nonelites.

A second factional split between "real" Menominees and "half-breeds" was based more on long-standing interfamily feuds than on any real distinction between "full-blood" Menominees and usurpers of that distinction. By 1950 the Menominee population on the reservation consisted of 97.3

[8]For a more detailed discussion of the governing elite and other Menominee "classes" see chapter 3.

[9]Much of the discussion of this and other pretermination divisions within the tribe is based on Ames 1958 and Ames and Fisher 1959. Ames used the term "Upper Crust" rather than "elite" and divided the nonelite into the "laboring class" and the "economically dependent class." It is with considerable reluctance that I note many of these tribal divisions, because to do so implies that some of the characteristics of the nonelite are singular characteristics of Menominees or, for that matter, that they are necessarily undesirable.

percent "mixed-bloods," with only eighty-two "full-bloods." The charge that someone was a half-breed was used mainly against political opponents and during implementation was repeatedly used to categorize any Menominee suspected of being in favor of termination.

Disaffection between non-Christians ("pagans") and Roman Catholics also contributed to tribal disharmony. Most of the Menominee elite were Roman Catholic, while the nonelite were Roman Catholics and non-Christians. The non-Christians tended to favor strongly the retention of native Menominee traditions and the weeding out of "half-breeds" from the tribal roles. Non-Christians were usually adamantly opposed to the implementation of termination.

David Ames offered an excellent description of a fourth ongoing tribal division between the "ins" and the "outs":

> The "outs" typically are aggressive and articulate and get elected to the advisory council or make themselves prominent by being the champions of the "little people" in the general council. But after a short period in office or as a spokesman for the "outs" they often obtain desirable positions on the payroll and become one of the "ins." The "little people" then look to someone else for leadership, someone else seizes the initiative, and the cycle repeats itself. [Ames 1958, p. 57]

During implementation the "ins" found themselves constantly embattled on two sides. On one side they faced relentless congressional pressure to get on with termination. On the other side they were continually reminded by the "outs" that the "little people" were totally opposed to termination.

A fifth distinction between the pro–Advisory Council group and the pro–General Council group closely parallels the division between elites and nonelites. The former group argued that the elite-dominated Advisory Council was the most effective governing body for the tribe. The latter group felt that the General council, with its membership composed of all eligible adult Menominee voters, should be the dominant decision-making institution. At one point immediately after the Termination Act became law, the General Council tried to abolish the Advisory Council but failed by a vote of 13 to 68 (Robertson 1961). The pro–General Council group was

more fundamentally opposed to progress on implementation.

The rivalry between the "radicals" and the "old men" represented a well-defined sixth tribal division, though both
groups supported the pro–General Council. Both saw themselves as defenders of the "little people." The "radicals" were
more interested in protecting the individual interests of tribal members (for example, the equitable, prompt distribution
of per capita payments from the tribe's savings accounts),
while the "old men" expressed a greater interest in preserving the tribal or communal interest of the "real Menominees."
Although both groups opposed termination, the "radicals"
exhibited a greater tendency for acceptance if it was accompanied by a per capita distribution of funds acquired from
the liquidation of tribal assets.

The "squaw men," a seventh tribal faction, were non-
Menominees, mostly whites, who were married to Menominee women. About one hundred families were within this
category. The squaw men had no voting rights in tribal
government and therefore had no way of directly advancing
their objectives or protecting the interests of their wives
and children during implementation of termination. There
is no record that this group took a position on termination.

Alienation between reservation residents and nonresident
Menominees provided the basis for yet another division between Menominee tribal members. Many reservation residents feared that nonresidents would be strongly in favor
of the sale of tribal assets and distribution of the proceeds
from that sale. They reasoned that nonresident Menominees
had little to lose from liquidation, since they had already
made a decision to leave the reservation. Although, as a
group, nonresidents did not actively seek liquidation, the
possibility of such action continued to concern tribal leaders
throughout implementation.

Thus it is clear that, while the Menominee people were
opposed to termination, they were also deeply divided among
themselves. These divisions, together with unrelenting congressional pressure to implement termination without delay,
made the political survival of any Menominee leader extremely precarious. Given this situation, elected leaders of

the tribe pursued four major objectives during termination: maintain their own political survival; preserve the tribe's liquid capital, land, and forest; stall final realization of termination as long as possible; and, when it appeared inevitable, implement a workable plan for termination. Leadership responsibility during these difficult years fell to the governing elite on the Menominee Advisory Council.[10]

In the earliest stages of implementation it soon became apparent that the Advisory Council had serious deficiencies. The first problem involved the General Council's power to override decisions of the Advisory Council. Under normal conditions before termination this power was seldom exercised and the governing-elite members of the Advisory Council were, in effect, policymakers for the tribe. The members of the governing elite were more knowledgeable about policy matters, and, since it was only a twelve-man group, the Advisory Council functioned more effectively as a decision-making group than the more unwieldy General Council.

Tribal politics during implementation were a different matter. From January, 1954, to April, 1965, ten of forty-eight Advisory Council resolutions were rejected by the General Council (Bureau of Government 1956, p. 15). This structural weakness in tribal government meant that elected leaders could not force necessary but unpopular decisions upon the reservation population.

A second problem involved the political vulnerability of the governing elite on the Advisory Council. The average member of the Advisory Council was forty-three years old, had served three previous terms, had completed about two years of high school, and held one of the better jobs at the tribal lumber mill (Bureau of Government 1956, p. 17). A seat on the Advisory Council was usually secure. In 1956 the pattern began to change. Four of twelve incumbents were defeated, and the old governing-elite majority was seriously weakened. Moreover, the campaign was unusually divisive, with charges of nepotism, needless spending of tribal money,

[10]For a description of the governing powers of the Advisory Council and the General Council see chapter 3. While some nonelite representation on the Advisory Council always existed, the governing elite tended to hold a majority of the twelve council seats.

and illicit love affairs and other smear tactics (Ames 1956d, p. 3). Under such volatile political conditions the already weak formal authority of the Advisory Council was even more seriously weakened by the deterioration of the individual political influence of the council members. This was happening when the tribe was most in need of forceful leadership.

The seriousness of the leadership crisis is clearly illustrated by the dissolution of the tribe's capital accounts. In 1954 the tribe had $10,437,000 in several savings accounts, with most of the money held in trust in the United States Treasury. By 1960 the tribe, in General Council resolutions, had voted itself a total of $9,265,424 in direct per capita payments from the capital fund and stumpage payments from earnings on the logging industry (Wisconsin Legislative Council 1966, pp. 18–19). The nearly complete dissipation of the capital accounts seriously depleted investment and operating accounts of the lumber industry and severely damaged the community's economic base.

Although aware of the critical fiscal problems generated by depletion of the capital accounts, the Advisory Council proved totally ineffective in its efforts to check the people's wish to pursue their immediate self-interest. Most of the Menominee people continued to vote according to their immediate self-interest throughout implementation of the Termination Act. In 1958 the Advisory Council presented to the General Council a motion for an assessment againt tribal members to help the tribe meet the costs of operating the reservation hospital and two parochial schools. In response the General Council passed a resolution by a vote of 117 to 0 stating, "The Menominee General Council is against any general assessment or partial assessment of the stumpage payment for the fiscal year 1958 for use in Tribal programs" (Robertson 1961). A later drive to solicit individual donations to keep the hospital open failed completely.

An observer of a 1956 Advisory Council meeting noted:

> The majority of the Council members indicated in the meeting that their constituents were applying terrific pressure on them to speed up the payments. . . . One of the Council members said, "We are all sitting on a powder keg . . . We better move

fast, after all the people have already directed us to make these payments in General Council." Most of the others joined him in urging that the payments be made as soon as possible and that the widest publicity be given to the fact that the Advisory Council had approved the release of these funds immediately, so that if there was any delay in making the payments, the onus would be shifted to the Agency. [Ames 1956b, pp. 1–2]

The members of the governing elite failed to protect the tribe's capital accounts. If they were going to protect other assets of the tribe from liquidation, they would have to find a way of soliciting the support of the general public or develop a mechanism to neutralize the negative power of the General Council. Moving toward the first goal, tribal leaders tried to keep the Menominee public informed on progress toward implementation by publishing a monthly newsletter *The Menominee News*. Although tribal leaders maintained that the newsletter was effective, many tribal members complained that it was "filled with legal and official terminology" and was "all Greek to them" (*Green Bay Press-Gazette*, December 6, 1958).

Partly because of their desire to avoid the General Council and partly because of a desperate feeling that they had to make some progress toward implementation or the tribe would soon find itself terminated with no plan for its own future,[11] the Advisory Council, in effect, admitted its own failure and convinced the General Council to elect a Coordinating and Negotiating Committee to implement termination. The new committee was composed of three members, but in reality the committee's business was run by George Kenote. Kenote, who had been serving with the BIA all around the country, was called back to the reservation because of his twenty-eight years' experience in the BIA and also because his long absence had left him free from association with any of the tribal factions. Kenote accepted the position of chairman of the Coordinating and Negotiating Committee with the understanding that he "was to have no connection with various

[11]The desperation was based on a provision of the Termination Act that provided for the secretary of the interior to appoint a trustee to handle Menominee affairs after termination if the tribe did not develop its own termination plan.

tribal cliques, and that he was to exercise real authority" (Orfield 1965, chap. 3, pp. 15–16).

Beginning its business on January 20, 1958, the committee, with considerable aid from tribal attorneys, completed a plan for implementation of termination in one year. Two law firms were involved, one from Milwaukee and one from Washington, D.C., plus an attorney from Shawano, Wisconsin. Many others contributed in some measure to completion of the final plan, including the MISC, the University of Wisconsin, and various state and federal officials. It is of interest to note that in 1974 the Menominees were divided in their opinion of the tribal attorneys' role in implementation. About half of the respondents considered the lawyers merely the helpful servants of the tribal leaders, while the other half suggested that the attorneys themselves acted as "leaders" and were key decision makers during this period.

On January 17, 1959, the General Council was faced with the decision either to approve the committee's plan or, by rejection of the plan, to surrender tribal responsibility for implementation to the secretary of the interior. With the creation of the committee the General Council had been effectively removed from direct involvement in implementation.

Creation of the Coordinating and Negotiating Committee did not automatically result in a trouble-free environment for smooth implementation of termination. The committee, like the Advisory Council, was unable to induce many of the Menominees to defer at least half of their per capita stumpage payments or accept discontinuation of free tribally financed health and education services to build up capital reserves in the lumber industry. Orfield has observed that, while "the committee was not afraid to make unpopular recommendations, it was unable to secure their adoption" (Orfield 1965, chap. 3, p. 16).

The committee also became the focus of continued pressure by the General Council to postpone termination as long as possible. The delaying strategy was clearly expressed by one tribal member: "I am for stalling it off as long as we can. We should appear to be preparing for it but really keep our wheels spinning" (Ames 1958, p. 6). The Coordinating and Negotiating Committee responded with continued recommendations to the state of Wisconsin and Congress for postponement of termination, even after the plan for implementing termination was complete and approved by the secretary of the interior.

Toward the end of implementation many of the governing elites finally became convinced that termination was inevitable. In January, 1959, the chairman of the Advisory Council told the General Council: "Cry as we may, we must present a (termination) plan and if we do not come up with a good, solid plan, we are all going to suffer" (*Green Bay Press-Gazette,* January 12, 1959). In 1974 a former leader who had been active in implementation recalled, "We all seduced ourselves into thinking termination would work."

Before, and especially after, the final date of termination was set many tribal members were heard to complain that the governing elite had "sold out" the Menominee people by accepting termination. Many other Menominees, however, have come to the conclusion that their former leaders at least thought they were making the right decisions. One former leader remarked, "It's so easy to say 'sold out.' The question is how? Would they have been happier if we would have just let the Secretary appoint the trustee of his choice?" Another Menominee remarked, "'Sold out' could only be said if they had originally supported termination, but they didn't."

It is certainly arguable that the governing elite, by grudgingly accepting termination and working for its implementation, was acting in what they perceived to be the best interests of the entire tribe. Congressional pressure for termination seemed insurmountable. Moreover, it is questionable whether the governing elite *could have* adjusted their thoughts and actions to conform to the demands of "the people." First, there was no clearly expressed alternative to implementation, beyond sincere nonelite fear and abhorrence of a new life without the reservation. Second, the members of the governing elite were among the Menominees least threatened by pending assimilation into white society.

Charles Lindblom has observed:

Elected and appointed proximate policy makers are overwhelmingly from the more favored classes. . . . To be sure, officials
do not see themselves as representing the interests of some classes
against others; rather it is that they see the general interest in
the light of their own group affiliations. . . . What is more, the
prestige of middle class attitudes and political preference is so
overwhelming in some countries, the United States included,
that many of the disadvantaged themselves subscribe to them,
thus endorsing and perpetuating the very bias in policy making
against which they might expect to protest. [Lindblom 1968, p. 68]

Lindblom's observation provides a plausible explanation for
the behavior of the governing elite. Perhaps the tribal leaders
could have pursued untried strategies to forestall or even
avoid termination. Yet, because of elite attitudes and values,
the leaders were not able to envision any alternative for the
Menominees' future beyond eventual assimilation into white
society. It may be true that, as one Menominee suggested,
the old leaders simply "didn't think 'Indian,' that is, like
Indian people." Yet, put in the context of the time, it is
difficult to suggest how the former leaders realistically could
have acted any other way than to proceed with the implementation of termination.

Every key decision made during the implementation of
termination was accompanied by a set of alternative actions.
One of the most important decisions centered on the choice
between alternative forms of government to replace tribal
government. In all, four options were seriously considered
(Bureau of Government 1956; Wisconsin Legislative Council
1957, 1959): (1) The reservation could be set up as an unorganized area with no formal county or local government but
still subject to the jurisdiction of the state. (2) The reservation could be divided between neighboring Shawano and
Oconto counties. (3) The reservation could be joined with
one of the three adjoining counties—Oconto, Shawano, or
Langlade. (4) The entire reservation could be transformed
into one new county.

The first alternative, transforming the reservation into
an unorganized area, was dismissed because of conflicts with
the state constitution and anticipated problems in selling

the unprecedented idea to the state legislature. Moreover, the fear existed that the state might unwittingly create a "state Bureau of Indian Affairs." That would hardly be in accord with the federal objective of Indian assimilation. The proposed division of the reservation between Shawano and Oconto counties was soon dismissed from active consideration because of an inability to reach agreement over equitable distribution of population and forest between the two counties. Shawano County complained that if the reservation was divided according to the then-current county boundaries Shawano County would receive nine-tenths of the Menominee population, but Oconto County would receive a disproportionate section of the tribe's forest lands. For this reason Shawano County remained adamantly opposed to such an alternative.

In 1958 the Coordinating and Negotiating Committee published a list of the advantages and disadvantages of the two remaining alternatives (see table 1). The list is informative, but it does not explain why the option of forming one new county prevailed over the possibility of merging the reservation with an adjoining county. Such an explanation is necessary, particularly in view of the several sound arguments against creation of a new county.

One argument centered on the small population of a separate new county. Wisconsin officials were seriously concerned by studies suggesting that a population of thirty-five to fifty thousand was the minimum desirable size for a county (Bureau of Government 1956, p. 67). The 235,000-acre Menominee Reservation had a population of about 3,500. Compared with the seventy-one existing Wisconsin counties, the new county would be seventy-second in total population, seventy-first in total assessed property value and density of population, and sixty-fourth in total land area (Bureau of Government 1956, pp. 56–57; "Menominee: Wisconsin's 72nd County," 1963, p. 3). The state and Menominee leaders also noted that if the BIA Relocation Program proved effective it would further reduce the new county's population.

The probable cost of government operations in the new county also troubled state officials. A 1956 estimate of expected expenditures strongly indicated that creation of a

TABLE 1. *Menominees' Assessment of Advantages and Disadvantages in Forming Local Government on the Reservation*

| Forming One County | Attaching to Another |
|---|---|
| **ADVANTAGES** | |
| 1. Better control of local taxes | 1. Government structures, including facilities, already established |
| 2. Better protection of tribal assets | |
| 3. Avoid unequal representation in County Government | 2. Availability of trained personnel, including lawyers, social workers, etc. |
| 4. Years of experience would provide better understanding of local problems | 3. Avoid responsibility of workout school problems (districting etc. by county school committee) |
| 5. Possibly avoid competing interests (agriculture v. forest affairs) | |
| 6. Possible representation in State assembly (legislation needed) | 4. Relieve ourselves of responsibility of governing |
| 7. No split of responsibility in County Government | 5. No split of responsibility in County Government |
| 8. Control of county ordinances | 6. Probably less expensive than having our own county |
| 9. One administration of tax kick-backs from state | |
| **DISADVANTAGES** | |
| 1. Lack of experienced personnel to begin with | 1. Need for action by state legislature to establish authority |
| 2. School districting problem to work out, alone or with other counties | 2. Need for referendum in county to which we propose to join (outcome unknown) |
| 3. Capital investment in setting up plant for County Government | 3. Unequal representation in County Government |
| 4. Assume responsibility for County Government | 4. Little voice in control of county and school district taxing |
| 5. Responsibility for collection of taxes | 5. Possible disinterest in forest affairs |
| 6. Probably more expensive than belonging to another county | 6. No local control of zoning and districting |
| 7. Need for legislative action to establish one county by state legislature | 7. No control of county ordinance making |
| | 8. No local control of administration of tax kick-backs from State |

Source: *Menominee News,* May 9, 1958.

separate county would be significantly more expensive than merger with an adjoining county (see table 2). The cost argument was particularly compelling for state officials already worried that the former reservation would cause a fiscal drain on state resources.

TABLE 2. *Estimated Expenditures for County Government*

| Budget Account | Placing Entire Reservation in An Existing County | Creating a Separate County |
|---|---|---|
| 1. General Government | $ 5,900 | $ 36,525 |
| 2. Protection of Person and Property | 11,500 | 25,345 |
| 3. Health | 18,375 | 17,375 |
| 4. Education | 5,850 | 15,500 |
| 5. Charities and Corrections | 71,275 | 75,275 |
| 6. Unclassified | 2,000 | 2,000 |
| Total | $114,900 | $172,020 |

Source: Bureau of Government, 1956.

The Menominees' lack of experience with self-government was a third argument against a separate county. State officials and Menominee leaders often noted that the BIA had not properly prepared the Menominees to take responsibility for their own affairs. Both groups felt that there would be a severe shortage of qualified people to run the new county. For example, no Menominees had the legal training required to be county judges or district attorneys (Ames 1958, pp. 80–84).

The possibility that the Menominee people lacked the political sophistication necessary to function as an informed electorate also worried state officials. Noting a chronic absence of quorums at General Council meetings, the domination of tribal politics by a small clique, and a lower Menominee voter turnout in Wisconsin general elections than that in surrounding counties,[12] the state argued that, as a product of one hundred years of dependence upon the federal government, the Menominee people were not prepared for meaningful political participation in their own government (Bureau of Government 1956, pp. 13, 62). State officials and several individual Menominees also feared that a separate county would perpetuate the power of the governing elite over tribal affairs and that nepotism and other undesirable characteristics of tribal politics would continue unabated.

Finally, many federal and state officials felt that a separate county might perpetuate the tribe's segregation and keep the Menominees "second class citizens" (Ames 1958, pp. 80–84). If, as a consequence, assimilation of the tribe was delayed, creation of the new county would frustrate the primary objective of termination.

All these objections to the formation of a separate county were well founded. Nevertheless, four arguments, both white and Menominee, were put forth in its favor. First, the state and Menominee governing elite argued that direct responsibility for their own affairs would enhance Menominees' self-reliance. As a low-status minority in an adjoining county, the Menominees could not effectively participate in the affairs of their own community. They would become apathetic "dropouts," lacking incentives to acquire skills and other attributes necessary for success in white society. Assimilation remained the objective, but with the creation of a separate county the likelihood of success would be greater because the Menominees could adjust to nonreservation existence at their own pace and would not be thrust into white-dominated counties as a disadvantaged minority.

Second, Menominee governing elites felt that their hope of forestalling individual Menominee demands for liquidation of tribal assets lay in maintaining the geographical integrity of the reservation. Much of their authority would be preserved as they assumed leadership positions in the new county government. Moreover, the state would be unable to implement necessary legislation for guaranteeing sustained-

[12]It was also noted at the time that the comparatively lower voter turnout might be attributable to the Menominees' lack of direct concern in local and state government issues (Bureau of Government 1956, p. 13).

yield management and protection of the Menominee forest unless it was wholly contained within a separate county.

The preservation of "Menomineeland" was a third, though unrealistic, argument for a separate county. Many Menominees feared that they would lose their land through tax delinquency and opposed the loss of some of the privileges of life on the reservation, particularly hunting and fishing rights (Ames 1958, pp. 40–44). Two MISC staff members observed that the Menominees' desire for a separate county was based in part on "a false expectation of being insulated from 'outside' demands." They reminded the Menominees that the new county "will not be 'Menomineeland,' but a unit of Wisconsin government . . . subject to the Wisconsin constitution and statutes" (Bowers and Fisher 1959, p. 2).

Finally, while it was not often mentioned publicly, a fourth argument for a separate county was white discrimination against Indians, particularly in counties adjoining the reservation. David Ames, an anthropologist, preferred to call discrimination and racism the "human factor." In a confidential report to the MISC he wrote:

> Excluding the human factor . . . a merger with a neighboring county would make for an easier transition from Reservation to Wisconsin governmental structure, and a more economical solution in terms of *over-all* efficiency. However, if the human factor is included, we must reckon with the heritage of differing Menominee and non-Menominee attitudes—toward each other and toward the same real or psuedo facts. Will it be too difficult or impossible to attain the minimum of mutual understanding, cooperation and good will between groups that is necessary to make a government function adequately for all of its citizens? I do not know . . . nor do I believe that there is any easy answer. [Ames 1958, p. 80]

The Menominees were sensitive about their status as Indians; many were distrustful of white men and feared the consequences of being a minority on a white-dominated county board. For their part, significant numbers of whites in the surrounding region felt that the Menominees had an "almost biologically inherent" inability to take care of themselves, were chronically dependent on free handouts from the government, preferred relief to work, and were unethical and dishonest or amoral, "like irresponsible children" (Ames 1959, pp. 63–74). Ames took pains to point out also that many instances of friendship existed between Menominees and their white neighbors. The fact remained, however, that enough discrimination and racism existed to make merger with an adjoining county impractical.

On September 9, 1958, a referendum was held on the reservation to determine the Menominees' preferences for local government after termination: 662 voters or 89 percent of the total votes cast favored a separate county. Voter turnout was 43 percent of the eligible voters (Robertson 1961). The low turnout might, in part, be because, if the members of the tribe had been given a real choice, they would have rejected all the reorganization alternatives and would have voted to continue their reservation as it was. Since the choice of voting to keep the reservation was not available, many Menominees just ignored the election and stayed home.

On January 17, 1959, the General Council approved implementation of a separate county as a part of the total termination plan. According to the plan that was devised, the new county would consist of a theoretical "town" with a county board of supervisors having joint membership on the town board. The single board was to consist of two members elected at large and one member from each of the county's five precincts (Fairchild, Foley, and Sammond 1959; Department of Interior, Bureau of Indian Affairs 1961). It was decided to merge the county and town governments to reduce administrative costs and the number of qualified personnel required to run the new county.

During the 1954 Termination Hearings, Senator Watkins offered his opinion that "the assimilation, or at least taking over by the state of Wisconsin and the local authorities, is almost complete as of now" (Joint Hearings 1954, p. 651). Senator Watkins's statement typified congressional ignorance of the Menominee Reservation and its people. Seven years later the implementers of termination faced a massive job of integrating the former reservation into the fiscal and governmental infrastructure of the state of Wisconsin.

Records for the Menominee Reservation are incomplete and often unreliable. On the basis of data available for 1960, however, a ranking of the reservation as a county among Wisconsin's other seventy-one counties provides a rough indication of the serious problems that would immediately face the new county government (see table 3).

TABLE 3. *Rank of Menominee Reservation Among Wisconsin Counties For Selected Characteristics, 1960*

| Characteristic | Rank |
|---|---|
| Total area | 64 |
| Total population | 72 |
| Population density per square mile | 71 |
| Percent increase in population, 1950–60* | 67 |
| Median age of population | 72 |
| Percent of labor force unemployed | 1 |
| Median family income | 72 |
| Percent of population 5–24 years old enrolled in school | 2 |
| Percent of population 25 years old and older who completed high school | 72 |
| Median school years completed | 72 |
| Percent of total housing units classed as sound | 72 |
| Total assessed valuation of all property (1961) | 71 |

*From 1950 to 1960 there was an actual net emigration of 342 people compared with a net increase of 195 and 260 people 1940–50 and 1930–40.

Source: "Menominee: Wisconsin's 72nd County," 1963, p. 3.

Early estimates of expected revenues and expenditures for government services after termination proved grossly optimistic. During the 1954 termination hearings the Wisconsin tax commissioner estimated that the cost of government operations and services would be approximately $250,000 a year. About $100,000 of the needed revenue would come from property taxes, the remaining $150,000 coming from interest on the tribe's capital accounts (Joint Hearings 1954, p. 659). During the formulation of the termination plan the Coordinating and Negotiating Committee remained optimistic, estimating that total annual government expenditures for the new county would be $380,000. They also estimated that profits from the tribe's logging mill and other industries would be $800,000 before taxes and interest. The committee concluded that "the available funds are thus more than twice the required budget" (Menominee Indian Tribe 1959, p. 7).

The search for the means to provide necessary government services in the new county led implementers of termination in several directions. Potential sources of support included federal and state aid, taxation, and contracts or agreements with other jurisdictions for the performance of services.

Both state and Menominee leaders hoped that the federal government would provide some financial assistance to the new county, at least for the first five or ten years after termination. The state realized that "a strong possibility" existed that in the first years of the county the value of taxable property would be less than the minimum amount required to provide sufficient revenues for government operations. State officials suggested that

> if it were possible to omit relief and categorical welfare costs for the Reservation from the county budget, the Reservation would no doubt have an adequate property tax base to meet its proportionate share . . . as a separate county. It is possible that the federal government might, at least for an initial period, be willing to assume all or part of the estimated total welfare costs. . . . It is also possible that if the federal government could not assume such costs, the State of Wisconsin could assume all or part of the welfare burden on much the same grounds as it presently makes payments to distressed counties. [Bureau of Government 1956, p. 49]

Unfortunately, Congress did not provide transitional aid for the new county, beyond a partial reimbursement of expenditures incurred during the tribe's preparation for termination.[13] The Wisconsin State Legislature also refused to extend aid to the new county. The end result was that no special federal or state aid was available to Menominee County at the outset of termination.

Orfield notes that the state of Wisconsin "simply assumed that the tribe must provide all services and meet all criteria

---

[13]Considerable aid was extended to the new county after the final implementation of termination, but it was authorized after termination had gone into effect.

imposed by state laws and do so with no sustained state assistance" (Orfield 1966, p. 8). State officials, with the reluctant approval of the Coordinating and Negotiating Committee, pressed for the maximum allowable local tax rates in the new county. With the adoption of sustained-yield management, however, the forest could not be assessed to full stumpage value. In order to achieve the highest possible tax base, the state urged that the forest be assessed at 40 percent of its market value, a higher percentage than that of any other sustained-yield forest in the state (Sammond 1959). The state was determined that the new county would pay its own way after termination.

The Menominee leaders also expected serious tax-collection problems. A newspaper reporter who attended a meeting by the Coordinating and Negotiating Committee to explain new termination plans noted that many elderly tribal members simply did not comprehend the meaning of the word "taxes." He observed wryly that "perhaps few things more painful to the Menominees will come out of this . . . than the real meaning of the word 'taxes'" (*Green Bay Press-Gazette,* January 15, 1959). The probable difficulties of tax collection had been illustrated by an earlier experience when an uproar erupted among parents of school children over assessment of a ten-cent-a-day charge for their children's school lunches (Ames 1958, p. 9).

The new county would also face problems in the delivery of services. Wisconsin statutes permitted counties to contract for or take joint action with adjacent counties to negotiate the delivery of required local services (Bureau of Government 1956, p. 59). Menominee leaders began seeking service contracts and other joint agreements with neighboring counties for several services, including education, law enforcement, health, and welfare.

The termination plan called for merger of the new county with the city of Shawano in a joint school district. The Coordinating and Negotiating Committee estimated that it would cost $150,000 a year to operate and maintain a public elementary school in the county and to pay tuition and transportation costs for children attending elementary schools and high schools outside the county.

The judicial system for the new county was joined with that of Shawano County. Although the new county would have its own sheriff, the district attorney, municipal court, juvenile court, and jail would be located in Shawano County. The Menominees would pay a portion of the district attorney's salary but would not participate in his election (Gordon 1971, pp. 13–14; Menominee Indian Tribe 1959, p. 9).[14]

The Coordinating and Negotiating Committee also planned to set up a contractual agreement with Shawano County for health and welfare services. Maintenance of health facilities, notably the reservation hospital, proved to be an insolvable problem, however. The reservation hospital was operated with tribal funds. The Coordinating and Negotiating Committee planned to transform the hospital into a corporation and operate it on a fee basis. To cover the transition the tribe would apply $50,000 of its funds with a matching amount from the federal government. The matching federal funds never arrived. When the hospital was given the additional burden of meeting state inspection standards, it was forced to close well before the final termination date.

The implementation of contractual and other service agreements helped the Menominees cope with problems of inadequately trained personnel and excessive administrative costs. A danger existed, however, that service agreements, particularly those for education and law enforcement, might be jeopardized by intercounty conflicts between Menominees and their white neighbors.

State and Menominee leaders made optimistic estimates of the costs of operating the new county. The estimate of the Coordinating and Negotiating Committee was $380,000 for expenditures with an expected income of $800,000 in the first year. The inaccuracy of their estimate became painfully obvious in the weeks before final termination. A severe recession in the timber industry decreased the demand for sawlogs and the sawmill was forced to lay off 150 of its 550 employees (*Capital Times,* May 6, 1961). The medical and hos-

[14]Although originally excluded from jurisdiction under Public Law 280, the tribe requested and was placed under the law in August, 1954. Public Law 280 allowed the state to administer law enforcement within the reservation.

pital insurance of the laid-off mill employees was suspended, and medical welfare costs went up $35,000. Many more Menominees became eligible to draw surplus farm commodities. Distribution costs totaled an additional $12,000. The Division of Children and Youth of the State Welfare Department was standing by with an unforeseen bill of $50,000 for the care of Menominee juvenile delinquents. In 1959 only four cases of tuberculosis were reported on the reservation. Immediately before the full implementation of termination twenty-one active cases were on record. The additional cost for medical care was $75,000. The estimate of the cost of government operations in the new county's first year was revised upward to $570,000. Total revenues were expected to be about $340,000 plus school taxes. The new county was going to be $170,000 short (Dadisman 1961). Little reason for optimism existed on the eve of termination.

The means for assuring successful management of the Menominees' resources and economy was another major area of concern to the state and tribe. Protection of the Menominee forest was seen by everyone as the key to successful termination. The forest represented continuing jobs and income for the Menominees, a stable property-tax base for local government services, and the basis for future industrial and recreational development. Without the forest the idea of a separate county was meaningless.

At least fourteen alternative futures for the Menominee forest-and-milling industry were considered by the implementers of termination (Knight 1956; Mackie et al. 1956; Brown 1957a, 1957b; Wisconsin Legislative Council 1958). By combining similar alternatives, the list can be reduced to seven options.

The first choice, sale of tribal assets and equal distribution of the proceeds, was the easiest alternative to understand and implement. It represented a clear step toward rapid assimilation. A strong indication also existed that many Menominees were in favor of it. One Menominee commented, "I'd rather get my $10,000 now than have only 10 cents later on" (Ames 1958, p. 90).

The state and most members of the governing elite, however, strongly opposed liquidation. It represented an irrevocable act that would in all likelihood mean subdivision and loss of the sole economic base of the area. The state feared that most of the Menominees would quickly spend their per capita payments and become economically dependent. Many Menominees, particularly the more conservative older people, were adamantly opposed to the sale of the reservation under any circumstances.

Some of the elite Menominee families developed fallback strategies in case liquidation occurred. Plans were made to pool money and buy a large block of the reservation for jointly managed recreational development or to sell part of the reservation, retaining the remainder for joint ownership by the tribe (Ames 1958, pp. 93–98). George Kenote recalled that when it became known that the Menominees "would only get thirty cents on a dollar for the value of the forest, mills, everything, [it] took the wind out of the movement to liquidate and divide Menominee assets." The state insisted on sustained-yield management, which severely depressed the forest's market value.

The sale of the forest to a non-Menominee corporation was a second option that was considered and rejected. If it had been adopted, it might have led to the institution of sound management of the forest as an industry, but it could also have led to the dissipation of tribal assets. Moreover, it was unlikely that a corporation could have been found to purchase the entire forest.

A third choice, ownership and operation of tribal assets by the new county, was considered but quickly discarded. Finding the financial means to permit county acquisition of tribal property was considered impossible.

Transfer of the reservation from federal to state trusteeship with the tribe retaining ownership of its assets gained some support as a fourth alternative. Under state trusteeship proper management could be guaranteed; however, a state reservation would require state enabling legislation and approval by the tribe and the secretary of the interior. The state eventually rejected the idea because it did not want to create a "state BIA" to administer the reservation. Moreover, state trusteeship was inconsistent with the objectives of termination.

Outright federal or state acquisition of the Menominees' timberland, with subsequent management of the land as a park or forest, was considered as a fifth option. For a time the idea of a national park was more popular among the Menominees than any other alternative (Ames 1957, p. 2). It was viewed as the best way to preserve the reservation and the Menominees' accustomed way of life. Ultimately the proposal was rejected because of the high cost of acquisition and because it would not provide for sustained-yield management and would endanger the continued operation of the tribe's forest-products industry.

The sixth alternative, ownership and management of tribal assets by the Menominees as either a private cooperative or a corporation, offered several advantages. The Menominees would have full control over their resources, keep all profits from their forest and industry, learn by experience to manage a major business, and retain many features of reservation life, including private hunting and fishing rights. It has been said that members of the governing elite supported this alternative because they could preserve their community status and avoid facing competition of white society (Gordon 1971, p. 23). In the end this alternative was rejected because the cooperative or corporation would be required to carry the full load of property and income taxes, separate economic and government functions would have to be maintained, and, most important, the state lacked confidence in the Menominees' ability to manage their own affairs.

The final option, continued ownership of assets by the Menominees with management provided under a private-trust agreement, won the approval of the state and tribe. Menominee ownership combined with a management trust offered many of the advantages of the preceding alternative. Moreover, it relieved the state's concern for high-quality professional management. Non-Menominee professional expertise could be employed through the trust agreement to safeguard tribal assets. The management trust also offered income-tax advantages not available to a corporate form of organization. After the long debate on all the alternatives, the new plan for managing the tribe's resources and economy moved rapidly.

Overall trust responsibility for Menominee assets after termination would be assigned to the Menominee Common Stock and Voting Trust (also referred to as the Board of Trustees and the "voting trust"). By a vote of 84 to 4, the General Council approved the voting trust. Four Menominees and three non-Menominees were elected to positions on the trust. The voting trust, in turn, selected five non-Menominees and four Menominees to serve on a board of directors, which would supervise management of a new corporation called Menominee Enterprises Incorporated (MEI).

Transferred to the voting trust were 327,000 shares of corporation stock valued at one dollar per share. The trust then issued voting-trust certificates — not shares — to the tribe. The former stumpage payments, based on annual timber cut, became income bonds. One bond, with an annual yield of $120 and a maturity value of $3,000 in the year 2000, was issued to each tribe member.

The adoption of a voting trust, the formation of a board of directors, and the use of voting-trust certificates and income bonds were all motivated by the desire of the state and tribal leaders to retain assets of the tribe intact within the corporation. Corporate decisions could be made with a two-thirds majority of the voting trust, not a two-thirds majority of MEI stockholders. All former reservation land was retained by MEI and must be purchased from the corporation by the occupants. The state passed legislation (the Trinke Amendment) which forbade sale or mortgage of any tribal property without approval by the Wisconsin Conservation Commission and the governor. An absolute restraint on alienation of voting-trust certificates was imposed for five years. Income bonds were nonnegotiable for three years after termination, and were then negotiable only with either the corporation or the state. The state argued that trade restraints and other restrictions on corporation assets were necessary if the new corporation and county were to have a chance for survival.[15]

The adoption of a non-Menominee majority for the new MEI Board of Directors was hotly debated in the General

[15]The management trust has been discussed in some detail because of its importance after termination was implemented. Much of the foregoing description of the corporate structure of MEI is based on Gordon 1971, pp. 24–29.

Council and finally gained approval by a close sixty-one to forty-nine vote (Van Ryzin 1959). Many Menominees did not want non-Menominees to have a controlling voice in tribal affairs. Prevailing Menominee attitudes, however, favored a non-Menominee majority on the board to protect the corporate management from becoming entwined in tribal politics. Many Menominees argued that difficult management decisions, such as the laying off of surplus personnel, would have to be made if the corporation was going to avoid bankruptcy after termination. This position was even advocated by several laborers who knowingly stood to lose their jobs as a result of such a policy (Ames 1958, p. 96). An even more compelling reason for a non-Menominee majority was the need to convince the state that the corporation had a stable management basis.

The Menominees just managed to beat, by a week, the final deadline for submission of a termination plan. The state legislature was threatening to delay or withhold approval of the plan, thereby making implementation of the termination the responsibility of the secretary of the interior. Under this pressure, the Menominees readily accepted a non-Menominee majority on the board of directors and many other state "recommendations."

Two additional aspects of the plan for management of tribal assets became extremely controversial after the implementation of termination was complete. The first was the decision to employ the First Wisconsin Trust Company to hold all voting certificates and income bonds of Menominee minors (youth under twenty-one) and incompetents. The decision to employ a single trust was based on a desire to save administrative and court costs involved in separate guardian agreements and was also a response to BIA and state pressure to set up a "competent" system to handle the assets of minors and incompetents. The ability of the trust company to exercise the certificate voting rights of the minors and incompetents and thereby exercise a controlling influence on corporate affairs was recognized as an inherent danger in the arrangement; however, tribal attorneys dismissed the danger and the trust was established (U.S., Senate, Hearings 1961, p. 131).

The planned recreational development in the new county

was another controversial subject. Arguments for recreational development were based on a desire to develop the natural resources of the area and broaden the tax base necessary to support county operations. Many Menominees, however, were strongly opposed to the sale of reservation land and the ensuing influx of non-Menominees into the new county. Studies of the possibilities for a commercial recreation industry were begun as early as 1956 (Loomer 1956), and in 1958 the Coordinating and Negotiating Committee was actively pursuing a plan for the construction of tourist cottages along the Wolf River and in other attractive areas (*Menominee News,* October 28, 1958; January 28, 1959). With the adoption of the MEI voting trust, the management of the new corporation could make decisions necessary to the pursuit of a recreational development program without a favorable majority vote of the tribal membership.

In sum, the plan finally implemented for management of the tribe's resources and economy had three significant characteristics. First, a genuine potential existed for operational conflicts between the new county and the corporation. Because MEI would be the single-largest source of tax revenue, conflict could arise in the maximization of county revenue and services, the maximization of corporate income for such purposes as plant expansion, and the payment of income to holders of corporate stocks and income bonds. Also, given the limited number of Menominees qualified to hold government and corporate positions, conflict was possible among the various county officials, who would be required to make welfare and taxation decisions which affected themselves and who also had probable roles as joint owners, officers, and employees of the largest taxable property (Bowers and Fisher 1959, p. 7).

Before termination the MISC was warned:

> The legislature is being asked to create a "company county," with one government, one landowner combined with one industrial corporation, and with one ethnic group dominant. Their boundaries would be exactly the same; their powers would be overlapping, not countervailing. Sizable conflicts of interest are latent in this situation, all of which call for the erection of safeguards of the legislature. [Bowers and Fisher 1959, p. 11]

Second, the plan for the management of the tribe's assets offered a mechanism for the governing elite not only to retain but to expand their control of tribal affairs. While they would share their authority with the non-Menominees on the MEI Board of Trustees and Board of Directors, they would not have to debate before and win the approval of the General Council for major decisions, such as land sales. Assuming that they could take most of the responsible positions in county government and maintain harmony with policy objectives of the state, the governing elite stood to remain entrenched in the public and private power structure of the new county.

Finally, the termination plan was, in effect, a collective series of private substitutes for the Bureau of Indian Affairs. Under the corporate plan the Menominee people would have considerably less to say about the management of their assets than they had had under the bureau. The First Wisconsin Trust would stand *in loco parentis* to Menominee minors, far more than the BIA had (Bowers and Fisher 1959, p. 4). Absolute control over sale of Menominee land would be exercised by the state rather than the federal government. With termination the Menominees would be freed of BIA supervision, but their property would remain outside their control.

*Menominees shopping after receiving $1,500 share payment, 1954.*
Milwaukee Journal *photo.*

*Governor Gaylord Nelson signing the bill which created Menomi-
nee County, July 31, 1959. Photo by* Capital Times. *Courtesy of
the State Historical Society of Wisconsin, Madison, Wis.*

*Menominee schoolchildren, 1960. Courtesy of Menominee Self-Determination Office.*

*Menominee Indian youth in ceremonial dance, 1961.* Milwaukee Journal *photo.*

# 6

# TERMINATION AND POLICY PERFORMANCE

*A review of developments in Menominee County since termination of
the Federal trust in 1961 makes clear how ill-advised were the terms
on which the Menominees were deprived of Federal services and
supervision. . . . The Department of the Interior sees no alternative to
combined State and Federal support of the county and its people, who
are in desperate circumstances. Continuation of the present trend will
threaten the existence of the corporation and lead to decline of county
services, to the detriment of the Menominee people and their non-Indian
neighbors in Wisconsin. To stand idly by and watch the further growth
of such a pocket of poverty is unthinkable.* — Department of the
Interior, Bureau of Indian Affairs, "The Status of Termination
of the Menominee Tribe," 1965, p. 6097

IN 1971, ten years after implementation, Menominees still
vigorously debated the success of termination. Many of those
who held elective office in county government or managerial
positions in Menominee Enterprises, Inc., argued that, in
spite of many obstacles, termination was going well. It was
giving members of the tribe more opportunities to prosper
and to grow away from dependency on the BIA and a reservation way of life. Others, however, argued that termination was a failure at its inception. Federal and state aid,
corporate diversification, and other survival strategies only
succeeded in reducing the size of the disaster. This chapter
examines the performance of termination policy in the first
decade after implementation of the Menominee Termination
Act.

Policy implementation and policy performance are two
distinct phases of the policy process. As pointed out in the
preceding chapter, policy implementation can be thought
of as building or setting up the "machinery" to carry out the
decisions of public policymakers. Policy performance, by
contrast, refers to the operation of that machinery once it
has been implemented. To assess the performance of the

political and administrative machinery set up to carry out
Menominee termination, this discussion will focus on government operations and services within Menominee County
and the role of Menominee Enterprises, Inc., as sole manager
of the county's economy. Performance of the county and
corporation in their first years of operation also provides
the basis for an appraisal of the early successes and failures
of Menominee termination.

When Menominee County was established on May 1, 1961,
it was the poorest county in Wisconsin. The new county was
immediately declared a "depressed area" to make it eligible
for federal grants and aids (*Appleton Post-Crescent*, September
2, 1962). More than ten years of termination did little to
change this bleak picture. In 1972 the Bureau of Indian Affairs declared:

> Upon termination the reservation became a county which today
> is the most poverty-stricken in the State of Wisconsin. Public
> expenditures which were to decrease over time soared from an
> annual figure of $160,000 before termination to almost $2,000,000
> thereafter. Yet despite the cost the county ranks at the bottom
> of Wisconsin counties in employment, income, education, health,
> housing, property values and other areas. [Department of the
> Interior, Bureau of Indian Affairs 1972, p. 7]

Because early records are often incomplete or compiled
in ways that make interpretation difficult, a systematic chro-
nological report on the first years of Menominee County's
existence is impossible. Nevertheless, a composite picture of
the county after termination can be drawn from available
information. An examination of personal income, employment, health and welfare, housing, and education tends to
lend support to the BIA's gloomy portrait of the new county.

Menominee County consistently ranked as the Wisconsin
county lowest in family and per capita income. In 1964, 74
percent of Menominee family incomes were under $3,000
($2,677 average), which was the highest percentage among
Wisconsin counties.[1] By 1970 the relative income of Menomi-

---

[1] The next highest percentage was 48.2 percent for Burnett County,
and the lowest percentage was in Waukesha County, where only 8.7 percent of family incomes were below $3,000 (Wisconsin Legislative Council
1966, p. 62).

nees had not changed. Per capita income in the county, at
$1,028 compared with a $3,158 state average, was the lowest
among Wisconsin counties. Family income in Menominee
County was $5,758 in 1969 versus $10,069 in the state (Wisconsin Legislative Council 1966, pp. 43, 62; Department of
the Interior, Bureau of Indian Affairs 1972, p. 3; Department
of Business Development 1972).

Employment statistics were as bleak. From 1964 to 1973
unemployment ranged from 18 to 28 percent with seasonal
highs reaching 40 percent. In 1970, 46 percent of Menominees aged sixteen to sixty-four were on the labor force, versus 59 percent for the state. Employment for women in the
county was all but nonexistent, and jobs for young Menominees who had completed college or vocational-education programs were extremely scarce. A large portion of well-educated Menominees moved outside the county to find employment (Wisconsin Legislative Council 1966, p. 43; 1973,
p. 5; U.S., Senate, Hearings, 1965–66, p. 219; *Milwaukee Journal,* November 7, 1971; Department of the Interior, Bureau
of Indian Affairs 1972, pp. 3–4)).[2]

The most spectacular rise in county expenditures after
termination was in the area of health and welfare. From
1962 to 1970 expenditures for these services rose from $72,740
to $605,700, for a total increase of $532,960, or 833 percent,
in eight years. Aid to Dependent Children rose from 91
cases, costing $2,828 in May, 1961, to 432 cases, costing $26,829
in 1967. The total amount of welfare assistance for Menominee County during one month in 1965 averaged $7.43 for
each person versus a state average of $1.85 per person. Fifty
percent of Menominee County residents were on welfare in
1968. Twenty-five percent of Menominee County families received public assistance in 1970 versus 3 percent for the state.
In the area of health 25 percent of the county's residents
had no health coverage in 1970. In 1966 tuberculosis treatment costs in the county were $23.82 per capita versus $1.10

[2] In 1971 the total labor force in Menominee County was 640: 210 were
employed in manufacturing, 240 in nonmanufacturing, nonfarm jobs, and
30 in farm-related jobs, 160 were unemployed, making an unemployment
rate of 25 percent (Northeastern Wisconsin Health Planning Council 1971,
p. 3).

in the state. Also in 1966, 93.5 percent of Menominee school children were in need of dental care. In 1964, 113 problem drinkers existed among the 496 families in the county. A doctor did not practice in the county from 1961 to 1972. Twenty-five percent of Menominees eligible for the labor force by their age, excluding inmates and students, were disabled in 1970 (Department of the Interior, Bureau of Indian Affairs 1972, pp. 3–4, 8, 64; Wisconsin Legislative Council 1966, p. 27; *Wisconsin Blue Book* 1968, pp. 648–53; U.S., Senate, *Congressional Record,* 1966, p. 24251; Fields 1965; Northeastern Wisconsin Health Planning Council 1971, p. 12; Deer et al. 1971, pp. 16–17; Blackwell 1972).

Housing conditions were the poorest in the state at the outset of termination and remained that way. In 1970 one-half of the homes in the county did not have complete plumbing and central heating. One-third had telephones, versus 90 percent for the state. In 1970 the value of Menominee County homes was $5,100 compared with $15,300 in the state (Department of the Interior, Bureau of Indian Affairs 1972, pp. 3–4).

In education the median grade completed for Menominees twenty-five and older rose from 8.4 years in 1964 to 9.2 years in 1970, but the state average in 1970 was 11.9 years. A pronounced shift from attending parochial schools to attending public schools occurred, which contributed to rising educational costs for county residents. Most Menominee students attended junior high and high school in Joint District Eight schools outside the county. In 1972 parochial and public elementary schools in the county ranged from 92 to 100 percent Indian, while junior high and high schools outside the county ranged from 15 to 30 percent Indian. Charges of discrimination were continuously voiced by Menominees against District Eight schools. The Menominees' complaints culminated in a Department of Health, Education, and Welfare, Office of Civil Rights, investigation, which concluded in 1972 that the district was in violation of the Civil Rights Act. The dropout rate for Menominees in grades nine to twelve was 69 percent versus 17 percent for non-Menominees. In 1971–72, 48 percent of the Indian students in District Eight schools were suspended, versus 5 percent of white students. (On the discrimination problem see Shames, ed., 1972, pp. 45–66; U.S., House, Hearings, 1973, pp. 76–78; Kreisman 1972; Mines 1972; *Milwaukee Journal,* March 11, 1973. For other data see Wisconsin Legislative Council 1966, p. 43; Department of the Interior, Bureau of Indian Affairs 1972, pp. 3–4.

Clearly termination did not improve the quality of life for Menominee Indians. In 1972 the Bureau of Indian Affairs accurately summed up the situation when it reported:

> A close examination of the data for Menominee County reveals that the socio-economic situation of the Tribe is most precarious. Any "progress" that has been achieved since termination has been accomplished largely by the massive infusion of public funds into the area. The slight improvement in average family income, for example, is largely due to increased welfare expenditures, expenditures of the anti-poverty programs of O.E.O., and other public spending. Little or no gains have been made in the private sector of the economy. . . . Almost without exception the economic and social indicators for the Menominees are considerably lower than those of any other population segment in the State of Wisconsin. [Department of the Interior, Bureau of Indian Affairs 1972, p. 3]

Expenditures for local government and services during the first years of termination were a major burden on the new county. From 1962 to 1970 the combined county, town, and school expenditures rose by an average annual increase of $102,730. Total expenditures of $663,614 in 1962 rose 239 percent in eight years to $1,588,217 in 1970 (see table 5). The performance of Menominee termination is reflected in part by the county's inability to raise sufficient revenues to meet local demand for government services. A brief glance at the sources of county revenues (see table 4) reveals that state and federal aids were largely responsible for keeping the county solvent after termination.

In the ten years before termination annual government assistance to the tribe ranged from $20,000 to $70,000 (U.S., Senate, Hearings, 1965–66). A 1971 state of Wisconsin study found that from 1961 to 1971 combined federal and state grants-in-aid (regular and special) totaled $19,127,650 (federal total, $11,702,584; state total, $7,425,066). Among the highest subtotals for the ten year period were $2,283,709 for federal aid for education, $2,401,811 for federal housing aid, $1,028,192 for state aid for welfare, $888,000 for federal aid for sewer and sanitation improvement, $463,774 for federal aid for health, and $358,527 for state highway aid (Moulin 1971a, p. 1).

The state of Wisconsin was extremely reluctant to grant special aid to Menominee County. State officials argued that, since termination was the idea of Congress, it was the responsibility of the federal government to provide the necessary funds to bring Menominee County up to state standards for government services.[3] During debate over a plan to aid the county's revenue problem, this attitude was reflected in one state official's warning that "it would be extremely unfortunate if Congress were given the impression that this problem is being solved by the state, and there is no need for federal assistance" (Wisconsin Legislative Council 1965a, p. 6).

State reluctance to aid the county is also reflected in the pattern of shared taxes and state aids to Menominee County compared with other Wisconsin counties. Menominee County was one of the least-subsidized counties in the state in its first four years of existence. In 1965 using

Aids and shared taxes as a percentage of state total
_____

Net property tax as a percentage of state total

as the criterion for allocating aids, "five counties, including Menominee County, subsidized the remainder of the state" (Harkin 1969, p. 8). Only Milwaukee County did more. With increased welfare costs Menominee County began to fare better in county competition for state aids, but by 1968 twenty-four counties were still more heavily subsidized according to this measure.[4] Local taxes in Menominee County were among

[3]Wisconsin officials argued that termination had placed a "special burden" on the state, a burden not held by other states and that, therefore, Wisconsin should receive special federal aid (Wisconsin Legislative Council 1965a, p. 8; 1966, p. 46).

[4]It should be noted that on a per capita basis Menominee County became one of the most heavily subsidized counties in the state, ranking sixth. The high per capita aid reflects the level of welfare payments in the county (Harkin 1969, p. 86).

TABLE 4. *Expenditures and Revenues: Menominee County, Town, and School, by Year, 1961–1970**

| | Budget Year, Dollars | | | | |
|---|---|---|---|---|---|
| | 1962 | 1964 | 1966 | 1968 | 1970 |
| Expenditures | | | | | |
| County and Town | | | | | |
| General government | 44,039 | 74,412 | 80,326 | 105,061 | 127,031 |
| Protection of persons and property | 62,744 | 75,498 | 86,731 | 96,880 | 123,821 |
| Health and social services (welfare) | 72,740 | 198,041 | 262,520 | 383,317 | 605,700 |
| Education and recreation | 12,002 | 12,921 | 11,961 | 19,999 | 26,463 |
| Highways, streets, and bridges | 229,576 | 185,336 | 267,678 | 271,226 | 319,028 |
| Sewer and water | ......... | 15,000 | 16,000 | 46,237 | 25,015 |
| Miscellaneous | 21,668 | 6,265 | 11,601 | 11,301 | 9,522 |
| Subtotal, county and town | 442,769 | 567,473 | 736,817 | 934,521 | 1,236,520 |
| Joint School District 8† | 220,845 | 246,571 | 252,450 | 297,094 | 351,637 |
| Total expenditures | 663,614 | 814,044 | 989,267 | 1,231,615 | 1,588,217 |

| Revenues | | | | | |
|---|---:|---:|---:|---:|---:|
| Property taxes—county and town | 296,394 | 339,453 | 300,824 | 280,653 | 139,845 |
| Property taxes—school | 845 | 114,571 | 208,450 | 147,094 | 201,637 |
| Total property taxes | 297,239 | 454,024 | 509,274 | 427,747 | 341,422 |
| Other taxes | 8,061 | 19,687 | 29,084 | 31,910 | 50,413 |
| Special federal aids—schools | 220,000 | 132,000 | 44,000 | 150,000 | 150,000 |
| Special federal aids—health and welfare | ......... | ......... | ......... | 221,632 | 224,913 |
| Other state-federal aids | 94,602 | 201,116 | 251,846 | 269,412 | 520,307 |
| Earnings and miscellaneous | 66,918 | 120,762 | 192,303 | 157,748 | 206,448 |
| Total revenues | 636,820 | 927,589 | 1,026,507 | 1,258,449 | 1,493,563 |
| Excess of revenues over expenditures | 23,206 | 113,545 | 37,240 | 26,834 | (−94,654) |
| Adjustments | (−2) | +175 | (−17,872) | +24,642 | +859 |
| Cumulated surplus, county and town | 288,817 | 357,799 | 357,364 | 514,498 | 477,595 |

*The years shown are not exactly the same for county, town, and school accounts. The county fiscal year is the calendar year. The town fiscal year runs from the latter part of March of one year to the latter part of March of the next. The school budget year coincides with the school year. Further, the school property tax shown in the table is for the year following the tax year. For example, the amount shown for 1970 is the school tax for the 1960 tax roll. The procedure used shows expenditures and revenues more nearly in accordance with the actual time of expenditures and collections and gives more meaningful comparisons.

†Menominee County share.

Source: Department of the Interior, Bureau of Indian Affairs, 1972, p. 63.

the highest in Wisconsin, and yet the state did not reward the county for its local tax effort.

The highest single category of state aid to Menominee County was for welfare. Welfare aid was, however, not without "strings" attached. Under state law, to become eligible for welfare, recipients must own no more than $500 in negotiable assets. Thus to qualify for welfare a Menominee was required to assign his or her $3,000 income bond to the state. A Menominee could also pledge the bond as collateral for a loan of up to $1,200. By 1971, Wisconsin had collected $1.2 million worth of income bonds, which continued to bear 4 percent interest. In effect, state collection of income bonds reduced direct aid for welfare and the tax load of Menominee County by having individual Menominees at least partly finance their own welfare payments (Gordon 1971, p. 26; see also Moulin 1971b; Shames, ed., 1972, pp. 39–40; Deer et al. 1971, pp. 22–23).

In addition to direct state aids and shared taxes Wisconsin, in 1964, organized "Project MAP" (Menominee Action Program), which was to incorporate many state agencies and organizations in an extensive aid program for Menominee County. Some actions were taken, such as the establishment of a $1 million loan fund for county residents, and other programs were planned; however, most of the "action" required additional funds. Requests to the state legislature for the required money were met with recommendations to seek either private capital or federal assistance. Wisconsin eventually abandoned Project MAP and placed its hope for the county on President Lyndon B. Johnson's "War on Poverty." In 1964 the state, on behalf of Menominee County, requested a total of $1,600,588 in aid from the Office of Economic Opportunity (OEO). Playing an all-out version of the grantsmanship game, the request included $96,200 for a demonstration project to reduce delinquency and crime through the use of a special police force, $177,840 for a pilot project of Aid to Dependent Children of Unemployed Parents, $120,700 for a youth work program, $38,450 for a preschool children's program, and $1 million for two community centers (Summary of Requests 1964).

The stopgap nature of the state's strategy for obtaining OEO funds is painfully apparent. Orfield noted:

> The majority of these necessary programs are requested not as continuing projects, but as pilot programs lasting from one to three years. Several of the "pilot projects," such as the provision of adequate police protection, are thinly papered-over basic services which the county is financially unable to provide. . . . None of the projects . . . contribute to the solution of the economic problems facing the Menominees. [Orfield 1965, chap. 6, p. 20]

Unfortunately for the Menominees, inadequate congressional appropriations for the War on Poverty were divided and subdivided so that at least a few dollars could be granted to every request for OEO funds. As a result of the intense competition for limited federal dollars, the Menominees received less than 9 percent of their grant request, or $138,295. Included were $75,200 for the development and administration of a Community Action Program (CAP), $42,145 for educational services in Joint School District Eight, $18,300 for six VISTA volunteers, and $2,650 for a day nursery for preschoolers. The CAP dollars were effectively used by the Menominees to fund a neighborhood youth corps, establish a county library, start an "Operation Headstart" program, promote the growth of a labor union for mill and highway employees, and initiate several other needed projects (Wisconsin Legislative Council 1966, pp. 40–42).

The most substantial sources of federal aid for Menominee County were the "Nelson-Laird" Menominee aid bills of 1962 and 1966. The first provided $1,674,000 for education, health and sanitation, and public welfare. The grant was distributed in declining annual payments from 1962 to 1967. The second bill provided $1,850,000 for tax relief for schools—offsetting welfare costs, health aids, and disease control—and for completion of water and sewage projects. The aid was again distributed over a four-year period ending in 1971 (U.S., House, Report 272; Menominee Enterprises, Inc., 1966, p. 8).

In 1962 requests for transitional aid for Menominee County received little opposition. Backed by the Menominees, the state of Wisconsin, and the BIA with endorsements from former President Eisenhower and several private organizations, Senator Nelson and Representative Laird were also able to secure passage of the 1966 aid bill. Scheduling of hearings for the requested aid before Senator Gaylord Nelson's Subcommittee on Employment and Manpower of the Committee on Labor and Public Welfare, rather than the protermination Senate Interior and Insular Affairs Committee, also helped assure the bill's passage (see U.S., Senate, Hearings, pp. 1965–66).

Federal and state grants-in-aid kept Menominee County financially solvent during its first ten years of existence. With outside aid the county was able to maintain its tax rates below the maximum local tax rates set by Wisconsin statutes. Although local tax rates were kept within acceptable limits, county officials still faced many taxation problems. One problem was in relation to the development of a tax base sufficient to support county operations and services. More will be said of this later. A second concern involved a chronic problem of tax delinquency.

The Menominee people did not pay property taxes on their reservation. When termination became effective, they were introduced to local taxes. On May 1, 1961, tax bills were mailed to raise funds to run the county for the rest of the year. Final payments were due on November 31, 1961. Within thirty days tax bills were mailed again, this time for 1962 (Clifford 1964). In 1962, 88 percent of the private taxpayers in the county were delinquent. In 1966 the tax delinquency rate fell to 40 percent, but in 1969 the rate was still 26 percent. Uncollected real-estate and personal-property taxes in 1969 totaled $72,592 (Department of the Interior, Bureau of Indian Affairs 1972, p. 74). Delinquent taxes not only directly deprived the county of badly needed revenues but excessive delinquency rates also jeopardized state willingness to provide special financial aids to the county (U.S., House, Hearings, 1973, p. 97). As late as 1973 the county was still considering court action to obtain about $33,000 in unpaid taxes (*Menominee County-Town News,* May, 1973).

While the balancing of revenues and expenditures was the most serious problem, other difficulties also hampered the performance of Menominee County. From one perspective government operations ran smoothly after termination. No indication was given that the county's administrative agencies were any less professionally managed than they were in any other rural Wisconsin county. Menominee County officials were highly regarded by state and surrounding county officials.[5] County officeholders generally won reelection in county elections. Although administratively well run, the county did have a serious operational weakness. It was almost totally subservient to the one dominant industry in the county, Menominee Enterprises, Inc. As Orfield noted in 1965:

> Menominee Enterprises literally owned most of the county and the county board was reluctant to oppose the corporation executives. The company was the only important source of employment and of tax revenue. Of the seven members of the 1964 board, six are directly dependent upon Menominee Enterprises for their livelihood. . . . The county, observes one board member is "pretty much like any other company town." Most board members, he says, "do not dare to oppose the Enterprise." [Orfield 1965 chap. 6, p. 17]

At the outset of termination the total assessed value of Menominee County was $16,354,870. The assessed value of MEI was $15,217,215 (Kenote 1971?, p. 3). MEI comprised 93 percent of the tax base of the county and, in 1962, paid $305,408 in property taxes. In the same year MEI paid $388,800 in interest on the Menominees' 4 percent income bonds (Boyd 1973). In 1965, MEI provided over 90 percent of the earned income of the 2,600 residents of the county (Knight 1965, p. 1). It also provided employment for 405 of the 570 employed people in the county (*Milwaukee Sentinel*, June 30, 1965).[6] The corporation controlled the county's economy.

[5] A rare exception to this generally positive evaluation of government operations in the county occurred in 1970, when the Menominee County Department of Social Services came under fire from the Menominee County Board and a state assemblyman for alleged administrative inefficiencies within the department. The director of the department was eventually dismissed (O'Donahue 1970).

[6] Other jobs included fifty county and town positions, fifteen to twenty teachers, fifty self-employed activities, and about fifty jobs outside the county (*Milwaukee Sentinel*, June 30, 1965).

MEI, not county government, inherited the political authority of the Menominee Advisory Council and the General Council. Before termination the Menominee people, either directly through the General Council or indirectly through elected representatives on the Advisory Council, exercised considerable decision-making authority over the Menominee lumber industry. This influence was exercised in the selection and tenure of the mill's business manager and the BIA superintendent and in the preparation of the mill's budget (U.S., Senate, Hearings, 1965–66, p. 308). After termination corporate decisions were made by the MEI Board of Trustees and Board of Directors (see chart). The average Menominee had only two ways of affecting corporate decisions: he could vote once a year for one member on the Voting Trust and once every ten years on the continued existence of the Voting Trust.

In practical terms the influence of the Menominee people over MEI was even further diluted by the Menominee Assistance Trust. The implementers of termination chose the First Wisconsin Trust Company to act as guardians for the assets of Menominee minors and those judged by the BIA to be incompetent to handle their own financial affairs. This, in effect, made all Menominee parents appear "incompetent" because, under normal trust arrangements, natural parents or legal guardians are automatically responsible for a minor's property, unless declared incompetent in court. In a like manner, the BIA assumed the role of the court when it arbitrarily declared a list of Menominee tribal members "incompetent."

From 1961 to 1968 the First Wisconsin Trust Company cast from 80 to 93 percent of the annual votes in trustee elections. This occurred while the percentage of voting certificates held by the trust declined from 42 percent to 21 percent (Deer et al. 1971, p. 25). The turnout of eligible Menominee voters for trustee elections during the same period ranged from 17.8 percent to a low of 3 percent (Wisconsin Legislative Council 1970, p. 16). By default of the Menominee shareholders the First Wisconsin Trust Company indirectly exercised a disproportionate influence over MEI.

Low voter turnout by Menominee certificate holders re-

*Structure of Menominee Enterprises, Inc.*

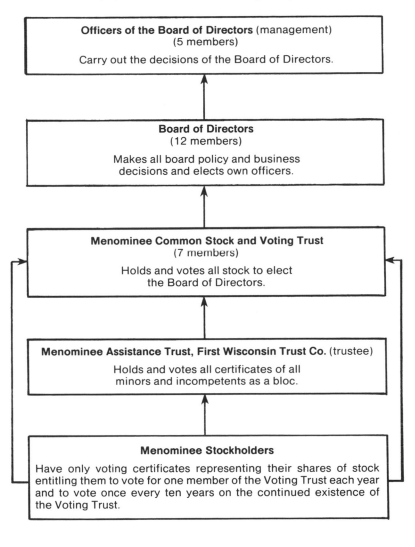

**Officers of the Board of Directors** (management)
(5 members)

Carry out the decisions of the Board of Directors.

**Board of Directors**
(12 members)

Makes all board policy and business
decisions and elects own officers.

**Menominee Common Stock and Voting Trust**
(7 members)

Holds and votes all stock to elect
the Board of Directors.

**Menominee Assistance Trust, First Wisconsin Trust Co.** (trustee)

Holds and votes all certificates of all
minors and incompetents as a bloc.

**Menominee Stockholders**

Have only voting certificates representing their shares of stock
entitling them to vote for one member of the Voting Trust each year
and to vote once every ten years on the continued existence of
the Voting Trust.

flected deep dissatisfaction with MEI in the early years after termination.[7] One of the most controversial corporate actions involved the sale of county land to the Menominee people. The termination plan had specified that title to all county land must be transferred to MEI but did not state how individual Menominee ownership of homesites was to be recognized. Less than two months after termination the MEI Board of Directors declared that land in use for residences or farms was to be appraised as bare land and offered to the occupants for purchase. Once individual Menominees purchased their land, however, they could not freely sell it. The corporation retained the right of first refusal (Orfield 1965, chap. 6, pp. 11–12).

MEI's land-sale policy was resisted by many Menominees and thoroughly detested by nearly all county residents. As many as 600 Menominees were forced to return their income bonds to the corporation to buy their homesites. The benefit to the corporation was twofold. It reduced MEI's annual payment of interest on income bonds and the corporation's share of the property tax. As a result of the transaction individual Menominees lost their share of the tax, their bond, and whatever they might have paid for their land over the income bond (Gordon 1971, p. 25).

By 1970 less than 60 percent of MEI income bonds were held by individual Menominees. In addition to being claimed by the corporation for land sales, the bonds were held by Wisconsin for welfare aid and as loan collateral, by local banks to back loans, and by a Shawano attorney as collateral for overdue legal fees (Department of the Interior, Bureau of Indian Affairs 1972, p. 6; *Appleton-Post Crescent,* April 4, 1965).

The unpopularity of MEI was reinforced by Menominee resentment over a non-Menominee majority on the Board of Directors and the presence of whites both on the Board of Trustees (three of seven members) and within corporate management. Repeated reports of a serious division between Menominees and whites within the corporate hierarchy were

[7]Other reasons for low turnout include an increasing dispersal of Menominees away from the county or surrounding area and a continuing lack of understanding by many Menominees of the corporation's structure and operations (Deer et al. 1971, p. 25).

heard. Charges of discrimination against Menominees for top management positions in the corporation were also made (*Green Bay Press-Gazette*, December 8, 1962; U.S., Senate, Hearings, 1965–66, p. 309).

In addition to unpopularity MEI had other problems. One of the most serious was the alleged incompetence of corporate management. In an effort to improve professionalism, top positions in MEI were filled by non-Menominee foresters and lumbermen hired for their experience with the lumbering methods used in Washington and Oregon. Unfortunately, western lumbering methods were not appropriate for the small-scale Menominee industry. A new technique of cutting timber by weight rather than by size led to excessive waste of usable lumber. MEI management purchased several new logging trucks that proved too wide and heavy for use on existing logging roads (Orfield 1965, chap. 5, p. 11). As a result of these and other management errors, many people, including several Menominee workmen of long experience, charged that most non-Menominee corporate leaders were grossly incompetent and unfit to run the corporation (U.S., Senate, Hearings, 1965–66, p. 309).

During the first five years of operation MEI was disliked and distrusted by most of the Menominee people, hampered by chronic internal divisions and dissention, and victimized by unsound management of its assets. Even more serious was a common realization that the termination experiment was failing. Both MEI and the county faced dissolution unless new strategies were found to strengthen the corporation and expand the county's tax base. Evidence for this bleak conclusion was abundant.

In its first four years MEI's operating profits increased 40 percent, yet the corporation ran at a net loss after payment of property taxes and bond interest. In 1966 it paid 48 percent of its net profit in property taxes and 43 percent in bond interest, leaving only $78,832 for corporate investment and expansion (Menominee Enterprises, Inc., 1966, p. 1).[8] From 1962 to 1966 property taxes for MEI rose 37 per-

[8]If just the net profits from the forestry and mill operations are considered (excluding land sales to Menominees, leases for summer homesites to non-Menominees, and so forth), the corporation actually lost $50,100 in 1966.

cent. The rate of increase was expected to continue or even accelerate. Another alarming trend was the rapid decline of corporate cash reserves. MEI reserves of $1,753,432 in 1962 had declined to $704,839 in 1966 (Menominee Enterprises, Inc., 1961; 1966). Before termination a BIA estimate of a minimum safe reserve for the tribe's lumber industry was $2 million (Orfield 1965, chap. 6, p. 14). The corporation could not continue to produce necessary tax revenues for county government operations and services and still survive, let alone expand and diversify operations.

Property taxes and bond interest were not the only factors limiting the growth of MEI. The Menominee forest was maintained under sustained-yield management. Timber could not be removed at a rate that would endanger the continued existence of the forest. In 1967 logging production was actually cut back from 30 to 22 million board feet because of earlier inaccurate estimates of potential production (Menominee Enterprises, Inc., 1967, p. 3). With sustained-yield management, no potential existed for an increase in logging production and the generation of investment capital. MEI could not finance industrial expansion, and outside financial interest displayed no attraction in industrial investment in Menominee County.

The pending expiration of transitional federal money ("Nelson-Laird" aid) in January, 1971, coupled with little likelihood of any additional government money to take its place, also darkened the future of the county and corporation. The aid had been used to subsidize county services and would have to be replaced with increased local taxes. A corresponding rise of $150,000 to $200,000 in MEI property taxes was expected.

Increasing demand for county services would make the need for more tax revenues even more acute. All socioeconomic trends, including low family income, high unemployment, high birth rates, and poor health, indicated that the fiscal strain on county resources to provide necessary aid and services would be overwhelming. The county found it difficult to take advantage of "Great Society" aids and grants because it could not produce minimum matching funds required for enrollment in many of the programs.

Finally, the possibility of adverse action by the state or by MEI stockholders on several important decisions affecting the corporation's and county's future also threatened the probable success of Menominee termination. In 1969 the Wisconsin state legislature was scheduled to make a final review of the progress of termination and decide whether to allow Menominee County to continue as a separate local government or to absorb it into surrounding counties.[9] In 1970, Voting Trust certificate holders would decide whether or not they wanted the Menominee Common Stock and Voting Trust to remain in operation. Many MEI officials feared that abolition of the Voting Trust would mean fragmentation of corporate assets and eventual collapse of the corporation. In 1971, MEI stock certificates would become negotiable, and Menominee stockholders could immediately sell their stock on the open market. A fear existed that the corporation's forest and other assets would be divided and sold to several different owners, many of them non-Menominees (Menominee Enterprise, Inc., 1967, pp. 3–14).

MEI sought several different strategies for strengthening the corporation and broadening the county's tax base. These strategies included the leasing of county scenic and recreational areas to the state, the adoption of a new "business philosophy" for the corporation, the expansion and diversification of MEI's forest-products industry, and the initiation of recreational land development and sales.

The state of Wisconsin was greatly concerned about the fiscal status of MEI but because of state law could not give direct aid to a private corporation. The state suggested several ideas to help the corporation's revenue situation, including purchase of Menominee land as a state park and sale of a large portion of the Menominee forest as a state forest (Wisconsin Conservation Department 1964; Wisconsin Legislative Council 1965a). MEI rejected both ideas and, instead, suggested that the state lease a portion of land along the Wolf River as a scenic and recreation area (Menominee En-

[9]The review was required by legislation passed before termination. The legislature eventually voted in favor of continuing the county, not because of a conviction that the county was sound but probably because they could think of no better government alternative for the Menominees.

terprises, Inc., 1965*a*). In exchange for public access to the river and fishing and hunting privileges, the state agreed, in a three-year contract, to pay MEI $150,000 per year. The amount was raised to $250,000 per year in 1969 (*Milwaukee Journal*, December 1, 1969; Wisconsin Legislative Council 1970, p. 60; Deer and Alston 1971). In effect, the leasing fee constituted direct state aid to MEI because no conditions were made on use of the money. The agreement also benefited MEI because it no longer had to pay property taxes on the leased land.

Before termination the Menominee mill was run under a "community service philosophy." The mill was organized to create employment; it provided a job for any Menominee willing to work. By strict profit-oriented standards the mill was frequently overemployed. After termination corporate leaders felt that, to compete in the lumber industry, MEI had to adopt a "business philosophy." Stress was put on modernization, cost effectiveness, efficiency, and automation (Shames, ed., 1972, p. 23). Unfortunately, a profit-oriented mill operation resulted in high county unemployment. By 1970, MEI could not provide as many jobs as it did in 1961 (Department of the Interior, Bureau of Indian Affairs 1972, p. 7). Moreover, mill layoffs and resulting high unemployment resulted in higher county taxes for welfare and other county assistance to the unemployed and their families.

A third strategy for strengthening the county's tax base involved expansion and diversification of MEI's forest-products production and generation of other kinds of industry in the county. By the mid-1960s, MEI was still almost totally dependent on saw-log production and lumber sales. The sawmill was over forty years old and nearly obsolete. Modest profits were possible before termination only because the mill operated with a tax exemption (U.S., House, Hearings, 1973, p. 159). Although MEI leaders developed plans for corporate diversification to "higher end-use products," such as veneer or plywood production, the corporation was unable to raise the capital necessary for plant expansion.

Menominee leaders were equally unsuccessful in attracting new industry to the county. Several factors worked against their best efforts (Ernst & Ernst 1967; Department of the Interior, Bureau of Indian Affairs 1965). Little or no investment capital or "seed money" was available from either government or nongovernment sources. High, unstable property-tax rates, together with insufficient revenues from a deficient tax base, made the provision of needed county services impossible. Also other amenities, such as retail trade and commercial service centers, were all but nonexistent. The Menominee labor force was dominated by people with little or no skills and had a reputation for poor worker dependability. Menominees with managerial skills or experience in commerce and industry were extremely scarce. Charges of discrimination by Menominees against non-Menominees, non-Menominees against Menominees, and Menominees against other Menominees were common in most areas of employment within the county. The potential for economic development was also weakened by prevailing tribal attitudes toward land use. Many Menominees wanted to prevent "encroachments" into the wild state of the land for industrial development or any other purpose. This attitude was reinforced by the "conservationist viewpoint" of various state officials and private interest groups. The sale of Menominee land to non-Indians was a particularly sensitive issue.

In 1967 a private consulting firm did a study of the potential for economic development in Menominee County. They suggested that the county's two greatest assets were abundant timber and "great natural beauty." They recommended (1) expansion of an already existing recreational homesite program, (2) construction of a year-round recreational resort complex on the Wolf River, and (3) rehabilitation and diversification of MEI (Ernst & Ernst 1967). The report stressed that realization of the third objective was dependent upon successful implementation of the first two recommendations. MEI subsequently chose the development and sale of recreational homesites and promotion of tourism as their principal strategies for achieving the survival of the corporation and county. Reflecting the immediate need for positive action, an MEI report argued that "recreational development offers the shortest and safest means of developing new income and tax resources" (Menominee Enterprises, Inc., 1967, p. 14).[10]

The consideration of at least limited commercial exploitation of the county's natural scenic beauty dates back to 1956 with a University of Wisconsin study, "Possibilities for Commercial Recreation Industry in the Menominee Indian Reservation" (Loomer 1956). In 1960, a year before termination, a state newspaper reported that the tribe was considering the development of a tourist industry in the new county (McMahan 1960). A somewhat covetous anticipation of such a prospect was scarcely hidden in the article, which described the "pristine grandeur" of the reservation as "a primeval wilderness of giant pine, swift streams, secluded lakes and roaring waterfalls" (McMahan 1960). In 1963 twenty-three lots were "leased" to non-Menominees for homes in Menominee County (U.S., Senate, Hearings, 1965–66, p. 199). Forty-two new leases were issued in 1964, and forty-four more in 1965 (U.S., Senate, Hearings, 1965–66, p. 199). The term "lease" was to become very controversial in later years because of MEI's reluctance to admit that it was actually selling the homesites to their new owners with the use of forty-year lease contracts. MEI clearly acknowledged that it was selling the land as early as 1965 in a memorandum to the Governor of Wisconsin (Menominee Enterprises, Inc., 1965b). In 1964, MEI reported to the Menominee Indian Study Committee that the corporation was considering the construction of six hundred homes, which would add $6 million to the county's tax base (Wisconsin Legislative Council 1964, pp. 10–11). In 1966 the corporation launched a program called "Menominee Forestedge" to develop and sell lakeshore lots for summer homes and cottages (U.S., Senate, Hearings, 1973, pp. 179–84).

In 1967, MEI transformed recreational development from a sideline business venture to a principle survival strategy. After a still-disputed advisory vote of the corporation's stockholders, MEI's Board of Directors began a partnership with a firm of recreational-land-developers to begin a major land-

[10] For additional discussion of expected benefits from homesite and recreational development see N. E. Isaacson & Associates, 1972, pp. 202–203.

development project called Lakes of the Menominees (LOM).

On September 23, 1967, Menominee stockholders were called together to vote on the advisability of what was to become the Lakes of the Menominees land-development project. The term "warranty deeds" was euphemistically used by MEI to refer to the sale of county land to non-Menominees for homesites. Years later supporters of MEI and the sale of Menominee land claimed that the advisory vote supported MEI, while land-sale opponents argued that the vote opposed the development project or would have been negative if the affirmative vote of the Assistance Trust had been excluded. A check of news coverage of the issue does little to clarify the dispute. The *Green Bay Press-Gazette* reported, "The majority of Menominee Enterprise stockholders present at the meeting here Saturday, voted against outright sale of Menominee lands to improve the county tax base" (September 25, 1967). The *Milwaukee Sentinel* covered the same meeting and noted, "Sale of Menominee Indian tribal land to the white man for the first time since 1848 was approved at a meeting of stockholders of the Menominee Enterprises Corporation" (September 25, 1967).

For the LOM projects the developer agreed to provide necessary skills and capital, and MEI provided the land. About 2.2 percent of the county's total area, or 5,170 acres of land, would be devoted to the project. Profits would be split on a fifty-fifty basis after deduction of a 5 percent "operating costs" fee for the developer. The developer guaranteed total sales of $6 million in the first four years of the project (O'Donahue 1971; *Minneapolis Tribune,* October 24, 1971). LOM was to add an estimated $20 million to the county's tax base (*Shawano Evening Leader,* February 4, 1970).

Along with land development and sales, plans were made for a recreational-resort complex, later called a Visitor Destination Center. The project was largely a combined venture of MEI and the North Eastern Wisconsin Regional Planning Commission (NEWRPC).

It is probably not a coincidence that the major designer of the Visitor Destination Center was the chairman of the Planning Commission, a member of the MEI Board of Directors, and, until 1967, chairman of the Advisory Committee to the State Department of Resources Development (Gordon 1971, p. 39). Financial assistance, of $1 million for the center was also granted by the Economic Development Administration.

Construction of the complex began in 1968, but because of cost overruns and other factors discussed in the next chapter, the complex was never completed (Shames, ed., 1972, pp. 27–28). Upon completion it would have included a Nature Awareness Center; a Cultural Center with library and museum; a tourist information center; a bank; a grocery store; a professional building for a doctor, dentist, lawyer, and realtor; an inn with one hundred to two hundred rooms; and an "authentic" logging-camp area with museum (Gordon 1971, pp. 45–50). An estimated 150 to 300 jobs would be provided by the center. The NEWRPC estimated that the center would become self-sustaining within three years of its completion (*Green Bay Press-Gazette,* May 22, 1970).

MEI signed the partnership agreement to build Lakes of the Menominees on July 9, 1968. The development and sale of lakeshore lots began immediately on Legend Lake, the first of three phases in the LOM project. By 1971 gross sales were already at $9 million. Sale price of the lots varied from $3,500 to $15,500 each. Over thirteen hundred lots were sold, and the new owners made improvements on 10 percent of the lots. Structures built on the lots ranged from modest "cabins in the woods" to $40,000 A-frame second homes. An estimated six thousand lots were planned for sale in the entire LOM project. Over $1 million was spent promoting LOM sales, especially in Milwaukee, Chicago, and other Midwestern cities (*Shawano Evening Leader,* June 28, 1971; *Minneapolis Tribune,* October 24, 1971).

The project was producing impressive economic gains for MEI and the county. By 1971, MEI had gained over $1.7 million in profits from LOM. The money went for new boilers for the sawmill, salaries, taxes, and bond interest (*Minneapolis Tribune,* October 24, 1971). The county's tax base rose dramatically. In 1965 the Menominee Indian Study Committee estimated that by 1971 the county tax base would be about $18 million (Wisconsin Legislative Council 1965*b*). In fact, the county's tax base rose to $32 million, largely because of LOM (U.S., Senate, Hearings, 1973, p. 73).

Superficially, Lakes of the Menominees was a financial success. Unfortunately, the trend toward fiscal prosperity was largely illusory. The primary goal of LOM was expansion of the county's tax base. With an accompanying decrease in MEI's share of county taxes, profits could be redirected toward corporate expansion and diversification. The county tax base did nearly double, and MEI's share of county property taxes dropped from 93 percent in 1962 to 54 percent in 1972. Yet while the percentage of taxes paid by MEI dropped, the amount paid steadily increased from $305,400 in 1962 to $527,500 in 1972 (Kenote 1971?, pp. 3–5; Menominee Enterprises, Inc., 1972a; U.S., Senate, Hearings, 1973, pp. 51, 56, 73). Combined with the end of "Nelson-Laird" funds, the Nixon administration's cutback of OEO and other forms of federal aid, and a growth in county expenditures directly attributable to LOM (for example, increased expenditures for roads, police, and fire protection), the precarious fiscal condition of the county and corporation remained unchanged. Years later a critic of land sales to non-Menominees remarked that the Lakes of the Menominees project did little more than "make a raft of the superstructure of a sinking ship."[11]

Because the sale of Menominee land was so persistently controversial, the motives of the corporate leaders of MEI in the land-sale decision became subject to continuous debate. With the establishment of MEI's Voting Trust and Board of Directors, members of the old tribal governing elite moved on to new positions of power in the corporation. The reorganization effectively removed the affairs of Menominee Enterprises, Inc., from the control of Menominee nonelites. First in an uneasy alliance with non-Menominee corporate officials, and then by themselves, tribal elites controlled decisions affecting the future of the corporation and county. Contrary to later accusations, they did not initiate land sales because they really wanted to sell the land or

[11]The former state official making the comment preferred to remain anonymous.

because they stood to profit personally from the sales. Rather they saw the sale of land as the only alternative available to raise the necessary income to keep the county and corporation from going under financially.[12] Menominee governing elites did not ask for termination, but, given the reality of its implementation, they were determined to find the means for achieving its success.

[12]The vast majority of tribal members interviewed in 1974 agreed with this conclusion.

*Sign at entry road to Menominee County, 1961.* Menominee Tribal News.

*Street scene in Neopit, Wis., 1963.* Milwaukee Journal *photo.*

*Housing in Menominee County.* Milwaukee Journal *photo.*

*Another example of housing in Menominee County.* Milwaukee Journal *photo.*

*Gray skies over Menominee County. Bruce M. Fritz, photographer,*
Capital Times.

*Interior view of house in Menominee County. Bruce M. Fritz, photographer,* Capital Times.

*Winter in Menominee County. George P. Kosholl, photographer,*
Milwaukee Journal.

*House constructed in Legend Lake land development project.* Menominee Tribal News.

*Saint Joseph's School in Keshena, Wis., 1969.* Milwaukee Journal photo.

*Menominee County sheriff, 1969.* Milwaukee Journal *photo.*

# 7

# IMPACTS OF THE MENOMINEE
# TERMINATION ACT

*You can rest assured that Menominee County will develop and will be economically and socially happy as a land where you will want to live with pride, where you'll always be proud of your heritage.* —State Senator Ruben La Fave, as quoted in *Green Bay Press-Gazette,* August 31, 1969.

*What's incredible is that all this crap is still going on. We read about it, the stealing from the Indians and all, and we think that happened 100 years ago. The hell it did. It's happening right today. If we could just show our people that they don't have to take this lying down.* — Jim White, as quoted in *Washington Post,* October 3, 1971.

THIS CHAPTER focuses on the intended and unintended impacts of the Menominee Termination Act. "Policy impacts" are the effects of a policy on "real-world" conditions.[1] They refer to changes that occur because a policy has been implemented and is in operation. The intended goal of Menominee termination was rapid assimilation of the tribe. "Intended" and "unintended impacts" respectively refer to changes brought about by the Termination Act that moved the tribe toward full assimilation or changes that made rapid assimilation less likely or even impossible. The most significant intended impact of the act was a movement by many Menominee individuals toward assimilation into the larger society. The most dramatic unintended impact was the rise of a new organization called Determination of Rights and Unity for Menominee Shareholders (DRUMS). The new political faction harassed, overthrew, and replaced the established Menominee govern-

[1]For additional discussion of policy impacts see Dye, ed., 1971; Dye 1972*b;* Freeman and Sherwood 1970; Dolbeare 1972; Johnson 1974; Carroll 1975; Gilmer et al. 1975.

ing elite. The primary goal of the new governing elite within DRUMS was repeal of the Termination Act. DRUMS instilled a new sense of pride and purpose in the Menominee people. Armed with a renewed self-confidence based on their Indian identity, the Menominees eventually were able to reverse the ill-conceived policy of termination.

Of individuals within the tribe the Menominee elites made the most rapid progress toward assimilation. Identification with white-middle-class society was already a characteristic of elites before passage of the Termination Act. Elites felt the least threatened by termination and were the most adept at turning termination to their advantage, even when, as was often the case, they had opposed implementation of the act. The evolving attitudes and behavior of Menominee elites represent the most convincing evidence that assimilation was an achievable policy objective.

Ten years after final implementation of termination many Menominee elites held a distinctly optimistic view of the future. For example, an upper-level manager of Menominee Enterprises, Inc., suggested:

> In the eight and a half years since termination there has been a remarkable about-face, not only in the economy, but in attitude. We are proud to be standing on our own feet. In the next eight and a half years we'll advance at an even faster pace. [Boyd 1969]

Others reacted strongly to suggestions that termination was unsuccessful or should be repealed. A former Menominee leader argued: "There is a growing belief among the Indians of the country . . . that our termination has been a failure. I don't believe it. I for one would not go back to the old system" (Frechette 1970). Another Menominee commented: "I don't understand how people can be so . . . well . . . they talk about 'reconsidering termination'—there's even a committee for it! But that's impossible. . . . We've gone this far, we can't go back now" (Spindler and Spindler 1971, p. 203).

Elite support of termination even extended to defense of the Lakes of the Menominees (LOM) recreational-development project and to the sale of county land to non-Menominees. The Council of Chiefs, whose membership was primarily drawn from pretermination governing elites, declared their "wholehearted support" for the LOM project (Council of

Chiefs 1969). Evidence also exists that the project enjoyed limited support by Menominees who had opposed termination and were not elites, at least not in terms of private wealth. One Menominee commented: "I never did like the idea [LOM], but I have to admit, they really made a pretty shoreline. It turned out a lot better than I thought. I wish I could afford a lot there myself" (Spindler and Spindler 1971, p. 204).

Besides verbal approval of tribal affairs after implementation of the Termination Act, other evidence of Menominee progress toward assimilation was also apparent. Because of the need to run their own affairs, many Menominees assumed positions of responsibility and leadership in Menominee Enterprises, Inc., and county government. The resulting acquisition of administrative skills and political sophistication increased self-confidence and made interaction with non-Indians much less threatening than had been the case under supervision of the tribe by the BIA (U.S., House, Hearings, 1973, pp. 179–80).

Other Menominees were branching out into new "nontraditional" ways of making a living. New commercial establishments, owned and managed by Indians, arose to accomodate non-Menominees who purchased lake lots developed by MEI for summer recreational homes and year-round residences. In 1969 the *Milwaukee Journal* reported:

Along the streets in Neopit and Keshena that ten years ago did not even have a lunch counter, there now are three grocers, three places to buy gasoline, a restaurant and a drive-in, a plumber and even three taverns. The Keshena branch of the Shawano National Bank has made $125,000 worth of loans and has had up to 150 savings accounts. [December 1, 1969]

Two population trends also indicated Menominee progress toward assimilation. The first was an accelerated movement into the county by non-Menominees. In 1956 only about 2 percent of the reservation's population of 3,157 residents was non-Indian.[2] By 1970, 11.5 percent of the county's population of 2,607 was classified by the United States census as non-Me-

[2]The percentage of non-Menominees on the reservation is a rough estimate based on imprecise data (for example, Ames 1958, p. 47). Menominees married to whites ("squaw men") are included in the 1956 estimate.

nominee. Also by 1973 approximately 2,300 non-Menominees owned recreational and permanent homesites in the county (U.S., House, Hearings, 1973, p. 347). While most of the homesites were undeveloped or used only as summer residences, the sales figures portended a much higher non-Indian population in the county and a corresponding integration of non-Menominees into the former reservation's nearly exclusive Indian population.

A second population trend indicating increased assimilation was a marked increase in the movement of Menominees out of the county and a very low rate of intermarriage between Menominees. In 1952 about 80 percent of the Menominee tribe lived on the reservation. By the early 1970s only 40 to 45 percent of the enrolled Menominee population still lived in Menominee County (see tables 5 and 6). Approximately 45 percent of the Menominees still maintained residences near the county, however, particularly in Milwaukee and Chicago and adjacent Wisconsin counties, Shawano, Oconto, and Langlade (see tables 5 and 6).

Because of the questionable accuracy of the two membership lists, tables 5 and 6 should be considered only an approximation of the true population distribution. Both lists are cited because they were compiled at two different times and yet reflect a similar distribution of the population. One might question whether migration out of the county might have occurred at the same rate without termination. Although it is a possibility, previous discussions by the Menominees of the performance of termination would make such a conclusion unlikely. As one Menominee cynically observed, "The only good effect that termination had was that it made us leave the county and pushed us into the mainstream of American life" (unpublished interview conducted for Shames, ed., 1972).

Unfortunately, no records are available to determine the rate of intermarriage between Menominees before termination. Obtainable data suggest, however, that by 1973 only about one-fourth of the Menominee population was married to other Menominees. This figure is a rough approximation. It indicates the percentage of Menominees who married other Menominees compared with all Menominees married and unmarried in the total list of tribal members. While the rate

TABLE 5. *Distribution of Menominee MEI Shareholders in 1971*

| Shareholders | Number | Percent |
|---|---|---|
| Enrolled Menominees, 1957 | 3,270 | |
| Enrolled Menominees deceased or unaccounted for, 1971 | 1,086 | |
| Distribution of the remaining 2,242 shareholders, 1971: | | |
| Living in Menominee County | 903 | 41.4 |
| Living in Wisconsin but not Menominee County | 549 | 25.1 |
| Living in Milwaukee, Wis. | 228 | 10.4 |
| Living in Chicago, Ill. | 228 | 10.4 |
| Living in other states and overseas | 276 | 12.6 |
| Total | 2,184 | 99.9* |
| Menominees intermarrying and percent of total | 580 | 26.5 |

*Error due to rounding percentages.


TABLE 6. *Distribution of Menominees Based on DRUMS Mailing List For Tribal Members, 1973*

| Distribution | Number | Percent |
|---|---|---|
| Living in Menominee County | 935 | 43.7 |
| Living in Wisconsin but not Menominee County | 528 | 24.7 |
| Living in Milwaukee, Wis. | 181 | 09.0 |
| Living in Chicago, Ill. | 196 | 09.2 |
| Living in other states and overseas | 290 | 13.6 |
| Total | 2,140 | 100.2* |
| Menominees intermarrying and percent of total | 568 | 26.6 |

*Error due to rounding percentages.

of intermarriage compared with total marrieds would have been more desirable, the data for such a comparison were not available. The low intermarriage rate represents still another indication of movement, through intermarriage, toward Menominee assimilation into non-Indian society.

This and other evidence of some progress toward Menominee assimilation are clearly present. Unfortunately, a direct link between termination and increased assimilation can only be inferred because of limited reliable data. For example, it is likely that some movement toward assimilation, such as the further acquisition by Menominee elites of nontraditional career patterns and administrative skills, would have occurred without termination. In addition, significant dispersal and intermarriage of Menominees into non-Indian society would still have existed without passage of the Termintion Act. Other possible reasons for Menominee dispersal include the BIA's Indian-relocation programs of the early 1950s. Moreover, unlike a large, relatively autonomous tribe like the Navajo, one would expect a high intermarriage rate when a small, more socially integrated tribe of 3,270 members maintains a comparatively high rate of day-to-day contact with members of the dominant society.

Migration and the subsequent potential for integration of whites into the county's predominantly Indian population were the most clearly defined impacts of the transition from reservation to county. It would not have been necessary to sell lakeshore property to non-Menominees if the Menominees' land had remained in trust with the federal government. Despite the lack of complete data it is reasonable to conclude that elite progress toward accelerated assimilation into the larger American society was the most significant intended impact of Menominee termination.

It has been asserted that the movement of non-Menominees into the former reservation, migration of Menominees out of the county, and the high rate of intermarriage with non-Menominees represent indications of rapid assimilation. This assertion has not gone unchallenged. Lurie argued that the movement of whites into the county does not necessarily correlate with more rapid Menominee assimilation. The presence of nonwhites only makes for abrasive coexistence and greater stiffening of Indian resistance to assimilation. She noted that, for example, less segregation is evident in housing in the South than in northern cities. Blacks often occupied the same blocks as whites, black servants facing the poor back street and whites the affluent main avenues. Propinquity, she suggested, does not necessarily lead to assimilation. As for the movement of Menominees out of the county, particularly to surrounding cities, Lurie suggested that, although some emigrants have lost their Indian identity, the more common effect has been new introspection afforded by intimate observation of white life-styles and a renewed desire to retain Indian ways. Finally, Lurie argued that because the tribe has remained phenotypically distinct, despite a high rate of marriages with non-Menominees dating back to the 1700s, the high rate of tribal marriages to non-Menominees does not signify greater assimilation (Lurie 1978).

Unintended policy impacts refer to the consequences of termination that worsened the general welfare of the Menominees or undermined Menominee movement toward full assimilation. Changes in the tribe falling under the category of unintended impacts[3] include increased economic instability, higher unemployment, decreased public services, aggravated racial discrimination, lower morale and personal self-esteem, deeper political alienation, and renewed factionalism, together with intensified opposition to tribal leadership.

Before termination the Menominee tribe was nearly self-sufficient. It maintained $10 million in cash reserves in the United States Treasury. Ten years after termination the new county was considered a "pocket of poverty." That does not mean that the reservation was a paradise before termination. Earlier chapters discussing life on the Menominee Reservation have described the poverty, illiteracy, and high infant-mortality rates. Thus in many respects termination only made the Menominees' lives more difficult or inhibited what might have been greater socioeconomic progress if tribal

[3]Other summaries of the unintended impacts of termination on the Menominee people can be found in U.S., House, Hearings, 1973; U.S., Senate, Hearings, 1965–66, 1973; Deer et al. 1971, pp. 14–16.

life on the reservation had been retained. Although many
Menominees argue that termination "caused" Menominee
poverty, many of the conditions of poverty were already
there. They became "visible" in part as a result of an increased national sensitivity to poverty characterized by the
"War on Poverty" programs of the mid-1960s.

After termination the tribe's narrowly based economy could
not provide sufficient local tax revenues to operate county
government operations and services. Corporate leaders at
MEI were compelled to develop and sell ancestral tribal
land as recreational homesites to non-Menominees to prevent fiscal collapse of the corporation and county. Summa-
rizing the condition of the Menominees after termination,
a local newspaper columnist pessimistically concluded:

> The Menominees cannot support themselves, at least not in the
> segregated culture and on their own lands as they apparently
> desire. In one way or another, they will again become wards of
> society. The question is whether they will be state dependents
> or will be supported by the national government which cut them
> adrift. [Wyngaard 1965]

Before termination the Menominee mill ran under a "com-
munity-service philosophy." Work was organized to create
employment, and anyone willing to work was hired. After
termination the new corporation stressed operational efficiency and a "business philosophy" for its employment practices. With the adoption of modern milling techniques, the
overall number of jobs available was also reduced. Unemployment reached annual rates of 18 to 28 percent, and seasonal rates approached 40 percent. By 1970 the corporation
had significantly expanded milling operations but could not
provide as many jobs as it had in 1961.

Despite major grants of federal and state aid to the new
county, several public-service programs were either halted
or reduced after termination. Free dental care, the reservation hospital, and a resident doctor were no longer available
to Menominee families. Free public utilities (electricity and
water) were discontinued. The resulting economic impact
on individual Menominees was often very severe. By 1970
over 40 percent of the Menominees had forfeited their MEI

income bonds to the state of Wisconsin or other non-Menominees to secure welfare and other supplemental aids and services (Department of the Interior, Bureau of Indian Affairs
1972, p. 6). The eventual expiration of special federal "transition aid" placed an almost overwhelming burden on the
county to provide necessary public services for its residents.

The provision of continued federal aid undoubtedly represented a serious dilemma for congressional policymakers
interested in achieving rapid assimilation of the Menominee
people. If, on the one hand, federal aid was generously provided for the county (for example, aid for public-service
improvement and economic development), it would tend to
support a continued Menominee communal identity. The
tribe, as a separate social unit, would be given continued
vitality. The pace of assimilation would, therefore, be slowed.
On the other hand, if aid was not provided, a real possibility
existed that the county would fail as a governing unit, and
MEI would become insolvent. Many Menominees, particularly those with the best education or skills, would leave the
county, while those least adaptable to non-Indian society
would stay. Assimilation would move rapidly for those who
departed, but the remaining population would become an
unsightly economic burden on the state and federal governments. In the end a middle policy course was chosen. Enough
aid was provided to forestall the complete collapse of the
county, but it was not enough to ensure a successful transition from reservation to county.

To provide necessary revenues, Menominee property taxes
were raised to near the maximum rate allowed by state statutes. For many tribal members the loss of their tax-exempt
status, enjoyed while on the reservation, was personally devastating. Tax evasion was a serious problem, and many individual Menominees were threatened with prosecution for
unpaid taxes.

In 1972 the BIA asserted, "Termination has resulted in
a generation of Menominees with little better than a ninth
grade education and an almost 75% dropout rate" (Department of the Interior, Bureau of Indian Affairs, 1972, p. 9).
Although insufficient data exist to support the BIA's conclusion that low Menominee educational achievement was

the result of termination (the average grade level attained actually increased slightly after termination), evidence is available to suggest that incidences of discrimination against Menominee school children increased with the merger of Menominee schools into Joint District Eight. A Menominee parent observed:

> One of our worst problems is the schools. We used to have our high school kids going to Shawano, Suring, and Antigo, whichever was nearest to their homes. Now they all have to go to Shawano. They don't like Indians there. Our kids don't feel at home there. . . . Lots of people here will deny there's any prejudice against Menomini [sic] in the schools, but they are most always people with no children in school. [Spindler and Spindler 1971, p. 199]

A 1972 report by the United States Office of Civil Rights concluded that fewer adequate and effective educational services are provided for Menominees than for white children in Joint District Eight schools (Mines 1972). Concentration of Indian students into a single school district, and particularly older Menominee students into the Shawano high school, increased the level of racial discrimination experienced by Menominee children and their parents.

In fairness it should be noted that not everyone agreed that racial discrimination was a problem in Joint District Eight schools. A former Wisconsin state assemblyman who was himself a graduate of Shawano High School said that he did not think "unusual discrimination" existed in Shawano High. In fact, he argued that Menominees have had unusual "breaks." They have become class presidents, sports team leaders, prom kings, and so on. In his opinion, "whether Menominee kids succeed or not is directly related to the kind of parents he has. Kids from good Menominee families have never had a problem. Kids from bad families are in trouble even before they get to school."

The weakening or eventual loss of Indian identity and historical traditions was naturally a part of the assimilation process and, therefore, was an intended impact of termination. A corresponding decline in morale and personal self-esteem evident in the tribe after 1961 was an unintended result of the policy, however. Closure of the tribal roles

in 1954 was a particularly severe blow to the tribe. It signi-
fied the eventual disappearance of the Menominees as a
distinct people or, as one Menominee leader put it, "Our
children born since 1954 have been legally deprived of their
birthright as Menominee Indians" (Deer et al. 1971, p. 15).
While many tribal traditions were already in decline or had
all but disappeared, termination accelerated the trend.

Like most other Americans, Menominees have never been
completely satisfied with every aspect of government in the
United States. The experience of termination, however, clearly
increased tribal dissatisfaction with the political system. Orfield noted:

> There can be few communities in America where the citizens so
> constantly and vigorously denounce state and local government.
> Viewed from the tribal villages, Government almost always seems
> negative. . . . Property taxation is set at the maximum allowable
> rate. . . . Impossible burdens are placed on large families with
> earnings well below the national poverty level. . . . Fathers are
> unemployed, and only very few can hope for admission to scat-
> tered retaining programs in the region. It is easy to think that
> all this must be the result of a plot by malicious Government
> officials. [U.S., Senate, Hearings, 1965–66, p. 315]

Although tribal factionalism has always been present in
Menominee society, divisions within the tribe after termination assumed a level of intensity rarely before experienced
on the reservation. Most of the controversy centered on MEI.
The corporation symbolized nearly all the widely disliked
features of termination. The widespread negative attitude toward MEI is illustrated by the comments of a Menominee
who observed that the corporation was "trying to make a
legislative flop work. It's common knowledge in Washington
that the termination bill was a bad piece of legislation. All
this work and money is just to make a legislative flop work"
(Spindler and Spindler 1971, p. 201).

The most intense negative attitudes toward MEI were held
by Menominee nonelites. Members of the tribal governing
elite generally were supportive of MEI and termination or
at least adopted a wait-and-see attitude toward the future of
the county (Spindler and Spindler 1971, pp. 197–98). Because
governing elites worked in the corporation or the county gov-

ernment, they had a direct personal stake in the success of termination. Although many of the elites had opposed termination before 1961, once it was a reality, they were determined to make the experiment work.

Nothing stimulated nonelite opposition to governing elites more than the development and sale of county land as recreational homesites for non-Menominees. In its most extreme form nonelite opposition assumed the character of a total denial of the legitimacy of MEI's existence. In the words of one Menominee:

> Treaty rights cannot be broken. To speak of this as a county is a lie. . . . [We] have *tribal* rights. Phony Enterprises, Inc., doesn't own anything. Yet you see signs around here saying "No Trespassing. Menominee Enterprises, Inc., Owner." But there's no law anywhere that gives them legal title to the land or to anything on it. But they're selling the land to Whites, and the Whites are ruining it. [Spindler and Spindler 1971, p. 202]

Besides being motivated by a repugnance to the further dissipation of the tribe's land assets to non-Menominees, the Menominees considered the possible loss of political control of county government an additional motivation for opposition to MEI's land sales. One concerned tribal member wondered:

> What do you think is going to happen when there's 2500 lots sold to Whites? Some of them are going to become permanent residents, and they'll have a vote in this county. Do you think they'll be satisfied to have the Menomimi [*sic*] run things? They're going to want their representatives to have a say. . . . It won't be long before outsiders are running Menominee County. The only thing left around here that's Menomini will be the name. [Spindler and Spindler 1971, p. 200]

Tribal opposition to MEI land sales is eloquently expressed in the emotion-laden testimony of a Menominee woman speaking before a congressional subcommittee in 1965:

> All we need is industry, but must it be recreation? Must the next thing be our land? Why must we entertain the white man? All over the State land is owned by counties, the State and Federal Government. Develop those lands first before you take any more from us. We do not want to be like the Negro who wants very

much to be your equal. We know we are of a different race and we want to stay that way. Our values are different. Your values are, when you see trees, your first thoughts are, "Boy, what money could be made from those trees." Our old people taught us, "Do not put a hatchet in that tree unless you are going to use all of it." And when you travel through this reserve, you can well understand the poem by Joyce Kilmer, "Only God can make a tree." As the Indian parent travels through this land of ours, we are grateful that we still own it and pray that the Great Spirit will keep it so. We think of our children who helped us to plant some of those trees and we . . . like to think that the Great Spirit held their grubby little hands in His. [U.S., Senate, Hearings, 1965–66, p. 228]

Opposition to the corporate policies of MEI and to almost all other facets of termination spawned several indigenous organizations, all expressing a common antipathy toward the dominant-elite leaders of the tribe. Among these groups were the Protest Delegation Fighting for Our Land and Homes (formed in 1964), Citizens' Association for the Advancement of Menominee People (1965), the Authentic Menominees (1969), the Menominee Information and Action Committee (1970), and the Citizens Association for the Advancement of the Menominee People (1968) (*Milwaukee Journal*, March 6, 1964; *Indian Voices*, September, 1965; *Green Bay Press-Gazette*, September 14, 1969, April 10, 1970; Shames, ed., 1972, p. 70).

Despite often-violent rhetoric none of the organizations had a significant direct impact on the policies of MEI or the progress of termination. In 1970 DRUMS was formed and presented the first effective political opposition to elite corporate and county leaders. Its creation was the most salient unintended impact of termination.

DRUMS did not originate in Menominee County but was organized outside the county, in Milwaukee and Chicago. Recruitment of Menominees in the county did not occur until after the two urban chapters of DRUMS were well established. Menominee opinion has been divided on the origin of DRUMS. About half of the Menominees interviewed in 1974 said that DRUMS was founded in Milwaukee and Chicago, while the other half argued that the organization was founded simultaneously in the cities and in Menominee County. Most evidence, however, seems to support the urban origin of DRUMS. The first newspaper account of DRUMS on July 13, 1970, referred to the organization as "a group of Menominees from Milwaukee" (*Green Bay Press-Gazette*, July 12, 1970). The first reported organizational meeting of DRUMS in the county was held over two months later (*Green Bay Press-Gazette*, September 1, 1970). DRUMS spokesmen have themselves stated that "the creation of DRUMS occurred simultaneously in Milwaukee and Chicago" (Shames, ed., 1972, p. 72). The urban origin of DRUMS was a particularly sensitive subject in the early years of the organization because of charges by MEI corporate leaders and other established county elites that DRUMS members were "outside agitators" who had no business meddling in county or corporate affairs.

The urban origin of DRUMS paralleled national patterns of rising Indian activism in the United States in the 1960s. Many new groups advocating "Red Power," such as the Amercan Indian Movement (AIM), began organizing in several major metropolitan areas (Bahr et al. 1972, pp. 506–32; Lurie 1973, p. iii). By 1970 a population base for Indian activist movements was already well developed in several cities:

> By the end of the 1960's several hundred thousand . . . perhaps more than half a million . . . Indians lived in Chicago, Minneapolis, Denver, Los Angeles, and other major cities. Many of them had been lured there by World War II defense jobs, others by the Bureau of Indian Affairs postwar relocation programs, and still others had gotten there on their own. [Josephy 1971, pp. 197–98]

Confronted with life in the cities, "urban Indians" became more sensitive to their status as a racial minority, and many of them, particularly the young and better educated, organized to fight for their rights as Native Americans. When questioned about the urban origin of his organization, a DRUMS member replied: "Menominee people outside the County were more aware of things going on with other Indians, for example, Red Power, self-determination. They were also more sophisticated or experienced with the outside world, slum lords, etc." Many nonresident Menominees were opposed to termination and were particularly angry about MEI sales of county land to whites. They considered tribal ownership of their ancestral land as the strongest surviving basis for their common Indian identity. They decided that they would do everything possible to prevent the further erosion of their Menominee identity.

Two of the first organizers of the Milwaukee and Chicago chapters of DRUMS were Ada Deer and Jim White. Both were to play key leadership roles in the new organization. Several non-Menominees were also involved in early DRUMS organizational efforts. They included Joseph Preloznik, the director of a legal-services agency funded by the Office of Educational Opportunity called Wisconsin Judicare; Nancy Oestriech Lurie, a professor of anthropology in the University of Wisconsin—Milwaukee; and two VISTA volunteers, who were particularly helpful during the DRUMS membership drive in Menominee County. Although these and other non-Menominees played important roles in the development of DRUMS, the organization was created and controlled by Menominee Indians.

Other Menominees centrally involved in the origin of DRUMS in Milwaukee and Chicago were Connie Deer, Joan Keshena-Harte, John Gauthier, Louise Kitchkume, and Georgianna Ignace (Shames, ed., 1972, pp. 72–73). Connie Deer is credited with originating the name DRUMS. In 1969, well before DRUMS was created, she raised questions about MEI operations and was told that the corporation's operations "were too complex for her to understand" (Lurie 1978). Menominee resentment of MEI's cavalier attitude toward its stockholders provided an additional issue around which DRUMS could rally tribal support.

Opponents of DRUMS are fond of an assertion that the organization was founded by Preloznik, Lurie, and the two VISTA workers. A DRUMS member responded to the assertion by noting that the charge was intended mainly as an attack on the legitimacy of DRUMS and that such assertions also reinforce "the stereotype that Indians don't have minds of their own."

Within a year of its founding, DRUMS had formed three chapters in Chicago and Milwaukee and in Menominee County. Each chapter was headed by a president, and the overall organization was guided by a DRUMS Council composed of members from each of the three chapters. Only five of the sixteen council members were residents of Menominee County.

At first organizational resources were mainly in the form of time and effort volunteered by DRUMS members. Later these resources were supplemented by money collected from various public fund-raising acitvities, private contributions, and a grant from the AKBAR Corporation of Chicago. This grant in 1972 from the AKBAR Foundation of $22,860 was designated as aid for Menominee socioeconomic self-improvement. Other significant contributions from October 1, 1971, to August 17, 1972, included $100 from the Council of Churches; $500 from American Friends Services, Inc.; $1,000 from Vine Deloria (a noted Indian author and national spokesman); $355 from the proceeds of lectures given by Nancy Lurie; $50 from the Robert F. Kennedy Youth Project in Washington, D.C.; and $453.08 in other cash donations. Additional money was also raised through rummage sales, dances, and fund-raising dinners. Although the lack of money was a chronic problem, DRUMS quickly initiated its campaign against MEI and the MEI policy of recreational land development and sales in the county.

Repeal of the Termination Act eventually became the primary goal of DRUMS, but it was not the immediate objective of the organization. Leaders of DRUMS concluded that the political climate in Wisconsin and in Congress was not receptive to a campaign to reverse termination. DRUMS decided, instead, to pursue a set of indirect strategies designed to overthrow governing elites in MEI and in county government and gain a controlling influence over Menominee affairs. A 1972 DRUMS newsletter stated the goals of the organization as follows:

> Our purpose is to stimulate and maintain active interest and unity among the Menominee people. Our specific goals are to:
>
> 1. Restore control over the corporation and its assets to the Menominee.
> 2. Stop the sale of land to non-Menominees.

3. Build socially and economically sound programs that will not destroy the land and culture of the Menominee.
4. Work to improve educational opportunities for Menominee children.
5. Encourage Menominees to participate in decisions affecting their land, their culture, and their future.
6. Work to keep the treaty rights to hunt, fish and trap exclusively for Menominees.[4]
7. Elect representative leaders who will be responsive to the needs and desires of the Menominee.
8. Reopen the tribal rolls so that our children will once more belong to the Menominee Tribe. [Shames, ed., 1972, p. 77]

DRUMS employed several tactics to achieve its objectives. It mobilized a loyal basis of support both within and outside the county. It launched repeated direct personal attacks against MEI corporate leaders and their policies. It organized public demonstrations to disrupt MEI's efforts to promote the sale of land to non-Menominees. DRUMS solicited favorable media coverage for its organization and objectives. Court actions were initiated to harass and delay the development and sale of county land. Finally, representatives of DRUMS lobbied in the Wisconsin state capital and in Congress to gain gradual state and federal support for the organization's goals.

Taken together, the tactics of DRUMS added up to a successful formula for confronting and eventually overthrowing the established elite leaders of MEI. Two authors, Saul Alinsky and Michael Lipsky, have written extensively on political protest movements in America (Alinsky 1969, 1971; Lipsky 1976).[5] Their ideas provide some useful insights into the internal operations and protest strategies of DRUMS.

Within months after organization of the Milwaukee and Chicago chapters of DRUMS, a membership drive was started

[4]In 1968 the Supreme Court decided that exclusive hunting and fishing rights on Menominee land were not terminated for the Menominees with the passage of the Termination Act. This case is discussed in detail in chapter 8.

[5]The close similarity between Saul Alinsky's "rules for radicals" and the actual tactics used by DRUMS strongly suggests that the leaders of DRUMS were familiar with Alinsky's works. Interviews with various DRUMS members did not, however, confirm that conjecture.

in Menominee County. The first DRUMS meeting in the county was disrupted by county and MEI corporate officials, who deputized MEI mill workers to break up the meeting (Shames, ed., 1972, p. 74). The leaders of DRUMS persisted, however, and with additional meetings, extensive door-to-door contacts with tribal members, and prodigal use of a mimeograph machine to publicize the nature and goals of the organization, DRUMS was able to establish a third chapter in the county.

With the three chapters of the organization separated by hundreds of miles, the leaders of DRUMS were immediately faced with the problem of keeping the new organization together. As Lipsky has warned: "Cohesion is particularly important when protest leaders bargain directly with target groups. In that situation, leaders' ability to control protest constituents and guarantee their behavior represents a bargaining strength" (Lipsky 1976, p. 78). The leaders of DRUMS made a special effort to coordinate policies and maintain cohesion within the organization. A policy was established to make telephone calls among the three chapters at least once a week. Moreover, procedures were adopted for replacing chronic absentees from the DRUMS Council (DRUMS Meeting Minutes 1971). The organizers of DRUMS understood that organizational cohesion was essential if they were going to confront elite corporate and county leaders successfully. They also knew that cohesion was essential to the long-range goal of DRUMS—to reverse termination. This fact was dramatically pointed out by Wisconsin's Governor Lucey. After noting that he was personally sympathetic to the long-range objectives of DRUMS, the governor went on to add, "Menominee Indians will not even have a chance to reverse termination of their former reservation status unless they unite and put aside tribal differences" (*Milwaukee Sentinel,* October 26, 1971).

With the joining of the county and the two urban chapters of DRUMS, an unusual coalition was formed. Menominee members from the cities were generally more socialized to the dominant American culture, better educated, and more politically sophisticated than county members. County members included many who were older, less well educated, and more attuned to the traditional Menominee culture and communal way of life. Although many Menominees from the county were strongly supportive of the objectives of DRUMS, they were afraid to confront tribal leaders openly, engage in demonstrations, or otherwise participate in other tactics employed by DRUMS in confrontation with tribal elites. Their behavior confirms Lipsky's observation that political or ethical mores or both may limit a protest organization's bargaining strength by diminishing the potential for maximum member participation (Lipsky 1976, p. 79). Governing elites often counterattacked DRUMS by equating the nonparticipation of many of the more tradition-oriented Menominees with weak tribal support or opposition to DRUMS and its objectives.

In his book *Rules for Radicals*, Alinsky argued: "Ridicule is man's most potent weapon. It is almost impossible to counterattack ridicule. Also it infuriates the opposition, who then react to your advantage" (Alinsky 1971, p. 128). The use of ridicule is an old, fine-honed technique of social control in Indian communities. "One of the few generalizations that can be made about tribes across the country is that they do not approve of punishing children by striking them. Discipline is accomplished by withholding attention or affection or ridiculing them. There is probably no situation where ridicule can be used to better effect than in an Indian setting" (Lurie 1978). The accuracy of Alinsky's views is clearly demonstrated by the method used by DRUMS against Menominee governing elites, particularly the corporate leaders of MEI.

In addition to attacking MEI corporate leaders, DRUMS also attacked the policies of the state of Wisconsin, especially its use of MEI income bonds as collateral for welfare assistance (Shames, ed., 1972, p. 40), the quality of education offered by Joint District Eight public schools (DRUMS Policy Committee Meeting 1971), and the decisions of Menominee County officials. The effectiveness of the tactics of DRUMS is exemplified by the following complaints contained in a letter from the Menominee County and town board chairman to the attorney general of Wisconsin. The chairman complained that DRUMS had "interfered with the proper procedures of my government, they have disrupted my committees and commissions to a point that we cannot in all fairness to our taxpayers, properly transact business" (B. Miller 1972).

DRUMS leaders waged their attack against MEI by denouncing corporate leaders at protest rallies, by disrupting regular official public meetings, and especially by publishing continuing attacks on the corporation in a monthly newsletter entitled *DRUMS*. They argued that MEI leaders were administratively incompetent and arrogant and that they had betrayed their entrusted obligation to maintain and protect Menominee assets. The Legend Lake (also called Lakes of the Menominees, or LOM) development project was a particular target of attacks by DRUMS leaders. They argued that the project was doing irreparable ecological damage to the environment and that the promised expansion of the tax base from the sale of lakeshore property would be consumed by demands for new, expensive services (such as police protection and road maintenance). They also argued that whites moving into the county because of the project would eventually outnumber Menominees and take political control of the county (*DRUMS,* March 25, 1972; Lurie 1970, p. 3; 1971*b*, p. 21; Deer et al. 1971, p. 22).

A real-estate development firm, N. E. Isaacson, Inc., entered into a partnership with MEI to develop the Legend Lake project and in the process also became a DRUMS target. DRUMS charged that Isaacson was "leaving MEI only the crumbs of the gross profits made on Lake sales." Moreover, they characterized Isaacson's campaign to promote the sale of redeveloped property as a "waste of hundreds of thousands of dollars of . . . gross profits on parties and fancy steak dinners for non-Menominees" (*DRUMS,* March 25, 1972, p. 1).

DRUMS resorted to some unusual methods of attacking its opponents. One was the following anonymous "Menominee Curse": "Let the bird of war circle ceaselessly over the camp of the enemy. Let them know no peace. Let their women grow barren and old before their time. Let their children deny them before their elders. The curse is on the building and on those who occupy it, Isaacson's house and office."

DRUMS leaders personalized their campaign against MEI,

directing many of their attacks against George Kenote, chairman of the board of the corporation. During the implementation phase of the Termination Act, Kenote was largely responsible for developing the termination plan finally adopted in 1961. He continued on as de facto leader of the tribe after termination. As such he was the target of the most vicious attacks by DRUMS. As part of its campaign DRUMS advocated the dissolution of the MEI voting trust and a return of control of the corporation "to the people." Kenote's opposition to the suggestions of DRUMS generated the following response from one DRUMS representative:

> And now our leader, George Kenote, does not want to terminate the voting trust but to enlarge it. Does he feel that the Menominee Indians are all little children who cannot make up their own minds as to what way they want to go? As a Menominee if I wish to sell myself down the river, then I, as a Menominee Indian and a U.S. citizen can do that for myself. I do not need the likes of Mr. Kenote or any other of those so-called leaders of Menominee Enterprises or the state or the federal government to do it for me. [Shames, ed., 1972, p. 79]

DRUMS also singled out Kenote for the "Apple of the Month Award" (an apple is an Indian who is "red on the outside but white on the inside").

Kenote and other members of the Menominee elite fought back through articles in the local press and in direct confrontations with DRUMS spokesmen (Kenote 1970*a*, 1970*b*, 1972; Menominee Enterprises, Inc., 1972*b*). They defended the sale of county land as necessary for the survival of the corporation and county. Unfortunately, many of their responses to the attacks by DRUMS were not understood or were ignored by tribal members. They also provided more material for the use of DRUMS in its efforts to ridicule county and MEI corporate leaders. As an example, Kenote, in "A Personal Memorandum for Menominee Youth," counterattacked DRUMS with the following argument:

> University life in the 60's — reddish tactic — sloganeering — hate targeting — underground press — big lie — racism — polarization — manipulation of the media — these have engulfed a simple people and ruined them. The Menominee Indians have paid a terrible

price. . . . For our people now to accept the philosophy and extreme negativism of an Alinsky, Preloznik, Lurie, Blackwell, the Revolutionary Youth Movement . . . and their like, is to reject the pride of achievement and to accept the rot of negativism and socialism in their worst effects. [Kenote 1972, pp. 1, 14][6]

Ironically, because of their successful assimilation into non-Indian society, Kenote and other members of the governing elite had lost contact with the average Menominee. DRUMS was not started by white infiltrators but arose from widespread rejection of termination within the tribe. The survival of MEI and the county did not interest Menominee nonelites. The LOM project and other MEI plans for economic development were viewed as strategies to make termination work and, therefore, were also rejected. Interestingly, evidence exists that many DRUMS members actually were not opposed to the basic idea of recreational land development in Menominee County.

At one point a former leader of DRUMS offered the following advice for the Menominees' future:

What we need is a major resort or complex of buildings owned and operated by Menominees. We could try to attract not local, but international tourism. . . . We could still enter into agreements with outside land developers, but they would be contracted by and under the direction of the Menominees. We could possibly fly people up here from Chicago and then have Menominees operating restaurants and hotels on the reservation. [unpublished interview conducted for Shames, ed., 1972]

Such development was, nevertheless, resisted because success for LOM would mean success for MEI and the county. If that were to occur, the long-range objective of DRUMS— the reversal of termination—would become impossible. MEI corporate leaders, of course, always argued that if their plans had not been disrupted by DRUMS then LOM and other forms of economic development could have made the county and corporation a success. In 1974 a DRUMS leader also stated (not for attribution) that he thought recreational development might have saved MEI and the county from fiscal

---

[6]Edward H. Blackwell, a reporter for the *Milwaukee Journal*, wrote articles sympathetic to DRUMS and its objectives.

collapse if DRUMS had not stopped the Lakes of the Menominees project.

From 1970 to 1972, DRUMS organized a continuous series of protest demonstrations against MEI and the Lakes of the Menominees (LOM) project. Picketing at the MEI land-sales office in Menominee County occurred nearly every Sunday. Pickets were stationed at LOM promotional dinners in restaurants in Milwaukee, Green Bay, and Appleton, Wisconsin, to discourage prospective property buyers from purchasing Menominee land. Demonstrators from DRUMS printed and distributed a pamphlet to potential purchasers of county land entitled *Why Are We Menominees Picketing Isaacson's Property Sale Dinners?*

The First Wisconsin Trust Company in Milwaukee was also picketed for its support of MEI corporate policies. The number of protesters involved ranged from a half-dozen sign carriers to over two hundred demonstrators assembled at a major rally in 1971.[7] With only a few exceptions the demonstrations were carried out nonviolently.[8] Their major purpose was to generate local, state, and national support for DRUMS and its objectives,[9] disrupt the sale of county land to non-Indians, and maintain constant pressure on the governing elite to submit to the demands of DRUMS.

On October 2, 1971, DRUMS launched its most dramatic demonstration, a 220-mile "March for Justice" from Menominee County to the state capitol in Madison, Wisconsin (Shames, ed., 1972, pp. 88–91; *Milwaukee Sentinel,* October 15, 1971; *Capital Times,* October 13, 1971; October 14, 1971). DRUMS published advance fliers publicizing the various

[7]For additional discussion of demonstrations by DRUMS see Wisconsin Legislative Council 1973, p. 10; White 1971; Shames, ed., 1972; Lurie 1971*b*, p. 23; *Green Bay Press-Gazette,* July 12, 1970, October 19, 1970; *Milwaukee Sentinel,* May 31, 1971; Blackwell 1971.

[8]In June, 1971, DRUMS demonstrators were arrested for violating a court injunction against demonstration opposed to MEI. A minimal amount of violence, including harassment of passing motorists, occurred in 1972 during a Memorial Day demonstration in Menominee County (*Green Bay Press-Gazette,* June 21, 1971; Wisconsin Legislative Council 1973, p. 10).

[9]Lipsky and Alinsky agree that one of the most effective uses of protest tactics is as a mechanism for building a protest organization's strength (Lipsky 1976, p. 93).

reasons for the march, issued press releases during the march, and presented a list of demands by DRUMS to Governor Lucey on the capital steps. The governor responded with a trip to Menominee County to assess the situation personally. The visit significantly strengthened the legitimacy and prestige of DRUMS. Former BIA Commissioner and Wisconsin Lieutenant Governor Philleo Nash concluded that the march successfully played on white guilt over the long history of injustice to American Indians. In his words, the march "played on John Q. Public's desire to be on the side of the Indians if they can figure out what it is."[10] Through demonstrations and other means of publicizing their demands, DRUMS eventually channeled diffuse popular sympathy into direct public support for the reversal of Menominee termination.

Lipsky has warned that "if protest tactics are not considered significant by the media, . . . protest organizations will not succeed. Like the tree falling unheard in the forest, there is no protest unless protest is perceived and projected" (Lipsky 1976, p. 81). The active campaign by the leaders of DRUMS to solicit favorable press coverage for their organization met with mixed results. Many newspapers, particularly local papers, were openly hostile or, at best, maintained a matter-of-fact stance when reporting demonstrations and other activities by DRUMS (for example, *Shawano Evening Leader, Appleton Post-Crescent, Green Bay Press-Gazette, Milwaukee Sentinel,* and *Chicago Tribune*). Others took a distinctly pro-DRUMS position (for example, *Milwaukee Journal, Capital Times, Washington Post,* and *New York Times).* DRUMS was also able to gain press coverage from the "CBS Evening News," several tribal newspapers (for example, the *Navajo Times*), and National Educational Television (NET). NET's coverage of DRUMS was particularly sympathetic. An NET station in Green Bay produced a program entitled ". . . and the Meek Shall Inherit the Earth," which portrayed the negative effects of termination and the efforts by DRUMS to reverse the policy. NET reporters were harassed and threatened by MEI mill hands during the first effort by DRUMS to organize a chapter in Menominee County in 1970. MEI's

[10]From a personal interview with Nash in 1974.

actions certainly did nothing to enhance NET's opinion of MEI or its policies (Shames, ed., 1972, p. 74).

Hostile press coverage also worked to the advantage of DRUMS. Stories critical of a group of disruptive Menominee troublemakers discouraged whites from buying property in the county. Moreover, extensive coverage, hostile or friendly, of Menominee protests and demonstrations supported the growing belief of many outside observers that termination would never be successful in Menominee County.

Lipsky argued that lawyers play extremely important roles in enabling protest groups to utilize the judicial process and avail themselves of adequate preparation of court cases (Lipsky 1976, p. 80). DRUMS was very fortunate. Wisconsin Judicare, a legal aid program funded by OEO, provided free legal assistance to DRUMS and helped the organization wage an unrelenting legal battle against MEI.

Judicare's first court action, in 1970, demanded that MEI make corporate records available to Menominee stockholders. Subsequently Judicare cited alleged environmental damages to obtain a series of restraining orders halting development of the LOM project. A stockholders derivative suit was filed, charging that MEI did not have the right to enter into a partnership with Isaacson to sell Menominee land without approval of two-thirds of MEI shareholders. Judicare also filed a class-action suit to release Menominee property held in trust by the First Wisconsin Bank of Milwaukee.[11]

By 1972 nearly all the suits had been lost after appeals through state courts, federal circuit court, and the Supreme Court. The various court cases had achieved their objective, however. By the end of 1971, MEI had already expended $20,000 in legal fees to fight DRUMS in court (Kenote 1972, p. 37).[12] The development of lake property was delayed sev-

[11]For further discussion of court actions filed by Judicare on behalf of DRUMS see Wisconsin Legislative Council 1973, pp. 11–13; Shames, ed., 1972, pp. 30–34, 70–71, 83–84; *Green Bay Press-Gazette*, August 28, 1970; Kenote 1972*a*, p. 44; *DRUMS*, August 23, 1972.

[12]The First Wisconsin Trust Company deducted $9,302 from the Menominee trust fund for legal fees incurred in its defense of itself from the suit by DRUMS. The bank's action provided additional ammunition for the attacks by DRUMS on the bank (*Milwaukee Journal*, December 12, 1971).

eral months by restraining orders. Despite the loss of all its major suits Judicare effectively used the judicial system to harass and cripple MEI and the Lakes of the Menominees project.

MEI's lawyers did eventually succeed in forcing the board of Wisconsin Judicare to remove the Judicare director and block further Judicare support of DRUMS; however, their action was too late to prevent the damage done to MEI and land development in the county (Foley and Lardner 1971; *Shawano Evening Leader*, September 14, 1970; *Green Bay Press-Gazette*, June 25, 1971; information also provided by an MISC staff member interviewed in 1974).

The leadership of DRUMS was informally divided among several Menominees; however, two leaders stood out during the campaign against MEI. Jim White assumed leadership of public demonstrations and protests against the corporation, while Ada Deer lobbied for the objectives of DRUMS among private organizations, and in state and federal government. Lipsky has suggested:

> Protest leaders can, in effect, divide up public roles so as to reduce as much as possible the gap between implicit demands of different groups for appropriate rhetoric, and what in fact is said. Thus divided leadership may perform the latent function of minimizing tensions among elements of the protest process by permitting different groups to listen selectively to protest spokesmen. [Lipsky 1976, p. 84]

Jim White provided the flamboyant leadership and inflammatory rhetoric necessary to maintain the enthusiastic support of the followers of DRUMS within the tribe and also of reporters interested in newsworthy stories. Ada Deer, on the other hand, waged a quiet but effective behind-the-scenes campaign to gain the confidence and support of important private-interest-group leaders, key state officials, members of Congress, and key personnel within the Nixon administration. In July, 1971, the value of the lobbying efforts by DRUMS became apparent when a delegation headed by Ada Deer was allowed to testify before the Senate Committee on

Interior and Insular Affairs on the failure of termination in Menominee County (Deer et al. 1971). The official contracts and private pledges of support she gained were to become particularly valuable in the subsequent drive by DRUMS to gain national support for the reversal of Menominee termination.

Taken together, the tactics of DRUMS against MEI had a devastating effect on the corporation and the LOM project. Litigation costs made severe inroads on corporate profits, LOM sales were depressed by buyer anxiety over dissension within the tribe, and potential outside investment in new business ventures within the county remained unobtainable because of the prevailing political instability.

In 1972, MEI stated that "a nationally known corporation" had voiced interest in locating in the county but after a personal visit had notified MEI it would not locate in the county "until the Menominee political dissention had settled" (Menominee Enterprises, Inc., 1972a, p. 1). Despite the success of these tactics by DRUMS, however, traditional Menominee elites remained in control of county government and the corporation. In 1971, DRUMS unsuccessfully attempted to dissolve the elite-controlled MEI board of trustees by gathering enough stockholder proxy ballots to vote the trust out of existence. Although DRUMS obtained a majority of the shares voted (119,320 to 118,516), it did not obtain the 51 percent majority of all outstanding shares required to dissolve the trust. The First Wisconsin Trust Company voted its 48,000 entrusted shares in favor of retention of the voting trust, thereby preserving elite control of the corporation (Shames, ed., 1972, pp.78–83).

When that effort failed, DRUMS adopted a new strategy. DRUMS candidates ran for positions on the trust as vacancies became available. The new strategy was a spectacular success. By the end of 1972, DRUMS held seven of eleven positions on the Board of Trustees and a majority on MEI's Board of Directors. Campaigns by DRUMS for county office were less successful. Because of MEI's controlling influence over county affairs, however, when DRUMS members took over management of the corporation, they, in effect, overthrew and replaced the traditional governing elite.[13] DRUMS became the new governing elite in Menominee County.

The significance of the emergence of DRUMS cannot be underestimated. It was founded by a new generation of well-educated, politically sophisticated Menominees who instilled in the tribe a new sense of political awareness and pride in their identity as Native Americans. DRUMS renewed Menominees' interest in tribal politics (*DRUMS*, February 17, 1972, p. 1). DRUMS also revived Menominees' interest in the affairs and future of the entire tribe by acting as a liaison among Indians living in and outside the county.

Most important, DRUMS provided Menominees with a new sense of individual pride and self-confidence. One DRUMS advocate summed it up most eloquently:

> The history of DRUMS' growth is the story of the rebirth of the Menominee people at the individual, family and tribal levels. For many tribal members who had been overawed and confused by the mechanisms of the Menominee termination, membership in DRUMS has spurred a growing comprehension of the nature and effects of that government policy. For other Menominees who had brooded or raged against the injustices of termination, DRUMS had provided an effective group forum through which they can take decisive action. For many Menominees, dependent upon MEI for employment and income, DRUMS has stimulated a courage to defy their corporate leadership. However, to all its members, DRUMS has demonstrated that mass, united tribal action is not only possible, but offers the tribe its only chance to end the oppression of termination. [Shames, ed., 1972, pp. 67–68]

Although agreement with this evaluation of DRUMS would not be unanimous, it represents the opinion of most of the Menominee people.

[13]Considerable evidence exists to indicate that DRUMS did not actively seek to gain control of county government because control of MEI would, of itself, assure control over tribal affairs (Wisconsin Legislative Council 1973, p. 16).

*Menominee March for Justice from Menominee County to Madison, Wis., 1971. Bruce M. Fritz, photographer,* Capital Times.

*James White, DRUMS activist, and Lester Voigt, secretary of Wisconsin Department of Natural Resources, meet during Menominee March for Justice, 1971. Bruce M. Fritz, photographer,* Capital Times.

*Ada Deer, DRUMS activist.* Post-Crescent, *Appleton, Wis.*

*Silvia Wilber, DRUMS activist. Courtesy of Menominee Self-Determination Office.*

*Shirly Daly, DRUMS activist. Courtesy of Menominee Self-Determination Office.*

*DRUMS occupation of Visitor Destination Center, Menominee County. Courtesy of Menominee Self-Determination Office.*

# 8

## POLICY INPUTS INTO THE MENOMINEE RESTORATION ACT

*State Senator Reuben LaFave, Oconto, chairman of the Menominee Indian Study Committee, said Saturday that the chance of reversing termination "is a myth." He noted that the Menominees have been terminated "by the law we all live under, the United States Congress. And the U.S. Supreme Court has declared that the Congress had the right to terminate the treaty."*—Green Bay Press-Gazette, August 31, 1969

*Mainly I want to show people who say nothing can be done in this society that it just isn't so. You don't have to collapse just because there is a federal law in your way. Change it!*—Ada Deer, as quoted by Patricia L. Raymer, "Cancelled Reservation," *Washington Post*, April 16, 1973

A COMBINATION of several policy inputs emerging from Menominee, state, and national policies eventually led to congressional adoption of the Menominee Restoration Act in 1973. One of the most important of these was the Menominees' own firm desire to restore their county to federal trust status, but not under the pretermination "paternalism" of the Bureau of Indian Affairs. The new governing elite of DRUMS demanded that Congress establish a new trust relationship characterized by Menominee "self-determination" over tribal affairs. The state of Wisconsin supported restoration but wanted the transition from county to reservation to occur without any short- or long-range hidden costs to the state. At the national level the primary objective of Congress was to halt the mistaken assimilation strategy of termination as quickly as possible. The central goal of the BIA was to reestablish a trust relationship with the Menominees that would conform with its administrative responsibilities for other Indian tribes. Finally, the widespread emergence of intensified Native American political activism (for example, the "Red Power" movement) provided additional pressure on Congress to respond to the Menominees' urgent demand for restoration.

The Menominees, led by DRUMS, exerted unrelenting pressure on Congress to reverse termination. The tribe insisted that rejection of termination would be complete and unmistakable only if Congress repealed the Menominee Termination Act. They argued:

> Repeal would eliminate any possibility that something less than complete restoration of the Federal trust relationship between the federal government and the Menominee Tribe and its members would [be established]. Repeal would provide the assurance that all rights and privileges which accrue to Indians because of their status as Indians shall again be available to the Menominees. In addition, to the Menominee people and to the Indian people throughout the country, repeal would be an important symbolic act indicative of the good faith of the United States Government in standing behind its announced anti-termination policy. [Menominee Indian Tribal Delegation 1972, p. 3]

The new governing elite of DRUMS insisted that Congress establish a new relationship between the BIA and the Menominees characterized by tribal self-determination over their own affairs. In the words of one DRUMS leader the "Menominees did not wish to go back to the paternalistic reservation system. The protection of the federal government is wanted but not its dictatorial powers as exercised before termination" (Wisconsin Legislative Council 1972, p. 4). To achieve self-determination, DRUMS demanded restoration of the entire county, intact, as their reservation and also the retention by the tribe of managerial control over Menominee assets (Black 1971; Shames 1972, pp. 93–94). Leaders of DRUMS argued that new restoration legislation should include specific provisions to

> 1) restore all Menominee to their *legal* status as American Indians, thereby entitling them to all the government services and benefits available to Indians;
>
> 2) re-open the Menominee tribal rolls, so that Menominee Indians born since 1954 can be legally recognized as Menominee, and regain their rightful share of tribal assets;

3) dissolve MEI and restore all its remaining assets to the status of tribal property, to be held in trust by the federal government;

4) purchase all Menominee land lost as the result of termination and restore it to the Menominee tribe;

5) award compensation to the Menominee tribe for the damages it suffered under termination; and,

6) establish an economic development program among the Menominee to attack the principal causes of our present poverty. [Deer et al. 1971, p. 32]

The Menominees presented several practical arguments to support their demands. First, they argued that restoration would save money. BIA reports revealed that the ten-year cost of operating Menominee County was $20 million, or $2 million a year. The bureau estimated that the cost of running the reservation after restoration would be $1.4 million a year; moreover, the tribe would pay part of the cost, as it had before termination (Department of the Interior, Bureau of Indian Affairs 1972, p. 8).

Second, the tribe pointed out that restoration would stop the further loss of the Menominee land base (Department of the Interior, Bureau of Indian Affairs, 1972, p. 8). This, in turn, would allow the tribe to preserve its forest-based economy and contribute to the operation of the restored reservation.

The need to preserve MEI assets (reorganized under another name) as the primary economic unit in the county was offered as a third argument for restoration.[1] No longer faced with the burden of local property taxes, the corporation could modernize and expand its facilities to become competitive again in the forest-product market (Boyd 1973, p. 3; Department of the Interior, Bureau of Indian Affairs, 1972, p. 6).

Finally, Menominee leaders argued that the reversal of termination would improve the tribe's standard of living.

[1] By 1973, MEI was approaching bankruptcy, with assets of about $36 million and liabilities of about $9 million (*Green Bay Press-Gazette,* December 8, 1973).

With renewed federal aid, a doctor and hospital could again
be provided for the tribe, educational opportunities could
be expanded, and inadequate housing conditions could be
improved on the restored reservation. Ironically the Menominees were arguing that the reestablishment of their reservation would bring the higher standard of living they were
supposed to enjoy after their termination as wards of the
federal government.

In the 1950s the Menominees were less effective in their
opposition to termination. The traditional governing elite,
although opposed to pending legislation, adopted a fatalistic
attitude that, no matter what their objections, Congress would
inevitably terminate the tribe. By the early 1970s, DRUMS
assumed the dominant role in a successful drive to achieve
restoration. Contrasting the two governing elites helps provide an explanation for the greater political effectiveness
demonstrated by the tribe during its restoration campaign.

After termination the center of power in tribal politics
transferred from the Menominee Advisory and General Council to the MEI Board of Trustees and Directors. By 1973,
DRUMS was in firm control of the policies and operations
of MEI. Members of DRUMS, like the traditional governing elite, held the most powerful positions of authority within the tribe. The new governing elite's greater success in the
pursuit of its policy objectives is not explained by the possession of varying degrees of formal or informal tribal authority. Since the DRUMS elite and the traditional elite had
about the same authority within the tribe, authority has little
relevance to an effort to explain why DRUMS' elite was more
successful.

Both sets of elite leaders also had similar access to tribal
funds. The leaders of the traditional elite had access to the
income of the tribe's sawmill, provided they could gain an
authorization to spend the money from the General Council.
After assuming control of MEI, DRUMS was able to gain
financial support from the corporation's treasury.[2] Additional
money was obtained from several outside public and private

[2] In fact, DRUMS had limited success gaining support for its lobbying
efforts before it gained a majority on the Voting Trust by persuading
nonaligned members of the trust to support the requests of DRUMS (Blackwell 1972).

sources. DRUMS formed a new organization called the Committee to Save the Menominee People and Forests to work specifically for restoration. The committee was supported by money from MEI, the Kennedy Youth Action Coalition, the Lutheran Council of the United States of America, and several other organizations. Contributions to the committee in 1972 totaled $8,707.30 (Committee to Save the Menominee People and Forests 1972). Although neither elite enjoyed unlimited resources, access to money does not appear to be an important distinction between the two sets of elites.

Both DRUMS and the traditional governing elite had access to skilled legal counsel. The traditional elite employed lawyers from Milwaukee and Washington, D.C. Legal counsel accompanied the Menominee delegation to Congress during the hearings on termination and helped draw up the final implementation plan. The DRUMS elite also relied heavily on lawyers, provided mainly by Judicare and the Native American Rights Fund (NARF).[3] Two lawyers from NARF estimated that in two years they had spent more than fourteen hundred man-hours working with the tribe on restoration (Native American Rights Fund 1973, p. 8).

Variations in such tangible factors as formal political power, money, or access to legal services are not sufficient to explain the greater political success of the DRUMS governing elite in relation to their traditional-elite predecessors. A combination of three additional factors, however, is important to an explanation of the success of DRUMS: strong determination, the "politics of conscience," and political sophistication.

In 1971, Ada Deer declared, "There comes a certain time in history when certain ideas are ready to be acted on, and now is the time for reversing termination" (from an unpublished interview from Shames, ed., 1972).[4] Two years later

[3]Much of the legal aid provided to the DRUMS elite was also free. Judicare was a federally funded program and NARF was funded by the Ford Foundation. After Judicare withdrew its services from the Menominees, the tribe retained and paid for the services of two former Judicare lawyers.

[4]The dominant role of Ada Deer in the restoration movement is illustrated by the following articles: Heinberg 1971; *Capital Times,* December 20, 1971; Austin 1972; M. Miller 1973; Raymer 1973.

when the drive for restoration was well under way, Deer's positive attitude was again apparent in the following statement to a newspaper reporter: "Mainly I want to show people who say nothing can be done in this society that it just isn't so. You don't have to collapse just because there's federal law in your way. Change it!" (Raymer 1973). Leaders of DRUMS like Ada Deer and Jim White were able to instill in the Menominees their conviction that Congress and the federal government would respond to Menominee demands if the tribe organized a unified, determined campaign to achieve restoration.

After DRUMS unified the tribe around a common dissatisfaction over MEI's decision to sell Menominee County land to whites, the new governing elite capitalized on what might be termed the "politics of conscience." Observing the strategies of the civil-rights movement, the migrant-workers' campaign, and other social-protest movements of the 1970s, DRUMS quickly realized the importance of the American conscience in American politics. By projecting themselves as a subjected minority who desired only the restoration of their rights as Native Americans, the Menominees successfully sought national support from many individuals and groups, such as the American League of Women Voters, who felt morally bound to help the tribe combat injustices caused by the policy of termination.

The political sophistication of the leaders of DRUMS is reflected in many of the specific strategies used by them on behalf of the Menominees in their drive for restoration. Beginning in 1971, these strategies included a petition to Congress calling for restoration; a letter-writing campaign to members of the Wisconsin congressional delegation; a "March for Justice" for Menominee County to Madison, Wisconsin; and, finally, a General Council meeting called so that the tribe could collectively confront the problem of achieving restoration (DRUMS Meeting Minutes 1971). By 1973, DRUMS had organized more than twenty-five meetings to discuss restoration in Menominee County, Chicago, and Milwaukee (Wilkinson 1973).

Outside the tribe, DRUMS leaders conducted an extensive lobbying effort. Contacts were established with Wisconsin public officials, other Indian tribes across the nation, key congressmen, the BIA, important members of the Nixon administration, and many private organizations throughout the nation. No reasonable opportunity to lobby for restoration was missed by DRUMS. Shirly Daly and Ada Deer, two DRUMS leaders, were selected as a McGovern delegate and alternate to the Democratic National Convention in 1972. While they were there, they successfully introduced an Indian minority plank into the Democratic platform and lobbied extensively for Menominee restoration (Austin 1972). The message carried to public officials in the state and in Washington was the same: "You told us to unify ourselves, and then come to seek help—we've done it, now help us."[5]

In sum, the DRUMS governing elite exercised a more effective voice in the national policy-making process than that of their traditional-elite predecessors because they displayed more self-assurance and determination in forwarding their objectives, possessed greater knowledge of the nature and uses of political power, and, finally, operated in a political climate more sympathetic than that of the 1950s to the unique rights of American Indians. Although many tribal members would agree with the opinion of one elderly Menominee that the "atmosphere was right and DRUMS stepped in at the right time," most would add the observation of another tribal member, who stated that, for restoration to occur, "it was necessary for an organization like DRUMS to point out the costs of termination to the state and federal governments." Menominees interviewed in 1974 were in nearly unanimous agreement that DRUMS was the most important component in the Menominees' campaign for restoration of their reservation.

Although it took an organization like DRUMS to focus tribal opposition into an effective campaign for the reversal of termination, something like restoration had been on Menominee minds for many years. As early as 1964 an anti-termination petition was signed by 788 Menominees which stated in part, "We the undersigned, members of the Me-

[5] The quotation is from a former leader of DRUMS, as noted in an unpublished interview conducted for Shames, ed., 1972.

nominee Indian Tribe, do respectfully petition the Congress of the United States to immediately enact legislation which will repeal Public Law 399 of the United States Congress" (Orfield 1965, chap. 6, p. 21; Department of the Interior, Bureau of Indian Affairs 1965, p. 6096). Again in 1969 members of the tribe formed the Indian Information Action Committee to organize another petition asking Congress to reverse termination (*Green Bay Press-Gazette,* September 9, 1969).

Agreement that restoration was desirable was widespread. Unity over what restoration actually meant was less apparent. A poll of the tribe in 1973 revealed that 98 percent of the Menominees returning mailed questionnaires favored the restoration of federal services to the Menominee Indians, however, the mailed questionnaire, distributed by Congressman Froehlich of Wisconsin, was returned by only 20 percent of the Menominees polled. Unfortunately the only available report of the survey's results fails to mention the total number of tribal members surveyed (*Shawano Evening Leader,* October 17, 1973). Although the reliability of the survey is questionable, its conclusions were also supported by interviews conducted for this book.

When restoration was interpreted to mean the return of Menominee County to its former status as a reservation, however, support for restoration declined to 83 percent of the total responses. A report on the survey also noted that "over 53 percent of the respondents felt individual Menominees should be permitted to turn their property into trust for themselves and family instead of turning over their property to the tribe for a common trust" (*Shawano Evening Leader,* October 17, 1973).

Several interrelated reasons existed for a less-than-total endorsement of restoration, particularly when it meant going back to life on a reservation.

Many Menominees, particularly those who had acquired land after termination, expressed concern over the future of individual property rights after reversion to a reservation. Others supported a return of the rights and privileges of trust status but were apprehensive about a return of BIA supervision over their lives. A third group simply felt that termination could not be "undone" (Wisconsin Legislative

Council 1973, p. 17). In the words of a former Menominee leader, "After all the damage that has been done to Indian tribes in the United States, the ability of those in power to correct bad situations must be taken with a grain of salt . . . [reversing termination is] just like giving Congress the job to unscramble eggs" (O'Donahue 1970). In a 1974 interview another Menominee argued that it was futile to believe that the Menominees could recapture and preserve their tribal identity:

> Intermarriage trends will make assimilation of the tribe inevitable anyway. Menominees can't really go back, but must learn to live and adapt in white man's society. Not only is the dilution of Menominee blood a factor, but also Menominees like many of the amenities of white man's culture, e.g., car, phone, TV, etc. Menominees aren't about to give these things up.

Fear of endangering the economic progress achieved after termination also prompted some resistance to restoration. In 1974 a Menominee woman, reflecting on the restoration movement, noted that "there were those who had achieved some economic stability, who had purchased some land. They felt that others should also have been able to 'succeed' under termination." The following comments of two other Menominees illustrate their opposition to the potential loss of personally achieved economic progress and independence. A service-station operator, who was also the owner of an excavating and landscaping service, stated that, being a business man, he would prefer not to see termination reversed: "Business is good now, but if we went back to reservation status my business would suffer" (O'Donahue 1970). Making her point a little more graphically, a Menominee woman said: "I own what I got now. I don't want to go back to the days when I have to get permission to get a tooth pulled or a new pair of shoes or a new roll of toilet paper. They're likely to tell me to get a corn cob" (Wilk 1972).

The possibility of a return to reservation life created a particularly troubling dilemma for many Menominees of the older generation. The nature of the dilemma is apparent from the comment of a Menominee woman surveyed in 1974: "There are still people today who aren't exactly against restoration, but are unsure of what is going to happen." The woman had lived under BIA supervision and had tried to "make it" after termination. She felt that she had done well in the white man's world while still retaining her Indianness. Although she thought that the Termination Act was wrong and should be repealed, she also stated that she did not want to relive the stigma associated with identification as a "ward" of the government. The woman also said that she feared that there would be a negative psychological impact on Menominee children who had grown up during the transition from reservation to termination and back to reservation. She wondered whether they might come away with the feeling that they had somehow failed in the white man's world.

A significant number of Menominees opposed restoration simply because it was supported by DRUMS. Many members of the deposed traditional governing elite continued to characterize DRUMS as a group of outsiders who had deceived the Menominee people and sabotaged the tribe's gradual progress toward assimilation. Several estranged members of DRUMS claimed that DRUMS leaders had "sold out" or compromised the true interests of the Menominee people during negotiations with state and federal officials.

Several issues existed on which alleged unauthorized compromises had occurred. For example, when DRUMS gained control of MEI, it failed to carry out its campaign pledge to cancel the state's lease on Wolf River because of an immediate need for the income derived from the lease. After one year the lease was canceled; however, the delay provided grounds for some tribal members to question the sincerity of promises made by DRUMS. Leaders of DRUMS also received criticism for continuing the hunting and fishing rights of non-Menominee property owners within the county. DRUMS argued that white opposition to a cancellation of those rights would jeopardize the support the tribe had achieved among the general public (Lurie 1978). A third issue centered on the failure by DRUMS to secure BIA educational benefits for Menominees not living on the reservation (U.S., House, Hearings, 1973, p. 59). One of the most prominent DRUMS dissidents was Jim White, former president of the Chicago chapter.

DRUMS dissidents were joined by the Menominee chapter of the American Indian Movement (AIM), despite the continued strong support of DRUMS by national AIM leaders. AIM was never strong in Menominee County. A local chapter was not formed until 1972, long after DRUMS was well established. Although it at first supported DRUMS, its few members later joined the opposition because they felt that DRUMS was ignoring the interests of a minority of resident Indians, many from other Wisconsin tribes, who were not officially represented on Menominee tribal rolls.[6]

The main line of resistance to the campaign by DRUMS for restoration emerged from three factions, the Menominee County Shareholders and Taxpayers Alliance, Menominees for Progress, and the Council of Chiefs. Membership in the organizations overlapped and generally consisted of traditional elite leaders or Menominees who owned personal property within the county or both. Although not officially opposed to the restoration of federal aids and services, they demanded that Menominees have an option between retaining individual ownership of their property and returning it to a common trust. They also wanted guarantees that sufficient federal funds would be available to provide county services to property owners after most of the county's land was restored to trust status. Finally, they argued (contrary to the position of DRUMS) that MEI should retain the authority to sell reservation land so that, in time of future need, additional revenue could be generated for the tribe (Kenote 1973a, 1973b; U.S., House, Hearings, 1973, p. 112; Council of Chiefs 1973a, 1973b; Native American Rights Fund 1973).

Tactics of the three organizations varied from direct attacks on the leaders of DRUMS and its policies to independent efforts to convince state and federal officials that their demands represented the legitimate demands of the Menominee people. The organizations formed an alliance with non-

---

[6] From an interview in 1974 with the president of the Menominee chapter of AIM.

Menominee property owners on the basis of their mutual concern over personal property rights and taxes after restoration. Finally, they sponsored candidates in various local elections (Council of Chiefs 1973a; Wisconsin Legislative Council 1973; DRUMS Meeting Minutes 1971).

In spite of their efforts, the opponents of DRUMS exercised only minimal independent influence on the outcome of the restoration campaign. DRUMS, for example, accepted their demand that Menominee property owners have an option of keeping their property (and paying property taxes) or returning it to the tribe to be placed in trust (*DRUMS*, June 1, 1973, p. 5). For the most part, however, DRUMS overcame its opponents' tactics and launched successful counterattacks on their demands. For example, in an attack on one of the opposition factions, DRUMS declared that "the Council of Chiefs has no legal right to act on behalf of or speak for the Menominee people and any person who claims to do so, does it falsely and illegally" (DRUMS, 2nd Annual Convention Minutes 1972).

The following quotation from the newsletter *DRUMS* illustrates one of the organization's methods of attack and its opinion of its opponents' motives:

> Many of the people who have profited from termination are now worried about the proposed restoration of the Menominee land and people. The special interest group is worried about their "vested interests" (i.e., the stocks and bonds issued at termination). They are saying "What about my property?," "I want to own the land," "I want to be able to sell my land!," "What about my three thousand dollar bond and my shares?"
>
> The only question that our people asked years ago was "what about our children and the old people?" The depth to which our tribe has deteriorated into white-thinking materialism in the past few years is appalling. [*DRUMS*, March 15, 1973, p. 6]

In sum, Menominee support for restoration was not unanimous but was strong enough to convince outsiders that the tribe genuinely wanted an end to termination. In fact, given the history of tribal factionalism going back to pretermination days, the comparative unity of the tribe behind DRUMS was remarkable. Despite their differences over the goals of restoration, most of the traditional elite agreed with DRUMS

that the policy of termination should never have been enacted by Congress. As George Kenote once noted: "Assimilation of the races is a biological and a personal thing. It
ought to be left to proceed at its own pace and not by allot-
ments and divestments of Indian property nor complete termination of the federal-Indian relationship" (*Green Bay Press-
Gazette,* July 22, 1971).

While less significant than internal tribal opposition to
restoration, the objections of non-Menominee county landowners to a reestablishment of the reservation also became
a factor in the Menominees' campaign to reverse termination.
The landowners' concern was for the future of more than
five thousand acres of recreational land owned by about
nineteen hundred non-Menominees. About two hundred of
the landowners were already permanent residents of the
county (Blackwell 1974). The landowners formed three prop-
erty-owners' associations to work for the protection of their
interests as residents and taxpayers in the county: the Legend
Lake Property Owners Association, the Moshawquit Lake
Association, and the LaMotte Property Taxpayers Association. Their influence became disproportionate to their numbers because the congressman representing the Menominees
in the House of Representatives was himself a landowner
in the county. In the words of a local newspaper reporter
Representative Harold Froehlich sought "to carry water for
both the Indians and the white landowners" (*Capital Times,*
October 18, 1973).

Representative Froehlich voiced the non-Menominee property owners' position on restoration, including the demand
for a two-year waiting period before MEI and individually
held land could be accepted into trust by the secretary of
the interior, assurances that federal aids would be forthcoming so that "the burden of financing local government
would not fall immediately and unfairly upon non-Menominee property owners," and a guarantee that hunting and
fishing rights would be available to the property owners.
Finally, the congressman also voiced opposition to a DRUMS
proposal to forbid the sale of tribal land after restoration
(Froehlich 1973). Representative Froehlich argued that the
ban on future land sales violated "the new spirit of self-

determination" sought by the Menominees (Froehlich 1973). He also sought the merger of property held by non-Menominees into a "taxable lands township" or inclusion of the property in a neighboring county; however, state officials declared his proposals unconstitutional (Smithson and Wilkinson 1973, p. 1; LaFave 1973).

Leaders of DRUMS considered an open confrontation with Representative Froehlich but, after debating the problem, decided to work with the congressman, if it was at all possible (DRUMS Membership Meeting 1973). To secure Representative Froehlich's support in Congress, DRUMS acceded to most of the landowners' demands. This action directly contributed to a charge by dissident DRUMS members that leaders of DRUMS had "sold out" the Menominee people by compromising the objectives of restoration (see U.S., House, Hearings, 1973, p. 59). They also appeased the landowners by successfully arguing that, although tax revenues would decrease because much of the county's land would be tax-exempt after restoration, expenditures would decrease proportionately. They argued that many expenditures (for example, educational costs) would be assumed by the federal government after restoration. The state of Wisconsin estimated that the county tax base would decrease about 51 percent after restoration; however, 61 percent of the county's tax bill would be erased when the federal government assumed educational costs with funds from the Johnson-O'Malley Act, Public Law 874 (Impact Aid Program), and various provisions of the Indian Education Act (*DRUMS*, June 1, 1973).

Although they secured significant concessions from the DRUMS governing elite, non-Menominee landowners continued to oppose restoration strongly. They remained reluctant to oppose the reversal of termination openly, however, since they considered restoration inevitable and were afraid of Menominee reprisals after the eventual passage of the Restoration Act. The best they could hope for was some assurance that their property rights would remain secure after restoration.

Overall, public and private opinion in the state of Wisconsin varied from unqualified support for restoration, to total opposition. One fact was agreed upon. Well before the restoration movement was under way, a state newspaper reported, "Virtually everybody in Wisconsin official circles is now convinced that the termination of U.S. government wardship for the Indians was a mistake" (*Green Bay Press-Gazette*, March 24, 1965). Over ten years after the implementation of the Termination Act, debate in Wisconsin was not over the merits of termination but over whether the Menominees should or could return to their former lives on a federal reservation.

Strong support for restoration was voiced by Wisconsin's two senators, several representatives, the governor, most of the state newspapers, the academic community, and a large block of the general public. The following excerpt from an editorial in Wisconsin's largest newspaper illustrates the prevailing state position on restoration:

> Obviously, the federal government must step back in. Its moral obligation cannot be overstated. Restoration of Menominee lands to federal tax-exempt trust [thus ending need for continued land sale], provision of federal services afforded other Indians, and establishment of a new mechanism for self-determination could provide long-term stability. Without that, the current tragic chapter in Menominee Indian history could be the last chapter. [*Milwaukee Journal*, November 7, 1971]

Antirestoration opinion within the state was generally based on the argument that a return to reservation status would be both impractical and unwise:

> In asking that termination of federal control of Wisconsin's Menominee Indians be reversed, certain Indian leaders are proposing, in effect, that the Menominees go back in time. Turn back the clock, and everything will be all right again, they seem to be saying. If such a change can be effected, it must also be accepted that what was wrong when termination went into effect in 1961 . . . will be wrong again, too.
>
> . . . No matter how peaceful the bygone days of the reservation status may be in memory, the Menominees should not allow any failures of the past 10 years drive them to seek out renewal of a stagnant pacification program. Continued efforts toward a successful Menominee County operation might right past failures, bringing a dignity that can never be achieved by going back to the reservation. Such dignity carries a much more valu-

able heritage than the attitude of dependency inherent in the
move toward restoration of federal control. [*Milwaukee Sentinel,*
July 27, 1971]

Some people, particularly whites living near Menominee
County, saw an underlying motive in the Menominees' campaign to achieve restoration. A state assemblyman from nearby Shawano made the following observation:

> To be called an Indian is a privilege in our society. Those Me-
> nominees who are unemployed, who don't want to work are the
> "Indians." Those who do want to work are treated like everyone
> else by surrounding whites. Many of the "Indians" are clever
> welfare loafers. Restoration will encourage the welfare Indian.
> Most Menominees would do alright for themselves if they were
> not given the alternative of regression to pre-termination days.
> [interview conducted in 1974 in Madison, Wis.]

Most of the officially expressed state concern over restoration centered on the question whether the county should
continue to exist after the reversion of Menominee land
and other assets to trust status (Wisconsin Legislative Council 1973, p. 18; Menominee Indian Study Committee 1973,
p. 8). Assuming that non-Menominee property owners within
the county would retain title to their land, several state officials were worried about the jurisdictional status of land
held by non-Indians and how welfare, road maintenance,
and other services would be provided for non-Menominee
residents after restoration. State officials, speaking for white
county residents, proposed the creation of a "supertownship"
or a merger of non-Indian property into adjacent counties;
however, the idea was declared a violation of the state constitution (U.S., House, Hearings, 1973, pp. 19–20). A few
state officials also called for a referendum to discover whether
the Menominees favored restoration and, if so, what they
wanted to do with the county after restoration (State of Wisconsin 1973).

The DRUMS governing elite dismissed state requests for
a referendum and time to study the implications of restoration as delaying tactics and evasive maneuvers (Menominee
Indian Study Committee 1973, pp. 12–14). They argued that
Menominee support for restoration was adequately demon-

strated by the successful election campaign of DRUMS for positions on the MEI Board of Trustees and Directors. DRUMS also asserted that an unnecessary delay of restoration would lead to a further dissipation of corporate assets because of the continued burden of property taxes. Many more families would have to divest themselves of their MEI stock and other assets to sustain themselves while the state conducted its studies (U.S., House, Hearings, 1973, pp. 50, 262, 297).

Hesitant state legislators and other officials soon found that they were faced with a policy situation largely out of their control. By the end of 1972 the leaders of DRUMS were in firm control of tribal government and had strong support within the state legislature, from the governor, and from a majority of the state delegation to Congress. Despite transition problems most state officials were convinced that restoration was preferable to continued state responsibility for a fiscally unstable county containing a large population of economically dependent residents.

The new DRUMS governing elite had clearly seized the political initiative over their own affairs. During the implementation of termination the traditional governing elite played a subservient role to the state's Menominee Indian Study Committee (MISC). The new Menominee elite's relationship with the MISC was characterized by boldness and determination. Facing the MISC in 1972, a DRUMS representative said, "What we want you to do is send a written message to the Interior Department in support of restoration" (*Shawano Evening Leader,* May 20, 1972). State officials, some despite their own opposition, complied with the demand of DRUMS for support.

Although it is not usually considered a part of the policymaking process, the federal judicial system also played a prominent role in the reversal of termination. At the local and state levels DRUMS made extensive use of the courts to obtain restraining orders to halt progress on the Lakes of the Menominees development project. Costs to MEI in terms of lost time in lake-lot development, loss of projected profits from a completed project, and lawyers' fees for the preparation of the corporation's defense and appeals to adverse de-

cisions severely undermined MEI's efforts to make termination work. Two years before the rise of DRUMS the United
States Supreme Court rendered an even more important decision affecting the eventual restoration of the Menominee
tribe. In 1968 it declared that Menominee hunting and fishing rights had "survived" termination. The decision immediately raised the question whether or not other Menominee
rights had also survived termination (Deer et al. 1971, p. 15).

In 1962 the state of Wisconsin declared that the Menominees were subject to its conservation regulations. The state
acted on the basis of Public Law 280 (1953), which gave the
state jurisdiction over offenses committed by or against Indians in all Indian country within the state. The state also
argued that the Termination Act had abrogated Menominee
hunting and fishing rights granted the tribe under the Treaty
of Wolf River in 1854. The Menominees brought suit against
the state, claiming that their treaty rights had not been nul-
lified by the Termination Act. The state's position was affirmed by the Wisconsin Supreme Court but was then overturned by the Federal Court of Claims. The Supreme Court
agreed to hear the case (*Menominee Tribe* v. *United States,*
391, US404, 1968) and in a six-to-two decision that both the
Termination Act and Public Law 280 provided that the tribe
should not lose any hunting and fishing privileges afforded
under any previous federal treaty or agreement (Washburn
1973, p. 2882).

Justices Potter Stewart and Hugo L. Black dissented, and
Justice Marshall was not involved in the case. The dissenting
opinion stated in part:

> The Termination Act by its very terms provides: "All statutes
> of the United States which affect Indians because of their status
> as Indians shall no longer be applicable to the members of the
> tribe. . . . The 1854 Treaty granted the Menominees special
> hunting and fishing rights. The 1954 Termination Act, by sub-
> jecting the Menominees without exception to state law, took away
> those rights." [Washburn 1973, p. 3887]

After the Supreme Court issued its decision, Vine Deloria
commented: "This decision is the first and major stepping
stone to a complete overthrow of the termination legislation

and to the reversal of federal termination policy. For, if nothing else, this case means that an Indian Tribe cannot be destroyed by an arbitrary act of Congress" (Deloria 1971, pp. 78–80). The Court's decision provided the first ammunition for the Menominees' upcoming battle against termination.

Early indirect support for restoration also emerged from the Nixon administration. On July 8, 1970, President Nixon sent a message to Congress outlining his opposition to the policy of termination. The president recommended that Congress adopt a new policy to provide for Indian self-determination "without termination of the special federal relationship with recognized Indian Tribes" (Nixon 1970). Although neither President Kennedy nor President Johnson supported the policy, President Nixon was the first chief executive to oppose termination strongly.

Other actions of the Nixon administration suggested a shift toward a more sympathetic Indian policy. The president recommended Indian eligibility for revenue-sharing funds and more tribal self-government. Although revenue sharing was considered desirable by most Indians, a cutback in funding for the Office of Economic Opportunity led to continued suspicions of federal intentions (Josephy 1971, pp. 155–57). Nixon also favored the decentralization of the BIA and a 15 percent increase in the bureau's budget (*Appleton Post-Crescent,* March 19, 1973). Vice-President Spiro Agnew took a special interest in the National Council on Indian Opportunity, and Leonard Garment, a presidential aide, was charged with the formulation of an Indian policy for the president (Josephy 1971, pp. 155–57).

An explanation for the administration's pro-Indian policy can only be speculated upon. It is possible that the president tried to compensate in part for the prevailing lack of black voter support for the Republican party. A strong antitermination policy was highly visible, and, even if it was intended largely as a symbolic gesture, it gained the support of a small but well-defined block of Indian voters.

Although the abandonment of termination as an official Indian policy was helpful, the Menominees were already a terminated tribe. Leaders of DRUMS needed specific administration support for restoration. They received it from two members of the president's staff, Bradley F. Patterson, a White House executive assistant in Indian affairs, and Melvin R. Laird, the counselor to the president for domestic affairs (*DRUMS*, July 15, 1973). Laird's role was confirmed by a senior BIA official, who commented that the former Wisconsin congressman "was the mover behind the scenes who formed the White House position on restoration." Former Congressman Laird's contacts both in the administration and with his former congressional colleagues opened many doors for Ada Deer and other restoration lobbyists. Twenty years earlier the Eisenhower administration had passively supported Menominee termination. By 1973 the role of the White House was clearly reversed with the antitermination efforts of Laird and other members of the Nixon administration.

Part of the Menominees' campaign for restoration included soliciting support from other Indian tribes across the country. The leaders of DRUMS accepted many speaking invitations from various tribes to publicize their drive for restoration. They mailed letters to other tribes requesting their support both in Congress and in the solicitation of financial support from private foundations and organizations, such as the Campaign for Human Development of the United States Catholic Conference, in Washington, D.C., (DRUMS Correspondence 1972).

By 1973 they had obtained the endorsement of more than fifteen Indian organizations and tribes.[7] A call for Menominee restoration was included among a list of twenty demands made by a group of Indians occupying the Washington offices of the BIA in 1972 (Raymer 1973), and the national conven-

---

[7] The list of Indian organizations and tribes endorsing restoration included National Congress of American Indians, Association on American Indian Affairs, National Tribal Chairman's Association, Great Lakes Inter-Tribal Council, National Indian Education Association, Western Tribes of Oklahoma, Indian Legal Information Development Service, American Indian Law Students Association, Native American Rights Fund, Native American Legal Defense and Education Fund, National Indian Youth Council, Americans for Indian Opportunity, Council of Chiefs of the Tuscarora Nation, Navajo Nation, and Flandreau Santee Sioux Tribe.

tion of the National Congress of American Indians in 1973 carried the theme "Restoration Now" (*Green Bay Press-Gazette,* August 20, 1973). Indian endorsements of Menominee restoration reflected a unanimous delight that at last a tribe had unified itself around a common goal, seized the political initiative, and was about to win a major policy dispute with the federal government.

The attack against termination followed two basic themes. First, Indian leaders argued that termination had impeded rather than helped progress toward greater self-sufficiency (N. Smith 1965, pp. 1–3; U.S., House, Hearings, 1973, p. 324). Vine Deloria suggested, "Tribes lost some ten years during the 1950's when all progress was halted by the drive toward termination" (Deloria 1969, pp. 33, 138–39). Others argued that the federal government in general and the BIA in particular raised the threat of termination well into the early 1970s whenever a tribe "became too pushy or demanding" (Lurie 1973, p. 26). One writer commented: "If the tribes complain too much, they foresee the withdrawal of [BIA] funds and services. If they are too successful in self-development, they foresee reduced funding before they can afford it. These conditions result in strong resistance and fear of change" (Muskrat 1973, p. 50). Indians were not opposed to socioeconomic progress, but they demanded that it occur at their own pace and without the loss of their cultural heritage and traditional identity with their land. If Congress sincerely wanted Indians to move toward greater self-sufficiency, Congress would have to abandon termination and remove it as a threat to the survival of the Indian's tribal way of life.

The second reason offered for a speedy approval of Menominee restoration evolved from a trend toward increased Indian militancy and an escalation of demands for direct participation in the formulation of policies and programs affecting Indians.[8] Speaking for the NCAI and other traditional Indian organizations, Deloria argued, "We very badly need an action by Congress, such as the restoration of the

[8]For additional discussion of "Red Power" and other Indian political movements see Svensson 1973 and Josephy 1971.

Menominees, to show the activists that you can work through the system" (U.S., House, Hearings, 1973, p. 327). The Native American Rights Fund echoed Deloria when it stated that restoration "has become a symbol for all Native Americans. Restoration "is not the first reversal in U.S. Indian policy, but it is probably the most important one. It provides the evidence needed to show that the American political system —imperfect as it has been and will continue to be—can be used as a tool to preserve Indian culture" (Native American Rights Fund 1973, p. 9).

In sum, other tribes and Indian organizations significantly aided the Menominees' campaign for restoration. They forcefully argued that restoration would accelerate the pace of tribal socioeconomic development and self-sufficiency and would improve relations between the federal government and all Indian tribes. Most important, their forceful, unified support of restoration transformed a relatively isolated policy issue involving a single terminated tribe into an issue of national political importance.

Several nationally based non-Indian organizations also contributed money, time, and publicity to the restoration campaign. Among the more prominent were the National Office of the League of Women Voters, the Friends Committee on National Legislation, and the Center for Community Change and Common Cause. Both the Democratic and the Republican parties inserted prorestoration statements into their 1972 party platforms. The list of individual non-Menominee supporters is too long to reproduce here; however, two people were particularly important as Washington lobbyists for restoration: LaDonna Harris, the wife of former Senator Fred Harris, and Philleo Nash, former lieutenant governor of Wisconsin and commissioner of the Bureau of Indian Affairs.

Twenty years earlier, the non-Menominee support for the traditional elite was all but nonexistent, partly because of prevailing national opinion favoring termination and partly because the old elite was too bound by traditional pride to solicit non-Menominee assistance. An individual who had long been familiar with the Menominee case characterized the traditional elite as "terrible snobs" who could have gained the help of outside private organizations but instead chose to go it alone. The Association of American Indian Affairs allegedly offered to help lobby against termination but their assistance was refused. The new DRUMS elite was favored by a more sympathetic political climate, and, more important, they appreciated and knew how to build political support beyond the boundaries of the reservation.

Building political support in the Congress was essential to the achievement of restoration. When DRUMS was organized, a total reversal of termination was considered impractical because Congress still appeared unwilling to halt its experiment in forced Indian assimilation. In 1970, Wisconsin Congressman David Obey reinforced this conclusion when he advised the Menominees that "as of now, I just don't see how we can reverse the federal law granting termination" (*Green Bay Press-Gazette,* July 16, 1970). Over a year later, conditions had not changed. Responding to a request by DRUMS for additional aid to combat the effects of termination, Senator William Proxmire advised the tribe that "any bill to provide effective help to the Menominees will have a difficult time passing. . . . The more the bill proposes to do on behalf of the Menominees, the less chance there will be to obtain committee hearings, let alone passage" (Proxmire 1971).

Although Congress did not appear ready to restore the Menominees to their reservation, strong indications existed that termination would not be applied to other tribes. As early as 1966, Senator George McGovern introduced a resolution in the Senate that in effect repudiated termination by calling for more federal aids and services to Indians living on established reservations and more Indian involvement in the development and management of their own programs (Josephy 1971, pp. 71–72). In 1971 the Senate went one step further by passing Senate Concurrent Resolution 26. The resolution reversed House Concurrent Resolution 108, passed twenty years earlier, and officially called for the abandonment of termination as a strategy for achieving Indian assimilation. Congress was gradually moving toward acceptance of a new Indian policy employing the principle of "self-determination." Reasons for the changing moods of Congress were eloquently summed up by Senator Edward Kennedy:

> First, we embarked on a policy of isolation, marching entire Indian nations to desolate reservations. Later, we turned toward assimilation, but for the wrong reason—to exploit and expropriate Indian land and Indian resources. We shouldered the "white man's burden" initially by herding separate Indian nations together against their will—then turned around and plunged them headlong into the white man's society, thereby helping to tear them apart. But in any case, so the feeling went, the Indians would be off our conscience, off our land, out of our pocketbooks. Well, it hasn't worked.
>
> Throughout the 1960's the Federal Government groped toward a more enlightened national policy. The results can be measured largely in terms of words rather than action. Numerous studies, reports and commissions have come forth with their "solutions" for the Indian problem. But the crucial ingredient that has always been missing is the concept that the Indian can speak for himself, can say what is wrong, what he wants and needs, and what our policies should be. . . . We might try turning to the American Indian himself. That's what he is asking. That's what he is demanding. And ultimately, that's what we must recognize as the best solution. [Kennedy 1972, pp. 534–35]

One additional factor also brightened the chances for Menominee restoration—the 1972 national election. Two long-term supporters of termination, Senator Gordon Allott, a Republican from Colorado, and Representative Wayne Aspinall, a Democrat also from Colorado, were defeated for re-election. Their respective departures from the Senate and House Committees on Interior Affairs meant that a restoration bill would have a much warmer reception in Congress.

The BIA had been receptive to restoration for several years, but because of its dependence on the goodwill of Congress, it was a less-than-effective Menominee ally. As early as 1965, bureau personnel interpreted Menominee requests for extensive additional federal aid as "an obvious sign that the experiment wasn't working."[9] Also in 1965, BIA Com-

---

[9]Quoted from the comments in 1974 of a BIA official based in Minneapolis, Minnesota.

missioner Nash discreetly implied that termination should be reversed when he combined his suggestion that the federal government should extend aid to the tribe with an additional recommendation "that if this is to be done, then there ought to be a resumption of the trust status; otherwise we are placed in the position of supervising people who are not beneficiaries of a trust" (*Wisconsin Rapids Tribune*, March 20, 1965). In 1972 the BIA became more bold and published a report on Menominee termination which stated that, although there had been some progress, the tribe would benefit from a restoration of their reservation (Department of the Interior, Bureau of Indian Affairs 1972).

Despite the bureau's positive recommendation, the report was attacked by DRUMS as, among other things, "inaccurate," "misleading," and a "surface rehash of census data" (Menominee Tribal Delegation for Restoration Bill 1972, p. 205). DRUMS was attempting to further restoration by arguing that conditions in the county were much worse than they were described by the BIA.

Although it supported restoration, the bureau differed with the tribe over the ultimate goals of restoration. The tribe envisioned the establishment of a new trust status founded on the basis of maximum Menominee self-determination over its own affairs. While the BIA agreed that "the only certain solution to the grim situation with which the Menominees are faced is to restore the trust relationship with them," they went on to say that they could not support the creation of a unique Federal relationship "with the Menominees whereby the secretary of the interior would play only a consulting role in the tribe's management of its trust assets: 'We believe that the normal trust relationship should apply to the Menominees'" (U.S., House, Hearings, 1973, p. 243). The bureau provided one basic reason for its reluctance to break with tradition. It argued that restoration of the "normal trust relationship" was the only way the secretary of the interior could "properly fulfill his duties toward the Menominees' trust assets" (U.S., House, Hearings, 1973, p. 243). Too much self-determination could result in the tribe's mismanagement of its own affairs, which could in turn lead to the bankruptcy of the lumber industry or the dissipation

of other tribal assets. Although the secretary would have
no control over the situation, he would still be responsible
to Congress for the declining welfare of the tribe.

The bureau's position was certainly reasonable. Still, three
other factors may also have affected the BIA's unwillingness
to part with past administrative practice. First, the bureau
was reluctant to delegate responsible decision-making authority either to Indian employees within the agency or to
tribes under its supervision. Tribal employees traditionally
occupied positions of "relatively second-rate status . . . by
comparison with federal employees" (W. Brophy et al. 1966,
p. 121). As for tribal participation in decisions directly affecting their interests, one observer of BIA operations has noted
that "the Federal Government annually appropriates almost
one-half billion dollars for BIA programs, yet no Indian or
Indian representative testifies before the budget committees
in Congress" (Muskrat 1973, p. 59). Among other things the
Menominees were seeking direct participation in budgetary
decisions of the BIA affecting the tribe after restoration.

Second, the BIA's primary allegiance has been to the House
and Senate Committees of Interior and Insular Affairs, not to
the bureau's Indian clients. One critic of the Bureau commented:

> In this age, when departments of government regularly get criti-
> cism for being 'slaves' to their constituencies, . . . the problem at
> BIA is just the opposite. The bureau pays lavish attention to the
> wishes of the House and Senate Interior Committees and rela-
> tively little to the voices of Indians that filter through the layers
> of the BIA bureaucracy. And it is because there are few rewards
> for the bureaucrat who listens to the Indians. [Maxey 1970]

Granting an unprecedented amount of self-determination to
the Menominees would encourage other tribes to demand the
same authority. The vision of an unpredictable, often hostile
Congress on one side balanced by a powerful, usually dis-
contented clientele on the other must have sent nervous
tremors throughout the bureau.

Finally, innovative action within the bureau was severely
constrained by unwieldy decision-making procedures and
bureaucratic inefficiency:

Over the years there has been accumulated a mass of 389 treaties, 5,000 statutes (many of which have been repealed by implication), 2,000 federal court decisions, more than 500 attorney general opinions, numerous Department of the Interior and solicitor rulings, 95 tribal constitutions, and 74 tribal charters, besides a conglomeration of administrative regulations—confusing and often contradictory—collected in a manual which is so large that if stacked volume upon volume, it would dwarf any person wanting to consult it. The delay and uncertainty caused by having to consult this unwieldy body of prescription and direction are costly and frustrating to all concerned, and management is so handicapped that many decisions are based on reinterpretation of laws or regulations instead of on the economic welfare or social needs of the tribes. [W. Brophy et al. 1966, p. 123]

Critics generally agree that most BIA personnel are genuinely interested in the Indians and their future. The agency's actions, however, are so severely constrained, both externally by Congress and internally by its own composition and decision-making procedures, that any innovative change in Indian policy is perceived as a threat to the bureau. Many BIA officials favored restoration. Addition of the terminated tribe to bureau supervision would increase the agency's administrative responsibilities and strengthen future claims for increased personnel and an expanded budget. For the Menominees bureau support was welcome but was treated with apprehension. The tribe envisioned the creation of a new relationship with the bureau based on the principle of self-determination.

Overall, several trends at the national policy-making level suggested that the time was right for Menominee restoration. Public opinion was moving toward greater sympathy for the problems and demands of several minority groups including blacks, Spanish Americans, and American Indians. The resulting supportive political environment made the task of DRUMS much easier. The press gave more publicity to the demands of DRUMS, and support from various non-Indian organizations and individuals was more easily obtainable. National Indian organizations and other tribes supported restoration because of their fear that the continuation of termination as a national Indian policy might eventually

result in their own termination, regardless of the outcome
of the Menominee experiment.

Although the Supreme Court's decision on hunting and
fishing rights was based on the faulty legality of the Termination Act and not on a negative reaction to the effects
of Menominee termination, it also provided a strong im-
petus for restoration. The prorestoration position of the Nixon
administration may have been conditioned in part by a desire to offset black support for the Democratic party by gaining the votes of Native Americans. Some of the BIA's support for restoration was based on a desire to reacquire the
terminated tribe and, thereby, enlarge their administrative
responsibilities and strengthen their claim for more personnel and an expanded budget. Finally, congressional support
for restoration was based on sympathy for the damaging
impacts of termination on the Menominees. It was also based
on other factors, including the departure of the most ardent
supporters of termination and a growing general disenchant-
ment with termination as a national Indian policy. Lingering
congressional support for the policy completely ignored the
impacts of Menominee termination and was based, instead,
on a determination to force continued assimilation, no matter what the consequences for Native Americans.

# 9

# TERMINATION, RESTORATION, AND
# INDIAN ASSIMILATION

*This morning on television they were showing this gimmick that they*
*recovered from space and mention was made that in the future they are*
*going to use perhaps mice or even a spider monkey, but it will be a*
*long time before they would attempt to use a human being. The same*
*principle could be applied to the Menominee Tribe in regard to*
*termination. We are actually the guinea pigs of the termination process.—*
Mrs. Irene Mack, a Menominee, U.S., House, Report 1842,
1960, p. 60

IN NOVEMBER, 1971, after DRUMS had clearly solidified
its position as the new governing elite, Governor Lucey
invited representatives of DRUMS, MEI, and the Menominee County government to discuss restoration legislation.
"Virtually every goal" sought by DRUMS was incorporated
into the proposed legislation (Shames, ed., 1972, p. 93). With
the help of lawyers from NARF (formerly from Wisconsin
Judicare), DRUMS leaders wrote the initial draft of the Restoration Bill (see appendix 3). The first draft was widely pub-
licized and debated in formal and informal tribal meetings.
   On April 20, 1972, the Menominee Restoration Bill was
introduced into both the House and the Senate. The House
Subcommittee on Indian Affairs held hearings on the bill in
Keshena, Wisconsin, on May 25 and 26, 1973, and in Washington, D.C., on June 28, 1973. Hearings were subsequently
held before the Senate Subcommittee on Indian Affairs on
September 17 and 26, 1973. Unlike the previous hearings on
termination, Menominee participants prevailed throughout
both hearings. After the hearings in Keshena three busloads
of persistent tribal members followed the House Subcommittee on Indian Affairs to Washington to appear again be-

fore that subcommittee (Native American Rights Fund 1973, p. 8).

Tribal support for restoration was nearly unanimous at both House and Senate hearings. Statements endorsing restoration were presented by the chairperson of MEI, members of the MEI Voting Trust and Board of Directors, the chairman of the Menominee County Board, and many other tribal members. The only adverse criticism voiced between the writing of the initial draft of the Restoration Bill and the conclusion of the hearings referred to various provisions of the bill, not to the principle of restoration itself. Menominee and non-Menominee property owners expressed concern over the future of their property after restoration. DRUMS dissidents alleged that the DRUMS governing elite had unnecessarily compromised several of the goals of restoration. They argued that the leaders of DRUMS had accepted an unnecessary provision to delay the implementation of restoration until two years after its enactment. They also objected to the extension of hunting and fishing rights to non-Indians and the failure of DRUMS to prohibit the sale of tribal land after restoration. Finally, they argued that the interests of all Menominees were not adequately protected in the restoration legislation. For example, they noted a failure of the bill to provide for educational benefits to Menominees not residing on the restored reservation. Despite their adverse testimony, the predominant tribal sentiment expressed during the hearings reflected overwhelming support for the Restoration Bill.

Menominee restoration passed the House on October 16, 1973, by a vote of 404 to 3. After some delay in the Senate Subcommittee on Indian Affairs the legislation was passed unanimously by the Senate Committee on Interior and Insular Affairs and passed the Senate on December 7, 1973. President Nixon signed the Menominee Restoration Act on December 22, 1973.

Considerable bitterness existed among Menominees when President Nixon signed the act without representatives of the tribe in attendance. DRUMS felt that a big public ceremony with the Menominee people present, particularly representatives of the growing factions in DRUMS, would help soothe some of the hurt egos and other wounds incurred during the campaign for restoration (Lurie 1978).

The Restoration Act reflected most of the provisions of the original legislation submitted to Congress a year and a half earlier (see appendix 4). One of the act's provisions, repeal of the Menominee Termination Act of 1954, was the cornerstone of the entire restoration campaign. It signaled the official end of the policy of termination. The Restoration Act also reopened Menominee tribal rolls. All Menominee children born after 1954 became eligible for admission to the rolls, provided they were of at least one-quarter Menominee blood. Reopening of the rolls was necessary to determine who was legally eligible for federal benefits and services after restoration. A third provision of the act reestablished federal-trust status for the tribe. The secretary of the interior was given the authority to receive and to hold in trust Menominee tribal assets, such as their forest and corporation, and the assets of individual Menominees who voluntarily elected to place their property in a common trust. The act did not adversely affect the property rights of non-Menominees owning land in Menominee County. They could retain title to their land as long as they wished. The state of Wisconsin retained the authority to provide public services for non-Menominee residents of the county after the majority of the county returned to trust status.

Before final passage of the Restoration Act, Congressman Froehlich argued that the transfer of Menominee assets to trust status should be delayed until two years after the enactment of restoration. Speaking mainly for non-Indian residents of Menominee County, he maintained that sufficient time should be allotted to study the potential economic impacts of restoration on the state and region surrounding the restored reservation. The Menominees successfully sought removal of the two-year-delay provision from the act. They argued that unnecessary delay would "result in additional economic damage, and loss of land, and [in any event] . . . the rights of private land holders in the area are fully protected by the Restoration Act" (Wilkinson 1973, p. 13).

Non-Menominee efforts to amend other provisions of the Restoration Act were more successful. The original legislation submitted by the tribe in 1972 included a statement that "no authority shall be granted to sell, or to mortgage or lease for a period exceeding 25 years, any of the land included within the limits of the reservation" (H.R. 14803, 92d Cong., 2d sess.). The provision was struck by Congress. Representative Froehlich and other opponents to the "no-sale" restriction argued that if adopted by Congress, not by tribal government, the provision would detract from "tribal sovereignty" and the principle of Indian self-determination.

The BIA resisted inclusion of a provision in the act which would have provided federal services to Menominees not residing on the reservation. The bureau persuaded Congress that the provision was superfluous because the Menominees would be treated like all other Indians after passage of the act. The BIA's action indirectly strengthened the position of DRUMS dissidents, who charged that the new governing elite failed to protect the interests of all Menominee tribal members.

Criticism from the opponents of DRUMS notwithstanding, the Restoration Act presented strong evidence that the bureau's renewed relationship with the tribe would be guided by the principle of self-determination. A provision of the act authorizing the tribe to form its own government and business organizations ratified the Menominees' demands for direct control over their own political and economic affairs. Another provision authorized the tribe to create the Menominee Restoration Committee (MRC). The new committee was given full authority to receive grants and make contracts with the Department of the Interior and the Department of Health, Education, and Welfare. Creation of the MRC reinforced the principle of self-determination because it meant that federal money for transition expenses would not be handled by the BIA but would be controlled directly by the tribe.

In retrospect, the speed of congressional action on restoration and the close conformity between the contents of the original Restoration Bill and those of the final Restoration Act dramatize the strength of congressional support for the reversal of termination. The list of congressmen endorsing Menominee restoration was impressive. Two key House supporters of the act were David Obey, the Menominees' former congressman,[1] and Representative Lloyd Meeds, chairman of the House Subcommittee on Indian Affairs. In the Senate bipartisan support for restoration was particularly noteworthy. Cosponsors of the Restoration Bill included Henry Jackson, chairman of the Committee on Interior and Insular Affairs; James Abourezk, chairman of the Subcommittee on Indian Affairs; Dewey Bartlett, a member of the Subcommittee on Indian Affairs; and Barry Goldwater, senator from Arizona (*DRUMS,* July 15, 1973).

Testimony of congressmen during both House and Senate hearings on restoration reflected nearly unanimous support for the reversal of termination. Senator Gaylord Nelson of Wisconsin declared flatly that "the experiment of termination was a failure" (U.S., House, Hearings, 1973, p. 2). Representative Meeds argued that "termination, as a means of fulfilling the obligations and commitments of the Federal Government to the Indian . . . [and] making the Indians first-class citizens . . . has, beyond question, proved a disaster to the Indian Tribes and people" (U.S., House, Hearings, 1973, p. 6). Representative John Saylor, ranking Republican on the House Interior Committee, characterized termination as a "monstrosity." Displaying a somewhat wry sense of humor, the congressman wondered, "What type of life must these people be living under if they think that life under the BIA would be better than the life they have now?" (*Green Bay Press-Gazette,* October 17, 1973).

In 1973 the magnitude of congressional support for Menominee restoration was the mirror image of congressional support for the tribe's termination twenty years earlier. In 1953, Senator Watkins of Utah held the policy-making initiative and was the driving force behind termination. His single-minded determination moved a Congress already in favor of the principle of termination to terminate the Menominee tribe.[2] In 1973 the DRUMS governing elite held the policy-making initiative. Their unrelenting campaign for restora-

[1]After a redistricting of Wisconsin's congressional districts, Representative Obey was replaced by Representative Froehlich.

[2]Ironically, former Senator Watkins died only months before enactment of the Menominee Restoration Act. One observer noted in passing that the policy of termination followed "its architect to the grave" (Native American Rights Fund 1973, p. 8).

tion moved a Congress already in favor of the principle of Indian self-determination to reverse Menominee termination and restore the tribe to its former reservation.

The respective roles of Senator Watkins and the DRUMS governing elite are important components in the Menominees' termination and restoration. Senator Watkins and DRUMS would command central attention in any account of the recent history of the Menominee tribe. This book, however, seeks to provide more than a descriptive history of the Menominee people. It incorporates many of the theories and concepts of political science into an explanation for termination and restoration. Incrementalism was used in earlier discussion to help explain the decision by Congress to terminate the Menominees. The model also provides a useful basis for explaining the tribe's subsequent restoration.

Incrementalists argue that man's capacity to make intelligent decisions is imperfect. Moreover, the national policy-making process is extremely complex, and policymakers lack the information necessary to make perfectly rational policy decisions. Under such uncertain conditions wholesale policy innovations are unwise. When faulty policy decisions are implemented on a broad scale, the resulting damage to society can be extremely costly or impossible to correct.

Because of the uncertainty involved in making public policies, congressional decision makers refused to terminate federal trust responsibilities for all tribes in 1954. Instead, termination was applied incrementally by experimentation with the Menominees and a few other smaller tribes who appeared to be ready for termination. If termination failed, Congress would not be committed to an unworkable policy, and the negative consequences would be limited. Remedial action would have been far more costly if the policy had been applied to all tribes at once.

Charles Lindblom noted: "Every policy decision is later judged to be in part mistaken. Policy is never exactly on target. . . . Hence in the actual play of power, policy making is in large part a process of remedying past errors in policy" (Lindblom 1968, p. 42). Herein lies much of the explanation for congressional approval of Menominee restoration.

When termination was recognized as a policy failure in the late 1960s, self-determination was adopted as a new strategy for achieving Indian assimilation. Congressional abandonment of termination meant that the reservation status of unterminated tribes was no longer in danger; however, the Menominees were already a terminated tribe. Adoption of Indian self-determination as the new national Indian policy did not directly affect them. Indirectly, it was a key input in the Menominees' drive for restoration. That is, the rise of public sympathy for minorities in the mid- and late 1960s, the Red Power movement, the Supreme Court's decision on Menominee hunting and fishing rights, as well as other inputs all combined with the decision by Congress to abandon termination and thus make the drive by DRUMS for restoration a realistic possibility. Menominee restoration occurred almost as a congressional afterthought, motivated by the felt obligation of Congress to remedy the negative consequences of its experiment with termination.

One additional factor also helps account for the successful restoration drive of DRUMS. For the last one and a half centuries the federal government has assumed a paternalistic responsibility for the welfare of Indians. Many of the harshest cycles in Indian policy, such as allotment and termination, were adopted by Congress and administered by the BIA in part because it was felt that, despite immediate hardships, forced assimilation was in the best long-term interests of the Indian's welfare. Ironically, this same sense of responsibility for the Indian helped make Menominee restoration possible. Because of it, Congress and the BIA, after the abandonment of termination as a national Indian policy, were vulnerable to the claim by DRUMS that the federal government had a special obligation to rectify the damaging effects of the policy on the Menominees. Congressional decision makers reasoned that the Menominees should be returned to their reservation and allowed the same privilege granted other tribes—to play a determining role in the choice of methods and the pace for achieving their own assimilation.

Although termination and other policies designed to promote rapid Indian assimilation have had consistently unfortunate consequences for Native Americans, Indian assimilation is likely to continue as a national policy goal for the forseeable future. "Cultural pluralism" has been suggested as an alternative to assimilation; however, the concept of Indians choosing to retain their treaty rights *to political autonomy* is simply too contrary to traditional American values and beliefs to be widely accepted.[3] Significant Indian assimilation continues to occur by individual choice. Yet the strength of Indian determination to maintain their cultural heritage and political autonomy separate from the dominant American society also shows little sign of weakening in the years ahead. The Menominee experience demonstrates that forced assimilation actually strengthens Native American resolve to maintain their tribal existence and Indian identity. Acceptance by white society of the Native American's desire to remain politically and culturally independent represents the only real, though improbable, solution to the "Indian problem."

[3]Indications exist that the melting-pot image of American society is losing popularity (for example, the continuing legacy of some of the counterculture experiments of the 1960s, rising ethnicity in general, and even the popularity of Alex Haley's *Roots* as a novel and on television). Nonetheless, desires for ethnic or racial identity are not the same thing as the Native American aspiration for political autonomy. While aspiration for ethnic or racial identity have met with growing acceptance in American society, Indian demands for political autonomy will meet with continued resistance.

*Interior Secretary Rogers Morton and Ada Deer sign deed conveying Menominee tribal land back to reservation status in Washington, D.C., ceremony, April 22, 1975. Wide World Photos.*

*Menominee Reservation clinic, early 1970s.* Menominee Tribal News.

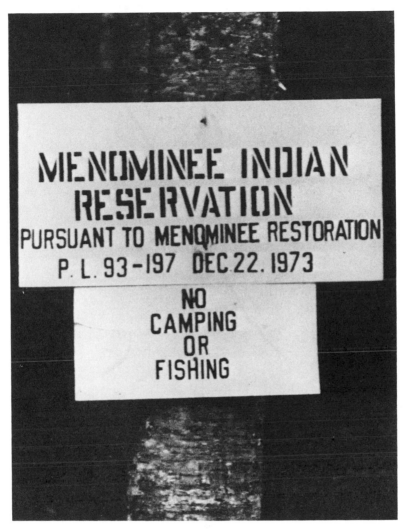

*Sign on Menominee Reservation.* Milwaukee Journal *photo.*

# APPENDICES

# Appendix 1

## PUBLIC POLICY AND POLICY CYCLES

THIS BOOK is written from the perspective of a political scientist. Although the specialized vocabulary of the profession has generally been avoided, the meaning or specialized use of certain terms in the text may be unfamiliar to the reader. Two such terms are "public policy" and the "cyclical policy-making process."

"Public policy is whatever governments choose to do or not to do" (Dye 1978, p. 3). For example, the decision by the federal government to create the Federal Communications Commission established the policy of government oversight of private use of the airways. Conversely, the government has not chosen to nationalize and operate all commercial radio and television stations in the United States. The decision not to act has established the government policy permitting private individuals and corporations to sell access to the airways to others for a profit.

Many public policies have the potential to affect the lives of all American citizens, including Native Americans, for example, changes in federal monetary policy that increase inflation or decrease inflation or a decision to declare war against another nation. "Indian policy" specifically refers to the actions the government chooses to take or not to take in relation to Native Americans. Since the early 1800s the choice of what to do or not do has been guided by the government's desire to assimilate American Indians into the larger American society.

The "policymaking process" is the mechanism responsible for changes in public policy. Subsumed within it are the activities of many public officials in all levels of government and an untold number of private citizens. Public policies that emerge from the process often seem to evolve in a cyclical pattern. That is, conditions in society are always changing, which creates new problems for society. Government responds by establishing a policy to deal with the new problems. A new agency is then set up to administer government programs to carry out the new policy. After programs are in operation for a time, they are examined to see how effectively they have dealt with the problem. After the examination changes may be made in existing policy, or an entirely new policy may be adopted to meet the goals.

Each cycle of the policymaking process consists of five phases—input, decision, implementation, performance, and impact. They are highlighted here because the organization of this book is roughly defined in terms of the five phases of the policymaking process.

1. *Input Phase.* Policy inputs are various factors that directly or indirectly bear upon a government decision to change an existing policy or develop a new policy. Within the general area of environmental policy examples of policy inputs include citizen demands for safe swimming beaches, the cleanup of disposal sites for toxic chemicals, and public concern for the protection of certain endangered species of plants and animals.

2. *Decision Phase.* This phase considers how a policy decision is developed by policymakers. Who favors and who opposes a proposed change in public policy? What factors account for a policymaker's position on a particular policy issue? In the example cited in 1 above, what was the policy position of the president, various congressmen, relevant interest groups, and others interested in the possible adoption of the Environmental Protection Act? What kinds of bargains and compromises were made between opposing policymakers before the act was finally signed into law?

3. *Implementation Phase.* The implementation phase involves setting up the machinery required to carry out a new public policy; for example, new agencies may be set up or old ones reorganized to carry out new responsibilities, new people may be hired or existing personnel may be retrained for newly created jobs, and so on. Implementation of the Environmental Protection Act mainly involved the creation of the Environmental Protection Agency (EPA). Specific implementation steps included the hiring of new people to staff the agency, the acquisition of space to house agency operations, and the development of a budget to manage agency funds.

4. *Performance Phase.* The performance phase is concerned with how well the newly implemented policy machinery works. Does the newly created or reorganized agency operate smoothly? Are the people assigned the responsibility of carrying out the policy decision doing their jobs? In the example of the EPA, this phase would include a look at how many complaints about pollution problems were received, processed, and acted upon by the agency. How enthusiastically do EPA personnel follow up on citizen complaints about environmental pollution?

5. *Impact Phase.* Policy impacts are the effects of a policy on "real-world" conditions. They are changes that occur because a policy has been implemented and is in operation. Has the amount of carbon dioxide or dust particles in the air decreased? How much?

Has the health of people improved because of improved water quality? What other changes in the environment have occurred as a result of EPA actions?

Phases of the policy-making process are linked in a circular fashion. The impacts of a policy often become inputs into a new policy cycle. For example, the EPA has banned certain pesticides used by farmers to protect their crops from insect infestation. Recently grasshoppers invaded and at least partly destroyed thousands of acres of crops in the Middle West. Farmers complained that all the pesticides effective against grasshoppers were banned by the EPA. An undesirable impact of the EPA policy banning the pesticides was low crop yields caused by grasshopper infestation. If the infestation continues and intensifies, a new cycle in environmental policy might occur. The ban might be lifted on certain pesticides, or the EPA might encourage farmers to employ an alternative solution to the grasshopper problem (such as various organic-farming techniques).

The use of policy phases and cycles to characterize the policy-making process provides a simplified description of a highly complex process. Unfortunately, simplicity usually leads to distortion. For example, although the phases are roughly sequential, the policy process is not as orderly as suggested by this discussion. Many policy impacts occur even before government policies are fully implemented. The congressional decision to create the EPA probably stimulated some industrial polluters to begin cleaning up plant emissions well before the EPA was fully funded, staffed, and in operation. Although some distortion of reality may occur, viewing public policy as the product of a cyclical policy-making process provides the reader with a useful framework for molding a diverse collection of complex facts and opinions into a plausible explanation for the termination and restoration of the Menominee tribe.

# Appendix 2

# MENOMINEE TERMINATION ACT

PUBLIC LAW 399, Eighty-third Congress, Second Session
(H.R. 2828)

AN ACT

To provide for a per capita distribution of the Menominee tribal
funds and authorize the withdrawal of the Menominee Tribe from
Federal Jurisdiction.

BE IT ENACTED BY THE SENATE AND HOUSE OF REPRESENTATIVES OF
THE UNITED STATES OF AMERICA IN CONGRESS ASSEMBLED. That the
purpose of this Act is to provide for orderly termination of Federal
Supervision over the property and members of the Menominee
Indian Tribe of Wisconsin.

SEC. 2. For the purposes of this Act—

(a) "Tribe" means the Menominee Indian Tribe of Wisconsin;

(b) "Secretary" means the Secretary of the Interior.

SEC. 3. At midnight of the date of enactment of this Act the roll
of the tribe maintained pursuant to the Act of June 15, 1934 (48
Stat. 965), as amended by the Act of July 14, 1939 (53 Stat. 1003),
shall be closed and no child born thereafter shall be eligible for
enrollment: PROVIDED, That applicants for enrollment in the tribe
shall have three months from the date the roll is closed in which
to submit applications for enrollment: PROVIDED FURTHER, That the
tribe shall have three months thereafter in which to approve or dis-
approve any application for enrollment: PROVIDED FURTHER, That
any applicant whose application is not approved by the tribe within
six months from the date of enactment of this Act may, within three
months thereafter, file with the Secretary an appeal from the failure of the tribe to approve his application or from the disapproval
of his application, as the case may be. The decision of the Secretary
on such appeal shall be final and conclusive. When the Secretary
has made decisions on all appeals, he shall issue and publish in
the Federal Register a Proclamation of Final Closure of the roll
of the tribe and the final roll of the members. Effective upon the
date of such proclamation, the rights or beneficial interests of each

person whose name appears on the roll shall constitute personal property and shall be evidenced by a certificate of beneficial interest which shall be issued by the tribe. Such interests shall be distributable in accordance with the laws of the State of Wisconsin. Such interests shall be alienable only in accordance with such regulations as may be adopted by the tribe.

SEC. 4. Section 6 of the Act of June 15, 1934 (48 Stat. 965, 966) is hereby repealed.

SEC. 5. The Secretary is authorized and directed, as soon as practicable after the passage of this Act, to pay from such funds as are deposited to the credit of the tribe in the Treasury of the United States $1,500 to each member of the tribe on the rolls of the tribe on the date of this Act. Any other person whose application for enrollment on the rolls of the tribe is subsequently approved, pursuant to the terms of section 3 hereof, shall, after enrollment, be paid a like sum of $1,500: PROVIDED, That such payments shall be made first from any funds on deposit in the Treasury of the United States to the credit of the Menominee Indian Tribe drawing interest at the rate of 5 per centum, and thereafter from the Menominee judgment fund, symbol 14S7142.

SEC. 6. The tribe is authorized to select and retain the services of qualified management specialists, including tax consultants, for the purpose of studying industrial programs on the Menominee Reservation and making such reports or recommendations, including appraisals of Menominee tribal property, as may be desired by the tribe, and to make other studies and reports as may be deemed necessary and desirable by the tribe in connection with the termination of Federal supervision as provided for hereinafter. Such reports shall be completed not later than December 31, 1957. Such specialists are to be retained under contracts entered into between them and authorized representatives of the tribe, subject to approval by the Secretary. Such amounts of Menominee tribal funds as may be required for this purpose shall be made available by the Secretary.

SEC. 7. The tribe shall formulate and submit to the Secretary a plan or plans for the future control of the tribal property and service functions now conducted by or under the supervision of the United States, including, but not limited to, services in the fields of health, education, welfare, credit, roads, and law and order. The Secretary is authorized to provide such reasonable assistance as may be requested by officials of the tribe in the formulation of the plan or plans heretofore referred to, including necessary consultations with representatives of Federal departments and agencies, officials of the State of Wisconsin and political subdivisions thereof, and members of the tribe: Provided, That the responsibility of the United States to furnish all such supervision and services to the tribe and to the members thereof, because of their status as Indians, shall cease on December 31, 1958, or on such earlier date as may be agreed upon by the tribe and the Secretary.

SEC. 8. The Secretary is hereby authorized and directed to transfer to the tribe, on December 31, 1958, or on such earlier date as may be agreed upon by the tribe and the Secretary, the title to all property, real and personal, held in trust by the United States for the tribe: PROVIDED, HOWEVER, That if the tribe obtains a charter for a corporation or otherwise organizes under the laws of a State or of the District of Columbia for the purpose, among any others, of taking title to all tribal lands and assets and enterprises owned by the tribe or held in trust by the United States for the tribe, and requests such transfer to be made to such corporation or organization, the Secretary shall make such transfer to such corporation or organization.

SEC. 9. No distribution of the assets made under the provisions of this Act shall be subject to any Federal or State income tax: PROVIDED, That so much of any cash distribution made hereunder as consists of a share of any interest earned on funds deposited in the Treasury of the United States pursuant to the Supplemental Appropriation Act, 1952 (65 Stat. 736, 754), shall not by virtue of this Act be exempt from individual income tax in the hands of the recipients for the year in which paid. Following any distribution of assets made under the provisions of this Act, such assets and any income derived therefrom in the hands of any individual, or any corporation or organization as provided in section 8 of this Act, shall be subject to the same taxes, State and Federal, as in the case of non-Indians, except that any valuation for purposes of Federal income tax on gains or losses shall take as the basis of the particular taxpayer the value of the property on the date title is transferred by the United States pursuant to section 8 of this Act.

SEC. 10. When title to the property of the tribe has been transferred, as provided in section 8 of this Act, the Secretary shall publish in the Federal Register an appropriate proclamation of that fact. Thereafter individual members of the tribe shall not be entitled to any of the services performed by the United States for Indians because of their status as Indians, all statutes of the United States which affect Indians because of their status as Indians shall no longer be applicable to the members of the tribe, and the laws of the several States shall apply to the tribe and its members in the same manner as they apply to other citizens or persons within their jurisdiction. Nothing in this Act shall affect the status of the members of the tribe as citizens of the United States.

SEC. 11. Prior to the transfer pursuant to section 8 of this Act, the Secretary shall protect the rights of members of the tribe who are less than eighteen years of age, non compos mentis, or in the opinion of the Secretary in need of assistance in conducting their affairs by causing the appointment of guardians for such members in courts of competent jurisdiction, or by such other means as he may deem adequate.

SEC. 12. The Secretary is authorized and directed to promulgate such rules and regulations as are necessary to effectuate the purposes of this Act.

SEC. 13. If any provisions of this Act, or the application thereof to any person or circumstance, is held invalid, the remainder of the Act and the application of such provision to other persons or circumstances shall not be affected thereby.

Approved June 17, 1954.

# MENOMINEE RESTORATION BILL

Ninety-second Congress, Second Session
(H.R. 14803)

A BILL

To repeal the Act terminating Federal supervision over the property and members of the Menominee Indian Tribe of Wisconsin;
to reinstitute the Menominee Indian Tribe of Wisconsin as a
federally recognized, sovereign Indian tribe; and to restore to
the Menominee Tribe of Wisconsin those Federal services furnished to American Indians because of their status as American
Indians.

Be it enacted by the Senate and House of Representatives of
the United States of America in Congress assembled, That this Act
may be cited as the "Menominee Restoration Act."

SEC. 2. For the purpose of this Act—

(1) "Tribe" means the Menominee Tribe of Wisconsin, as determined by the membership roll prepared pursuant to section 4 of
this Act;

(2) "Secretary" means the Secretary of Interior;

(3) "Menominee Restoration Committee" means that committee
of nine Menominee Indians, who have been elected at a General
Council meeting open to all living persons on the final roll of
the tribe published pursuant to the Act of June 17, 1954 (68 Stat.
250; 25 U.S.C. 893) (hereinafter referred to as the "final 1954 roll"),
and their descendants. The Secretary shall approve the membership of the committee if he is satisfied that the above requirements
of this section have been met. Immediately upon the enactment
of this Act, the Secretary shall publish the names of the membership of the Menominee Restoration Committee in the Federal
Register. The Menominee Restoration Committee shall be the en-
tity which shall represent the Menominee people in coordinating
and negotiating the implementation of this Act prior to the restoration date, as described in section 8 of this Act. The Menomi-

nee Restoration Committee shall have no powers other than those given to it by the Act.

Sec. 3. Effective on the restoration date established pursuant to section 8 of this Act, the Act of June 17, 1954 (Public Law 399 of the Eighty-third Congress, 25 U.S.C. 891-902) is repealed and shall be of no further force and effect.

Sec. 4. As soon as practicable, the Secretary shall establish a membership roll of the tribe (hereinafter referred to as the "membership roll"). The roll shall contain the ages and quantum of Indian blood and, when approved by the Secretary, shall constitute the legal membership of the tribe for all purposes. The membership roll shall include all persons listed on the final 1954 roll who are still living on the date of the enactment of this Act. The membership roll shall also include all descendants of persons listed on the final 1954 roll, if such descendants have at least one-quarter Menominee blood and if such descendants are living on the date of the enactment of this Act. Applications for inclusion in the membership roll may be filed with the Secretary for a period of four months after the enactment of this Act. Within thirty days after the enactment of this Act, the Secretary shall notify in writing all persons who were listed on the final 1954 roll for the purpose of ascertaining the names of all descendants of such persons. The Secretary shall also make all reasonable independent efforts to ascertain the identity of all persons entitled to be included on the membership roll. For a period of three months after the closing of the period for applications, the Secretary shall provide a reasonable opportunity for any person to protest against the inclusion or omission of any name on or from the roll. During such period of three months, the Secretary shall permit the examination of the applications by the Menominee Restoration Committee for the purpose of lodging protests in regard to the inclusion or omission of any name on or from the roll. The Secretary shall publish the membership roll in the Federal Register within thirty days after the last day on which protests may be filed pursuant to the above provisions of this section. After the restoration date, as described in section 8 of this Act, the Secretary shall make additions, deletions, and modifications to the membership roll, based upon written notice from the governing body of the tribe, according to tribal rules and regulations which have been approved by the Secretary.

Sec. 5. All persons on the membership roll shall be eligible, as of the restoration date as described in section 8 of this Act, to receive all Federal services furnished American Indians because of their status as Indians. Such services shall include, but shall not be limited to, all health, education, employment, welfare, loan, financial, and other assistance and services which are provided to American Indians because of their status as American Indians.

SEC. 6. (a) Subject to the approval of the Secretary, as set forth in section 7(a) of this Act, the tribe shall organize a governing body for the tribe's common welfare and shall adopt an appropriate constitution and bylaws, which shall become effective pursuant to the provisions of sections 7 and 8 of this Act. Such constitution and bylaws shall be revocable by an election open to the same voters and conducted in the same manner as provided in section 7 of this Act. Amendments to the constitution and bylaws may be ratified and approved by the Secretary in the same manner as the original constitution and bylaws. In addition to any powers which were vested in the tribe before the termination of Federal supervision and in addition to any powers which may be vested in any Indian tribe or tribal governing body by existing law, the constitution adopted by the tribe may vest in the tribe or its governing body the following rights and powers: to employ legal counsel, including the choice of counsel and fixing of fees; to prevent the sale, disposition, lease, or encumbrance of tribal lands, interests in lands, or other tribal assets without the consent of the tribe; to purchase property, real and personal; to create a tribal corporation or corporations to conduct all or some of the economic activities of the tribe, subject to the provisions of subsection (b) of this section; and to negotiate with the Federal, State, and local governments; except that no authority shall be granted to sell, or mortgage or lease for a period exceeding twenty-five years, any of the land included within the limits of the reservation. The Secretary shall advise, and consult with, the governing body of the tribe concerning all appropriate estimates of Federal projects for the benefit of the tribe prior to the submission of such estimates to the Office of Management and Budget or to the Congress.

(b) Subject to the approval of the Secretary, the tribe may organize a tribal corporation or corporations to conduct all or some of the economic activities engaged in by the tribe. The corporation or corporations may be organized pursuant to the laws of any State. In addition to all powers which may be vested in any corporation pursuant to the laws of the State in which the corporation is incorporated, the tribal corporation or corporations may be granted the following rights and powers: to purchase, take by gift or bequest, or otherwise own, hold, manage, and operate property of every description, real and personal; to purchase property, real and personal; to exchange interests in corporate property for any property, real or personal, acquired by the corporation; to dispose of personal property; to sue and be sued for matters involving such economic activities engaged in by the corporation or corporations, as may be incidental to the conduct of corporate business; and such further powers, not inconsistent with law; except that no authority shall be granted to sell, or to mortgage or lease for a period exceeding twenty-five years, any of the land included in the limits of the reservation.

SEC. 7. (a) The Secretary shall conduct an election by secret ballot, pursuant to the provisions of this section, for the purpose of determining the tribe's constitution and bylaws. Within fifteen days after the publication of the membership roll, the Secretary shall announce the date of the election. The date of the election shall be within sixty days after the publication of the membership roll. All adult members on the membership roll shall be entitled to vote in the election, either in person or by absentee ballot. The constitution and bylaws shall be adopted if they receive a vote of the majority of those actually voting and if they receive the approval of the Secretary, who shall give his approval or disapproval within thirty days after the date of the election. The Secretary shall approve any constitution and bylaws chosen by the tribe if he finds that the constitution and bylaws will treat with reasonable equity all persons on the membership roll and that they conform to applicable Federal and State law.

(b) The texts of the constitution and bylaws which shall be on the ballot at the election shall be determined by the Menominee Restoration Committee, after consultation with the Secretary. The Menominee Restoration Committee shall distribute to all persons entitled to vote in the special election, at least thirty days before the special election, a copy of the constitution and bylaws which will be presented at the election, along with a brief, impartial description of the constitution and bylaws. The Menominee Restoration Committee shall freely consult with persons entitled to vote in the special election concerning the texts and description of the constitution and bylaws.

(c) If the constitution and bylaws presented at the election are not adopted, pursuant to the provisions of subsection (a) of this section, a second election shall be held. The Secretary shall announce the date of the second election within fifteen days after the proposed constitution and bylaws failed to receive the requisite number of votes or, if applicable, within fifteen days after disapproval by the Secretary. The date of the second election shall be within sixty days after the proposed constitution and bylaws failed to receive the requisite number of votes or, if applicable, within sixty days after disapproval by the Secretary. Such election, and any subsequent election, shall be conducted in accordance with the provisions of this section in all other respects.

SEC. 8. Within fifteen days after the Secretary approves the tribe's constitution and bylaws, as provided in section 7 of this Act, the Secretary shall announce a restoration date. The restoration date shall be within ninety days after the Secretary approves the constitution and bylaws. The Secretary shall promptly publish the restoration date in the Federal Register. On the restoration date, the following events shall occur:

(1) Subject to the approval of the shareholders as required by the laws of the State of Wisconsin, the board of directors of Menominee Enterprises, Incorporated, or the appropriate officers at the direction of the board of directors, shall execute all necessary and appropriate documents to transfer to the Secretary all assets held by Menominee Enterprises, Incorporated. Such assets shall be held in trust by the Secretary, on behalf of the United States, for the tribe. Such assets shall include, but shall not be limited to, all cash, buildings, personal property, lands, waters, and interests therein owned by Menominee Enterprises, Incorporated, as of the restoration date. The transfer of assets shall be exempt from Federal, State, and local taxation. All such assets, while held in trust by the Secretary, shall be exempt from Federal, State, and local taxation.

(2) The land which is transferred pursuant to paragraph (1) of this section shall become a federally recognized Indian reservation.

(3) All provisions of the constitution and bylaws selected by the tribe and approved by the Secretary pursuant to section 7 of this Act shall become effective. The governing body selected by the tribe at the election and approved by the Secretary pursuant to section 7 shall begin operation and shall be the official governing body of the tribe in all respects.

(4) The tribe shall be a federally recognized Indian tribe.

(5) All persons on the membership roll shall be eligible to receive the Federal services set forth in section 5 of this Act.

SEC. 9. The Secretary is hereby authorized, in his discretion, to acquire for inclusion in the Menominee Reservation through purchase, relinquishment, gift, exchange, or assignment, any interest in lands, water rights, or surface rights to lands, within or without the Menominee Indian Reservation as those boundaries were established by the treaties of 1854 and 1856, except that land within the present boundaries of the Stockbridge-Munsee Reservation shall not be acquired by the Secretary pursuant to this provision. The Secretary is further authorized to receive on behalf of the United States from the governing body of the tribe, or from any person on the membership roll, voluntarily executed deeds to such lands as the tribe or person may own in fee simple free from all encumbrances. Any property purchased, or received from the tribe, pursuant to this section shall be held in trust by the Secretary, on behalf of the United States, for the benefit of the tribe. Any property received from any person on the membership roll pursuant to this section shall be held in trust by the Secretary, on behalf of the United States, for the benefit of such person. Any land or rights transferred under this section shall be exempt from Federal, State, and local taxation.

SEC. 10. The governing body of the tribe, after full consultation with the Secretary, shall make rules and regulations for the operation and management of the tribal forestry units on the principle of sustained-yield management. The governing body of the tribe, after full consultation with the Secretary, shall make such other rules and regulations as may be necessary to protect the lands of the tribe from deterioration. The governing body of the tribe, after full consultation with the Secretary, may regulate hunting, fishing, and trapping on the reservation.

SEC. 11. This Act shall reinstitute all, and shall not abrogate any, water, hunting, fishing, and trapping rights or privileges, and any other rights and privileges of the tribe and its members enjoyed under Federal Treaty or otherwise.

SEC. 12. The Secretary is hereby authorized to make such rules and regulations as are necessary to carry out the provisions of this Act.

SEC. 13. There are hereby authorized to be appropriated such sums as may be necessary to carry out the provisions of this Act.

# Appendix 4

## MENOMINEE RESTORATION ACT

PUBLIC LAW 93–197
Ninety-third Congress, First Session
(H.R. 10717)
December 22, 1973

AN ACT

To repeal the Act terminating Federal supervision over the property and members of the Menominee Indian Tribe of Wisconsin;
to reinstitute the Menominee Indian Tribe of Wisconsin as a
federally recognized sovereign Indian tribe; and to restore to
the Menominee Tribe of Wisconsin those Federal services furnished to American Indians because of their status as American
Indians; and for other purposes.

BE IT ENACTED BY THE SENATE AND HOUSE OF REPRESENTATIVES
OF THE UNITED STATES OF AMERICA IN CONGRESS ASSEMBLED, That
this Act may be cited as the "Menominee Restoration Act."

SEC. 2. For the purposes of this Act—

(1) The term "tribe" means the Menominee Indian Tribe of Wisconsin.

(2) The term "Secretary" means the Secretary of the Interior.

(3) The term "Menominee Restoration Committee" means that
committee of nine Menominee Indians who shall be elected pursuant to subsections 4(a) and 4(b) of this Act.

SEC. 3. (a) Notwithstanding the provisions of the Act of June 17,
1954 (68 Stat. 250; 25 U.S.C. 891–902), as amended, or any other law,
Federal recognition is hereby extended to the Menominee Indian
Tribe of Wisconsin and the provisions of the Act of June 18, 1934
(48 Stat. 984; U.S.C. 461 et seq.), as amended, are made applicable
to it.

(b) The Act of June 17, 1954 (68 Stat. 250; 25 U.S.C. 891–902),
as amended, is hereby repealed and there are hereby reinstated
all rights and privileges of the tribe or its members under Federal
treaty, statute, or otherwise which may have been diminished or
lost pursuant to such Act.

(c) Nothing contained in this Act shall diminish any rights or privileges enjoyed by the tribe or its members now or prior to June 17, 1954, under Federal treaty, statute, or otherwise, which are not inconsistent with the provisions of this Act.

(d) Except as specifically provided in this Act, nothing contained in this Act shall alter any property rights or obligations, any contractual rights or obligations, including existing fishing rights, or any obligations for taxes already levied.

(e) In providing to the tribe such services to which it may be entitled upon its recognition pursuant to subsection (a) of this section, the Secretary of the Interior and the Secretary of Health, Education, and Welfare, as appropriate, are authorized from funds appropriated pursuant to the Act of November 2, 1921 (42 Stat. 208; 25 U.S.C. 13), the Act of August 5, 1954 (68 Stat. 674), as amended, or any other Act authorizing appropriations for the administration of Indian affairs, upon the request of the tribe and subject to such terms and conditions as may be mutually agreed to, to make grants and contract to make grants which will accomplish the general purposes for which the funds were appropriated. The Menominee Restoration Committee shall have full authority and capacity to be a party to receive such grants to make such contracts, and to bind the tribal governing body as the successor in interest to the Menominee Restoration Committee: PROVIDED, HOWEVER, That the Menominee Restoration Committee shall have no authority to bind the tribe for a period of more than six months after the date on which the tribal governing body takes office.

SEC. 4. (a) Within fifteen days after the enactment of this Act, the Secretary shall announce the date of a general council meeting of the tribe to nominate candidates for election to the Menominee Restoration Committee. Such general council meeting shall be held within thirty days of the date of enactment of this Act. Within forty-five days of the general council meeting provided for herein, the Secretary shall hold an election by secret ballot, absentee balloting to be permitted, to elect the membership of the Menominee Restoration Committee from among the nominees submitted to him from the general council meeting provided for herein. The ballots shall provide for write-in votes. The Secretary shall approve the Menominee Restoration Committee elected pursuant to this section if he is satisfied that the requirements of this section relating to the nominating and election process have been met. The Menominee Restoration Committee shall represent the Menominee people in the implementation of this Act and shall have no powers other than those given to it in accordance with this Act. The Menomi-

nee Restoration Committee shall have no power or authority under
this Act after the time which the duly-elected tribal governing
body take office: PROVIDED, HOWEVER, That this provision
shall in no way invalidate or affect grants or contracts made pursuant to the provisions of subsection 3(e) of this Act.

(b) In the absence of a completed tribal roll prepared pursuant
to subsection (c) hereof and solely for the purposes of the general
council meeting and the election provided for in subsection (a)
hereof, all living persons on the final roll of the tribe published
under section 3 of the Act of June 17, 1954 (25 U.S.C. 893), and all
descendants, who are at least eighteen years of age and who possess
at least one-quarter degree of Menominee Indian blood, of persons
on such roll shall be entitled to attend, participate, and vote at
such general council meeting and such election. Verification of
descendancy, age, and blood quantum shall be made upon oath
before the Secretary of his authorized representative and his determination thereon shall be conclusive and final. The Secretary shall
assure that adequate notice of such meeting and election shall be
provided eligible voters.

(c) The membership roll of the tribe which was closed as of June
17, 1954, is hereby declared open. The Secretary, under contract
with the Menominee Restoration Committee, shall proceed to make
current the roll in accordance with the terms of this Act. The
names of all enrollees who are deceased as of the date of enactment of this Act shall be stricken. The names of any descendants
of an enrollee shall be added to the roll provided such descendant
possesses at least one-quarter degree Menominee Indian blood.
Upon installation of elected constitutional officers of the tribe, the
Secretary and the Menominee Restoration Committee shall deliver
their records, files, and any other material relating to enrollment
matters to the tribal governing body. All further work in bringing
and maintaining current the tribal roll shall be performed in such
manner as may be prescribed in accordance with the tribal governing documents. Until responsibility for the tribal roll is assumed
by the tribal governing body, appeals from the omission or inclusion of any name upon the tribal roll shall lie with the Secretary and his determination thereon shall be final. The Secretary
shall make the final determination of each such appeal within
ninety days after an appeal is initiated.

SEC. 5. (a) Upon request from the Menominee Restoration Committee, the Secretary shall conduct an election by secret ballot,
pursuant to the provisions of the Act of June 18, 1934, as amended,
for the purpose of determining the tribe's constitution and bylaws.

The election shall be held within sixty days after final certification of the tribal roll.

(b) The Menominee Restoration Committee shall distribute to all enrolled persons who are entitled to vote in the election, at least thirty days before the election, a copy of the constitution and bylaws as drafted by the Menominee Restoration Committee which will be presented at the election, along with a brief impartial description of the constitution and bylaws. The Menominee Restoration Committee shall freely consult with persons entitled to vote in the election concerning the text and description of the constitution and bylaws. Such consultation shall not be carried on within fifty feet of the polling places on the date of the election.

(c) Within one hundred and twenty days after the tribe adopts a constitution and bylaws, the Menominee Restoration Committee shall conduct an election by secret ballot for the purpose of determining the individuals who will serve as tribal officials as provided in the tribal constitution and bylaws. For the purpose of this initial election and notwithstanding any provision in the tribal constitution and bylaws to the contrary, absentee balloting shall be permitted and all tribal members who are eighteen years of age or over shall be entitled to vote in the election. All further elections of tribal officers shall be as provided in the tribal constitution and bylaws and ordinances adopted thereunder.

(d) In any election held pursuant to this section, the vote of a majority of those actually voting shall be necessary and sufficient to effectuate the adoption of a tribal constitution and bylaws and the initial election of the tribe's governing body, so long as, in each such election, the total vote cast is at least 30 per centum of those entitled to vote.

(e) The time periods set forth in subsections 4(c), 5(a), and 5(c) may be changed by the written agreement of the Secretary and the Menominee Restoration Committee.

SEC. 6. (a) The Secretary shall negotiate with the elected members of the Menominee Common Stock and Voting Trust and the Board of Directors of Menominee Enterprises, Incorporated, or or their authorized representatives, to develop a plan for the assumption of the assets of the corporation. The Secretary shall submit such plan to the Congress within one year from the date of the enactment of this Act.

(b) If neither House of Congress shall have passed a resolution of disapproval of the plan within sixty days of the date the plan is submitted to Congress, the Secretary shall, subject to the terms and conditions of the plan negotiated pursuant to subsection (a) of this section, accept the assets (excluding any real property not located in or adjacent to the territory, constituting, on the effective date of this Act, the county of Menominee, Wisconsin) of Menominee Enterprises, Incorporated, but only if transferred to him by the Board of Directors of Menominee Enterprises, Incorporated, subject to the approval of the shareholders as required by the laws of Wisconsin. Such assets shall be subject to all valid existing rights, including, but not limited to, liens, outstanding taxes (local, State, and Federal), mortgages, outstanding corporate indebtedness of all types, and any other obligation. The land and other assets transferred to the Secretary pursuant to this subsection shall be subject to foreclosure or sale pursuant to the terms of any valid existing obligation in accordance with the laws of the State of Wisconsin. Subject to the conditions imposed by this section, the land transferred shall be taken in the name of the United States in trust for the tribe and shall be their reservation. The transfer of assets authorized by this section shall be exempt from all local, State, and Federal taxation. All assets transferred under this section shall, as of the date of transfer, be exempt from all local, State, and Federal taxation.

(c) The Secretary shall accept the real property (excluding any real property not located in or adjacent to the territory constituting, on the effective date of this Act, the county of Menominee, Wisconsin) of members of the Menominee Tribe, but only if transferred to him by the Menominee owner or owners. Such property shall be subject to all valid existing rights including, but not limited to, liens, outstanding taxes (local, State, and Federal), mortgages, and any other obligations. The land transferred to the Secretary pursuant to this subsection shall be subject to foreclosure or sale pursuant to the terms of any valid existing obligation in accordance with the laws of the State of Wisconsin. Subject to the conditions imposed by this subsection, the land transferred shall be taken in the name of the United States in trust for the Menominee Tribe of Wisconsin and shall be part of their reservation. The transfer of assets authorized by this section shall be exempt from all local, State, and Federal taxation. All assets transferred under this section shall, as of the date of transfer, be exempt from all local, State, and Federal taxation.

(d) The Secretary and the Menominee Restoration Committee shall consult with appropriate State and local government officials to assure that the provision of necessary governmental services is not impaired as a result of the transfer of assets provided for in this section.

(e) For the purpose of implementing subsection (d), the State of Wisconsin may establish such local government bodies, political subdivisions, and service arrangements as will best provide the State or local government services required by the people in the territory constituting, on the effective date of this Act, the county of Menominee.

SEC. 7. The Secretary is hereby authorized to make such rules and regulations as are necessary to carry out the provisions of this Act.

SEC. 8. There are hereby authorized to be appropriated such sums as may be necessary to carry out the provisions of this Act.

Approved December 22, 1973.

# REFERENCES

Alinsky, Saul
1969    *Reveille for Radicals.* New York: Random House.
1971    *Rules for Radicals.* New York: Random House.
Ames, David W.
1956*a*  Memorandum to Rebecca C. Barton, Vernon W. Thompson, and Earl Sachse, February 5.
1956*b*  Memorandum to Rebecca C. Barton, Vernon W. Thompson, and Earl Sachse, November 9.
1957    Memorandum to Rebecca C. Barton, Vernon W. Thompson, and Earl Sachse, September 23.
1958    "Report to the Wisconsin State Legislative Council," April 18.
1959    "Some Social and Cultural Problems Related to the Withdrawal of The Menominee People from Federal Supervision." Paper presented to the Central States Anthropological Society Symposium on Indian Termination Problems, n.d.
Ames, David W., and Burton R. Fisher
1959    "The Menominee Termination Crisis: Barrier in the Way of a Rapid Cultural Transition." Reprinted from *Human Organization* 18 (Fall).
Anderson, James E., ed.
1976*a*  *Cases in Public Policy-Making.* New York: Praeger.
1976*b*  *Public Policy-Making.* New York: Praeger.
"Annual Report of the Secretary of the Interior."
1933    Washington, D.C.: U.S. Government Printing Office.
*Appleton Post Crescent*
1962    September 2.
1965    April 4.
1973    March 19.
Austin, Dorothy
1972    "Plank OK Aided by Indian Women." *Milwaukee Sentinel,* July 13.
Bachrach, Peter
1967    *The Theory of Democratic Elitism: A Critique.* Boston: Little, Brown & Co.
Bahr, Howard M., B. A. Chadwick, and R. C. Day

1972    *Native American Today: Sociological Perspectives.* New York: Harper & Row.

Bailey, John J., and Robert J. O'Connor
1975    "Operationalizing Incrementalism: Measuring the Muddles," *Public Administration Review* 35 (January–February): 60–66.

Barton, Rebecca
1956    Memorandum to Vernon Thompson, chairman, MISC, July 31.

Blackwell, Edward H.
1971    "Indians, Supporters Picket Bank Here." *Milwaukee Journal,* April 26.
1972    "Menominees' Great Leap Fell Short." *Milwaukee Journal,* September 17.
1974    "Menominee County's Future." *Milwaukee Journal,* March 3.

Bowers, John H., and Burton R. Fisher
1959    "Report and Recommendations to Menominee Indian Study Committee," April 20.

Boyd, Theodore S.
1969    Quoted in the *Antigo Daily Journal,* November 1.
1973    "A Review of Financial and Operating Analysis During the Years of Menominee Tribal Termination (1961–1973)." Submitted to the U.S. Senate Sub-Committee on Indian Affairs, September 14.

Braybrooke, David, and Charles E. Lindblom
1932    *A Strategy of Decision.* New York: Free Press.

Brophy, Byron
1945    "The American Indian and Government." In Francis J. Brown and Joseph S. Roucek, eds. *One America.* New York: Prentice-Hall.

Brophy, William A., et al.
1968    *The Indian: America's Unfinished Business.* Norman: University of Oklahoma Press.

Brown, Ray A.
1957a   "Transfer of Tribal Properties to a Corporation." MIAE Program.
1957b   "Memorandum on Legal Problems Concerning Control of Property on Menominee Indian Reservation," August 1.

Bunker, Donald R.
1972    "Policy Sciences Perspectives on Implementation Processes." *Policy Sciences* 3:71–80.

Bureau of Government, University of Wisconsin Extension Division
1956    Memorandum to Menominee Indian Study Committee of the Joint Legislative Council, State of Wisconsin.

Burnett, Donald L., Jr.
1972    "An Historical Analysis of the 1968 'Indian Civil Rights'
        Act." *Harvard Journal of Legislation* 9:149–76.
Butler, Raymond V.
1978    "The Bureau of Indian Affairs: Activities Since 1945." *An-
        nals of the American Academy of Political and Social Science* 436
        (March): 50–60.
*Capital Times*
1961    May 5.
1971    October 13, October 14, December 20.
1973    October 18.
Carroll, Michael A.
1975    "The Impact of General Revenue on the Urban Planning
        Process—An Initial Assessment." *Public Administration Re-
        view* 35 (March–April): 143–149.
Clifford, Paul
1964    "Menominee County Success or Failure?" *Stevens Point Daily
        Journal,* June 2.
Cohen, Felix A.
1960    *The Legal Conscience: Selected Papers of Felix S. Cohen.* New
        Haven: Yale University Press.
1971    "Indian Self-Government." In Alvin M. Josephy, ed. *Red
        Power: The American Indians' Fight for Freedom.* New York:
        American Heritage Press.
Coleman, James S.
1971    "The Development Syndrome: Differentiation-Equality-
        Capacity." In Leonard Binder et al. *Crises and Consequences
        in Political Development.* Princeton: Princeton University
        Press.
Collier, John
1943    Commissioner's Circular 3537, November 15.
1953    "The Genesis and Philosophy of the Indian Reorganization
        Act." In William H. Kelley, ed. *Indian Affairs and the Indian
        Reorganization Act: The Twenty Year Record.* Tucson, Ariz.:
        American Anthropological Association.
Commission on Organization of the Executive Branch of the Government: Social Security and Education
1949    *Indian Affairs: A Report to the Congress by the Commission on
        Organization of the Executive Branch of the Government.* Wash-
        ington, D.C.: U.S. Government Printing Office.
Committee to Save the Menominee People and Forests
1972    Financial Statement, November 20.
Congressional Debate on the Menominee Termination Bill
1953    July 18 and August 1. In Wilcomb E. Washburn, *The Ameri-*

can Indian and the United States: A Documentary History. vol. 3, New York: Random House.

Council of Chiefs
1969    "A Resolution," January 4.
1973a   "Resolution," June 13.
1973b   Correspondence to Hon. Harold Froehlich, June 24.

Dadisman, Quincy
1961    Untitled article in *Milwaukee Sentinel*, April 10.

Dahl, Robert
1961    *Who Governs?* New Haven: Yale University Press.

Davis, Otto A., M. A. Dempster, and A. Wildavsky
1966    "A Theory of the Budgetary Process." *American Political Science Review* 60 (September):529–547.

Debo, Angie
1970    *A History of the Indians of the United States.* Norman: University of Oklahoma Press.

Deer, Ada, et al.
1971    "The Effects of Termination on the Menominee." Testimony on Senate Concurrent Resolution 26, submitted to the Senate Committee on Interior and Insular Affairs, July 21.

Deer, Robert E., and Farnum Alston
1971    "A Case Study of a Resource Issue: The Menominees and the Wolf River." Mimeographed.

Deloria, Vine, Jr.
1969    *Custer Died for Your Sins.* New York: Avon Books.
1971    *Of Utmost Good Faith.* San Francisco: Straight Arrow Books.
1978    "Legislation and Litigation Concerning American Indians." *Annals of the American Academy of Political and Social Science* 436 (March):86–96.

Department of Business Development
1972    "Economic Profile: Menominee County." Madison, Wis.

Department of the Interior, Bureau of Indian Affairs
1961    "Plan for the Future Control of Menominee Indian Tribal Property and Future Service Functions," April 29.
1965    "The Status of Termination of the Menominee Indian Tribe." In *Congressional Record—House,* March 30, pp. 6093–97.
1972    "The General Economic Situation of the Menominee Indian Tribe of Wisconsin." Report to the House Committee on Appropriations and Interior and Insular Affairs Committee, March 31.

D'Ewart, Hon. Wesley A.
1953    *Congressional Record.* Vol. 99, pt. 7, 83d Cong., 1st sess., p. 8460.

Dolbeare, Kenneth M.
1972    "The Impacts of Public Policy." Mimeographed.
Dozier, Edward P., G. E. Simpson, and J. M. Yinger
1957    "The Integration of Americans of Indian Descent." *Annals
        of the American Academy of Political and Social Science* 311
        (May): 158–65.
Dror, Yehezkel
1968    *Public Policymaking Re-examined.* San Francisco, Calif: Chand-
        ler.
*DRUMS*
1972    February 17, March 25, August 23.
1973    March 15, June 1, July 15.
DRUMS Correspondence
1972    Form letter to Indian organizations appealing for support,
        June 14.
DRUMS Meeting Minutes
1971    Milwaukee, December 7.
DRUMS Membership Meeting
1973    April 7.
DRUMS Policy Committee Meeting
1971    Menominee Chapter, February 8.
DRUMS Second Annual Convention Minutes
1972    August 26–27
Dye, Thomas R., ed.
1971    *The Measurement of Policy Impact.* Proceedings of the Con-
        ference on the Measurement of Policy Impact, Florida State
        University.
1972a   "Policy Analysis and Political Science: Some Problems at
        the Interface." *Policy Studies Journal* 1 (Winter): 103–7.
1972b   *Understanding Public Policy.* Englewood Cliffs, N.J.: Prentice-
        Hall.
1978    *Understanding Public Policy.* 3d ed. Englewood Cliffs, N.J.:
        Prentice-Hall.
Dye, Thomas R., and L. Harmon Zeigler
1970    *The Irony of Democracy.* Belmont, Calif.: Wadsworth Pub-
        lishing Co.
Ernst, Roger
1959    Correspondence to James G. Frechette, chairman of the
        Menominee Advisory Council. January 16.
Ernst and Ernst
1967    "Opportunities for Economic Development, Menominee
        County, Wisconsin." Economic Development Administra-
        tion Technical Assistance Project, U.S. Department of Com-
        merce, Final Report. March.

Fairchild, Foley, and Sammond
1959    "Plan for Termination of Federal Control of Menominee
        Indian Tribe," January 26.
Fenno, Richard F., Jr.
1973    *Congressmen in Committees.* Boston: Little, Brown & Co.
Fields, Larry
1965    "Poverty of Menominees an Assault on Senses." *Milwaukee
        Sentinel,* March 22.
Foley and Lardner
1971    Correspondence to Douglas S. Moodie, chairman of the
        Board of Wisconsin Judicare, August 12.
Frechette, James G.
1957    Statement Before the Indian Subcommittee of House Com-
        mittee on Interior and Insular Affairs on H.R. 6322, July 15.
1970    Quoted in *Green Bay Press-Gazette,* August 18.
Freeman, Howard E., and Clarence C. Sherwood
1970    *Social Research and Social Policy.* Englewood Cliffs, N.J.:
        Prentice-Hall.
Freeman, J. Leiper
1965    *The Political Process: Executive Bureau Legislative Committee
        Relations.* 2d ed. New York: Random House.
Froehlich, Hon. Harold
1973    *Congressional Record.* Reprint. Vol. 119, no. 66, 93d Cong.,
        1st sess., May 2.
Gawthrop, Louis C.
1971    *Administrative Politics and Social Change.* New York: St. Mar-
        tin's Press.
Gilmer, Jay, et al.
1975    "The Impact of Federal Programs in State-Local Relations."
        *Public Administration Review* 35 (special issue, December):
        774–79.
Goodwin, George, Jr.
1970    *The Little Legislatures.* Amherst, Mass.: University of Massa-
        chusetts Press.
Gordon, Anne
1971    "The County Not Being Organized for That Purpose."
        Master's thesis, University of Wisconsin—Madison. Mimeo-
        graphed.
*Green Bay Press-Gazette*
1958    December 6.
1959    January 12, January 15.
1962    December 8.
1965    March 24.
1967    September 25.

1969    August 31, September 9, September 14.
1970    April 10, May 22, July 12, July 16, August 28, September 1,
        October 19.
1971    June 21, June 25, July 22.
1973    August 20, October 17, December 8.
Grodzins, Morton
1961    "Centralization and Decentralization in the American Fed-
        eral System." In Robert A. Goldwin, ed. *A Nation of States.*
        Chicago: Rand McNally & Co.
Haas, Theodore H.
1947    *Ten Years of Tribal Government Under I.R.A.* Extract. Wash-
        ington, D.C.: U.S. Indian Service, Tribal Relations, Pam-
        phlet 1.
1957    "The Legal Aspects of Indian Affairs from 1887 to 1957."
        *Annals of the American Academy of Political and Social Science*
        311 (May):12–22.
Harkin, Duncan A.
1969    "Forest Resources in the Future Development of Menomi-
        nee County." Mimeographed.
Harrison, William H.
1953    *Congressional Record.* Vol. 99, pt. 7, 83d Cong., 1st sess., p.
        9263.
Heinberg, Nancy
1971    "Ada Deer: A New Hope for the Menominees." *Capital
        Times,* December 27.
Honeck, Stewart G.
1957    Correspondence to Hon. James A. Haley, chairman, Sub-
        committee on Indian Affairs, Committee on Interior and
        Insular Affairs, U.S. House of Representatives, Washing-
        ton, D.C., July 15.
House, Charles
1959    "Absorption of Menominees by Whites Already Started."
        *Green Bay Press-Gazette,* August 19.
*Indian Voices*
1965    September.
Johnson, Ronald
1974    "A Taxonomy of Measurement Objectives for Policy Impact
        Analysis." *Policy Studies Journal* 3 (Winter): 201–6.
Joint Hearings Before the Subcommittees of the Committees on
        Interior and Insular Affairs
1954    "Termination of Federal Supervision over Certain Tribes
        of Indians." Pt. 6, 83d Cong. 2d sess., March 10–12.
Jones, Charles O.

1970    *An Introduction to the Study of Public Policy.* Belmont, Calif.:
        Wadsworth Publishing Co.
Josephy, Alvin M.
1971    *Red Power: The American Indians' Fight for Freedom.* New
        York: American Heritage Press.
Kappler, Charles J., ed.
1904    *Indian Affairs, Laws and Treaties.* Washington, D.C.: U.S. Gov-
        ernment Printing Office.
Keesing, Felix M.
1939    *The Menomini Indians of Wisconsin: A Study of Three Centuries
        of Cultural Contact and Change.* Philadelphia, Pa.: American
        Philosophical Society.
Keller, Suzanne
1963    *Beyond the Ruling Class.* New York: Random House.
Kenote, George W.
1970a   "Leader Defends Menominee Enterprises." *Milwaukee Jour-
        nal,* September 20.
1970b   "Working, Not Marching, Needed for Menominees' Uphill
        Struggle." *Green Bay Press-Gazette,* October 4.
1971?   "Discourse and Decision." Mimeographed.
1972    "A Personal Memorandum for Menominee Youth." Mim-
        eographed.
1973a   "Information Bulletin — Menominee Restoration Bill." Me-
        nominee County Shareholders and Taxpayers Alliance, Oc-
        tober 29.
1973b   "Statement and Comments on Draft Bill for Menominee
        Restoration," February 16.
Kennedy, Hon. Edward M.
1972    "Let the Indians Run Indian Policy." In Howard M. Bahr
        et al., eds. *Native Americans Today: Sociological Perspectives.*
        New York: Harper & Row.
Kickingbird, Kirke, and Karen Ducheneaux
1973    *One Hundred Million Acres.* New York: Macmillan Co.
Kornhauser, William
1959    *The Politics of Mass Society.* New York: Free Press.
Knight, W. D.
1965    "Preliminary Report to the Menominee Indian Study Com-
        mittee, Wisconsin Legislative Council on Economic Aspects
        of the Menominee Indian Reservation: Forest and Mill,"
        July 31.
1965    "Menominee Enterprises, Inc.," April 24. Mimeographed.
Kreisman, Irwin
1972    "Menominee Suit Charges Bias in Shawano Schools." *Capital
        Times,* May 30.

LaFarge, Oliver
1957    "Termination of Federal Supervision: Disintegration and
        the American Indians." *Annals of the American Academy of
        Political and Social Science* 311 (May):41–6.
LaFave, Ruben
1969    Quoted in *Green Bay Press-Gazette,* August 31.
1973    Correspondence to Hon. Harold V. Froehlich, March 12.
Larson, Andrews, and Milsap
1954    "Informational BRIEF re Menominee Indians in Connec-
        tion with the Program of Withdrawal from Federal Juris-
        diction and Control," January 22.
Lasswell, Harold, and Abraham Kaplan
1950    *Power and Society.* New Haven, Conn.: Yale University Press.
Lees, John D.
1967    *The Committee System of the United States Congress.* London:
        Routledge & Kegan Paul.
Lindblom, Charles E.
1959    "The Science of Muddling Through." *Public Administration
        Review* 29 (Spring):79–88.
1965    *The Intelligence of Democracy: Decision Making Through Mu-
        tual Adjustment.* New York: Free Press.
1968    *The Policy-Making Process.* Englewood Cliffs, N.J.: Prentice-
        Hall.
Lipsky, Michael
1976    "Protest as a Political Resource." In Stephen M. David and
        Paul E. Peterson, eds. *Urban Politics and Public Policy: The
        City in Crisis.* 2d ed. New York: Praeger Publishers.
Loomer, C. W.
1956    "Possibilities for Commercial Recreation Industry in the
        Menominee Indian Reservation," July 15.
Lurie, Nancy Oestreich
1957    "The Indian Claims Commission Act." *Annals of the Ameri-
        can Academy of Political and Social Science* 311 (May):56–70.
1961    "The Voice of the American Indian: Report on the Ameri-
        can Indian Chicago Conference." *Current Anthropology* 2
        (Spring):71–81.
1970    "Menominee." *Milwaukee Journal,* September 6.
1971a   "The Contemporary American Indian Scene." In Eleanor
        Burke Leacock and Nancy Oestreich Lurie, eds. *North
        American Indians in Historical Perspective.* New York: Ran-
        dom House.
1971b   "Menominee Termination: Reservation to Colony." Mim-
        eographed.
1973    "Forked Tongue in Cheek of Life Among the Noble Civ-

ilages." Mimeographed.
1978    Personal communication, February 26.
Mackie, Donald, et al.
1956    "The Forest Resources of the Menominee Indian Reserva-
        tion." In Citizens' Association of Wisconsin, Inc., *Menomi-
        nee Report.* Mimeographed. Pp. 38–47.
Matthews, Donald R.
1960    *U.S. Senators and Their Worlds.* New York: Vintage Books.
Maxey, David
1970    *Green Bay Press-Gazette,* May 31.
McKay, Douglas
1955    Correspondence to Oliver LaFarge, New York Association
        of American Indian Affairs, Inc., November 30.
McMahon, J.
1960    *Milwaukee Journal,* April 17.
*Menominee County-Town News*
1973    May.
Menominee Enterprises, Inc.
1961    *Annual Report,* September.
1965*a*   Memorandum to Hon. Warren P. Knowles, governor, state
        of Wisconsin, May 27.
1965*b*   *Annual Report,* September.
1966    *Annual Report,* September.
1967    "A Status Report—Menominee Indians, 1967."
1972*a*   "A New Report to our Certificate Holders," April 21.
1972*b*   "What Should We Do?" March 14.
Menominee Indian Study Committee
1973    "Summary of Proceedings," February 16.
Menominee Indian Tribal Delegation
1972    Correspondence to Louis R. Bruce, commissioner, Bureau
        of Indian Affairs, August.
Menominee Indian Tribe
1959    "Questions and Answers on Proposed Legislation." Pre-
        pared by attorneys for the tribe, May 25.
*Menominee News*
1955    January 27, May 13.
1956    April 25.
1958    May 9, October 28.
1959    January 28.
Menominee Tribal Delegation for Restoration Bill
1972    Correspondence to Louis R. Bruce, commissioner, Bureau
        of Indian Affairs, June 1.
*Menominee Tribal News*
1977    October, December.

*Menominee Tribe of Indians et al.* v. *United States*
1967    "Plaintiffs' Requested Findings of Fact and Brief," p. 1.
1973    "Plaintiffs' Requested Findings of Fact and Brief," p. 1.
"Menominee: Wisconsin's 72d County."
1963    April. Mimeographed.
Miller, Benjamin
1972    Correspondence to Robert W. Warren, attorney general, state of Wisconsin, July 31.
Miller, Mike
1973    "Menominees Seek Return to Reservation Status." *Capital Times*, March 12.
*Milwaukee Journal*
1958    July 17.
1959    June 22.
1964    March 6.
1969    December 1.
1971    November 7, December 12.
1973    March 11.
*Milwaukee Sentinel*
1965    January 30, June 30.
1967    September 25.
1971    May 31, July 27, October 15, October 26.
Mines, Kenneth A.
1972    Correspondence to Arnold A. Gruber, superintendent, Shawano Board of Education, October 4.
*Minneapolis Tribune*
1971    October 24.
Moulin, Faith
1971a   "Menominee County Aids and Grants." Menominee Indian Study Committee, November 17
1971b   "Report to the Menominee Indian Study Committee on the Menominee Enterprises, Inc. 4% Income Bonds." Menominee Indian Study Committee, December 29.
Muskrat, Joseph
1973    "Thoughts on the Indian Dilemma." *Civil Rights Digest* 6 (Fall):46–50.
Myer, Dillon S.
1953    "Annual Report, Commissioner of Indian Affairs, 1952." Washington, D.C.: U.S. Government Printing Office.
Natchez, Peter B., and Irvin C. Bupp
1973    "Policy and Priority in the Budgetary Process." *American Political Science Review* 67 (September):951–63.
Native American Rights Fund

1973    *Announcements* 2 (October–December).
N. E. Isaacson & Associates, Inc.
1972    "Brief and Appendix of Appellant in the Case of Henry L. Tomrow, Sr., et al. v. Menominee Enterprises, Inc., et al. and N.E. Isaacson & Associates, Inc., before the Supreme Court of the State of Wisconsin," August Term, no. 508.
*New York Times*
1950    March 6.
Nichols, Phebe Jewell
1956    "It Happened in Wisconsin." In Citizens' Natural Resources Association of Wisconsin, Inc. *Menominee Report.* Mimeographed. Pp. 7–34.
Nixon, Richard M.
1970    "Message from the President of the United States Transmitting Recommendations for Indian Policy." House of Representatives, 91st Cong., 2d sess., Document 91–363, July 8.
Northeastern Wisconsin Health Planning Council
1971    "Application to National Health Service Corps for National Health Service Corps Personnel," October 19.
O'Donahue, Pat
1970    *Green Bay Press-Gazette,* March 5.
1971    "Legend Lake Development Is Joint Effort to Reduce Indian Taxes." *Green Bay Press-Gazette,* July 11.
Orfield, Gary
1965    *A Study of the Termination Policy.* Denver, Colo.: National Congress of American Indians.
1966    "The War on Menominee Poverty," May. Mimeographed.
Otis, D. S.
1973    *The Dawes Act and the Allotment of Indian Lands.* Norman: University of Oklahoma Press.
Parenti, Michael
1978    *Power and the Powerless.* New York: St. Martin's Press.
Pressman, Jeffrey L., and Aaron Wildavsky
1973    *Implementation.* Berkeley: University of California Press.
Proxmire, Hon. William
1971    Correspondence to Ada Deer, December 7.
Prucha, Francis Paul
1962    *American Indian Policy in the Formative Years: The Indian Trade and Intercourse Acts, 1790–1834.* Cambridge, Mass.: Harvard University Press.
*Racine Journal*
1959    June 11.
Ray, Verne F.

1971    "The Menominee Tribe of Indians, 1940–1970." United
        States Court of Claims Docket no. 134–67. *Menominee Tribe
        et al.* v. *United States of America,* Plaintiff's Exhibit no. 1,
        Washington, D.C., November 1.
Raymer, Patricia L.
1973    "Cancelled Reservation." *Washington Post,* April 16.
Rieselbach, Leroy
1973    *Congressional Politics.* New York: McGraw-Hill Book Co.
Ripley, Randall B.
1975    *Congress: Process and Policy.* New York: W. W. Norton & Co.
Rittel, Horst W. J., and Melvin M. Webber
1973    "Dilemmas in a General Theory of Planning." *Policy Sciences*
        4:144–69.
Ritzenthaler, Robert E.
1951    "The Menominee Indian Sawmill: A Successful Community
        Project." *Wisconsin Archaeologist* 32 (June):69–74.
Robertson, Melvin L.
1961    "Chronology of Events Relating to Termination of Federal
        Supervision of the Menominee Indian Reservation — Wis-
        consin," May 31. Mimeographed.
Roosevelt, Theodore
1901    "Break Up the Tribal Mass," First Annual Message, Decem-
        ber 3. In Virgil J. Vogel, *This Country Was Ours.* New York:
        Harper & Row, 1972.
Sady, Rachel Reese
1947    "The Menominee: Transition from Trusteeship." *Applied
        Anthropology* 6 (Spring): 1–14.
Sammond, Frederic
1959    Correspondence to Hugh M. Jones, Wausau, Wis., March
        16.
Schusky, Ernest
1970    *The Right to Be Indian.* San Francisco, Calif.: Indian His-
        torian Press.
Seaton, Fred A.
1958    Transcript of a radio broadcast over Radio Station KCLS,
        Flagstaff, Ariz., September 18.
Shames, Deborah, ed.
1972    *Freedom with Reservation.* Madison, Wis.: National Commit-
        tee to Save the Menominee People and Forests.
Sharkansky, Ira
1970    *The Routines of Politics.* New York: Van Nostrand Reinhold.
*Shawano Evening Leader*
1952    June 19, June 26.
1970    February 4, September 14.

1971     June 28.
1972     May 20.
1973     October 17.
Simon, Herbert A.
1966     "Political Research: The Decision-making Framework." In
         David Easton, ed. *Varieties of Political Theory.* Englewood
         Cliffs, N.J.: Prentice-Hall.
Smith, Michael
1973     "The Constitutional Status of American Indians." *Civil
         Rights Digest* 6 (Fall):10–16.
Smith, Niki
1965     "Report to the Menominee Indian Study Committee on the
         National Congress of American Indians' Convention, No-
         vember 1–6, 1965, Scottsdale, Arizona." Menominee Indian
         Study Committee. Mimeographed.
Smithson, Thomas L., and Charles F. Wilkinson
1973     Correspondence to Hon. Harold Froehlich, March 28.
Spindler, George D.
1955     *Sociocultural and Psychological Processes in Menomini Indian
         Acculturation.* Berkeley: University of California Press.
Spindler, George, and Louise Spindler
1971     *Dreamers Without Power: The Menomini Indians.* New York:
         Holt, Rinehart and Winston.
1978     "Identity, Militancy, and Cultural Congruence: the Me-
         nominee and Kainai." *Annals of the American Academy of
         Political and Social Science* 436 (March):73–85.
State of Wisconsin
1973     Assembly Bill 892, April 24, 1973.
Summary of Requests
1964     Submitted to the Office of Economic Opportunity (Anti-
         Poverty Program) in Behalf of Menominee County, Sep-
         tember.
Svensson, Francis
1973     *The Ethnics in American Politics: American Indians.* Minne-
         apolis, Minn.: Burgess Publishing Co.
Tax, Sol
1958     "A Positive Program for the Indian." *American Indian* 8
         (Spring): 17–26.
Truman, David B.
1951     *The Governmental Process.* New York: Alfred A. Knopf.
Tyler, S. Lyman
1964     *Indian Affairs—A Work Paper of Termination: With an Attempt
         to Show Its Antecedents.* Provo, Utah: Institute of American
         Indian Studies.

U.S. House Committee on Interior and Insular Affairs Report 642
1951    "Authorizing a Per Capita Payment to Members of the Me-
        nominee Tribe of Indians." To accompany H.R. 3782, 82d
        Cong., 1st sess.
U.S. House, Concurrent Resolution 108
1953    83d Cong., 1st sess.
U.S. House of Representatives, Hearings
1973    Committee on Interior and Insular Affairs. Subcommittee
        on Indian Affairs. *Hearings on H.R. 7421.* 93d Cong., 1st sess.,
        May 25–26 and June 28.
U.S. House Report 2503
1947    *Report with Respect to the House Resolution Authorizing the
        Committee on Interior and Insular Affairs to Conduct an Investi-
        gation of the Bureau of Indian Affairs.* 80th Cong., 2d sess.
U.S. House Report 1034
1953    *Report to accompany H.R. 2828.* 83d Cong., 1st sess.
U.S. House Report 1824
1960    *Amending the Menominee Termination Act: Report to accom-
        pany H.R. 11813.* 86th Cong., 2d sess.
U.S. House Report 272
1962    *Lessening the Impact of the Termination of Federal Services to
        the Menominee Indian Tribe of Wisconsin: Report to accompany
        H.R. 4130.* 87th Cong., 1st sess.
U.S. Senate Committee on the Post Office and Civil Service, Hearings
1947    *Officers and Employees of the Federal Government. Hearings on
        S. Res. 41.* 80th Cong., 2d sess., February 8, pt. 3, p. 547.
U.S. Senate—*Congressional Record*
1966    89th Cong., 2d sess., p. 24251.
U.S. Senate, Hearings
1954    Hearings Before the Subcommittee on Indian Affairs of the
        Committee on Interior and Insular Affairs. 83d Cong., 2d
        sess., on H.R. 303, May 28–29.
1961    Committee on Interior and Insular Affairs. Subcommittee
        on Indian Affairs. *Hearings on S. 869 and S. 870.* 87th Cong.,
        1st sess., April 18–19, 24.
1965–   Committee on Labor and Public Welfare. Subcommittee on
   66   Employment and Manpower. *Hearings on S. 934.* 89th Cong.,
        1st sess., November 10–11, 1965, and February 17, 1966.
1973    Committee on Interior and Insular Affairs. Subcommittee
        on Indian Affairs. *Hearings on S. 1687.* 93d Cong., 1st sess.,
        September 17 and 26.
U.S. Senate Report 1116
1957    *Report to accompany H.R. 6322.* 85th Cong., 1st sess.
Van Meter, Donald S., and Carl E. Van Horn

1975    "The Policy Implementation Process: A Conceptual Frame-
work." *Administration and Society* 6 (February):445–88.
Van Ryzin, Jerry
1959    *Green Bay Press-Gazette,* January 19.
Vogel, Virgil J.
1972    *This Country Was Ours.* New York: Harper & Row.
Warne, William E.
1948    "The Public Share in Indian Assimilation." Speech before
the Annual Meeting of the Home Missions Council of North
America, Inc., January 6.
Washburn, Wilcomb E.
1973    *The American Indian and the United States: A Documentary
History.* 4 vols. New York: Random House.
*Washington Post*
1954    April 12.
1971    October 3.
Watkins, Arthur V.
1957    "Termination of Federal Supervision: The Removal of
Restrictions Over Indian Property and Person." *Annals of
the American Academy of Political and Social Science* 311 (May):
47–55.
*Weekly News Letter of the Menominee Tribe*
1954    January 25.
White, Jim
1971    "DRUMS Statement to All Menominee," December 15.
Wildavsky, Aaron
1964    *The Politics of the Budgetary Process.* Boston: Little, Brown &
Co.
Wilk, Stuart
1972    "Menominees Asked Little, Feel They Received Less." *Mil-
waukee Sentinel,* November 23.
Wilkinson, Charles F.
1973    Correspondence to Hon. Lloyd Meeds, September 6.
Wilkinson, Charles F., et al.
1973    "The Menominee Restoration Act: Legal Analysis." On
H.R. 7421 and S. 1687. 93d Cong., 1st sess.
*Wisconsin Blue Book*
1968    Madison, Wis.
Wisconsin Conservation Department
1964    "A Proposal for the Establishment of the Wolf River—
Menominee State Park," Madison, Wis.: State Parks and
Recreation Division.
Wisconsin Legislative Council

1957   "Menominee Indian Study Committee." *General Report,*
       nos. 2, 5. Madison, Wis., January.
1958   "Alternatives for Ownership and Management of Menom-
       inee Resources." Madison, Wis., June.
1959   "Analysis by Sections of Proposed Legislation on Menom-
       inee Indian Tribe: LRL 330 Creating Town and County
       Governments." Madison, Wis., April 29.
1964   Menominee Indian Study Committee, Minutes, March 25.
1965a  Menominee Indian Study Committee, Executive Commit-
       tee Minutes, April 23.
1965b  "Financial Information on Menominee County." Madison,
       Wis., March 1.
1966   "Report of Menominee Indian Study Committee." Submitted
       to the governor and the 1965 legislature, Madison, Wis.,
       April.
1970   "Report of Menominee Indian Study Committee. Submitted
       to the governor and the 1969 legislature, Madison, Wis.,
       January.
1972   Menominee Indian Study Committee Advisory Meeting,
       Minutes, Keshena Public School Library, Keshena, Wis.,
       May 19.
1973   "Report to the 1973 Legislature on the Activities of the
       Menominee Indians Committee," September.
Wisconsin Peace Action Committee
1970   "Wisconsin Enquirer." Milwaukee, Wis.
*Wisconsin Rapids Tribune*
1965   March 20.
Wyngaard, John
1965   "Solution Must be Found for Plight of Menominees." *Green
       Bay Press-Gazette,* March 23.
Yinger, Milton, and George Eaton
1978   "The Integration of Americans of Indian Descent," *Annals
       of the American Academy of Political and Social Science* 463
       (March):137–51.
Zimmerman, William, Jr.
1957   "The Role of the Bureau of Indian Affairs Since 1933."
       *Annals of the American Academy of Political and Social Science*
       311 (May):31–40.

# INDEX